Some Very Special Men

Some Very Special Men

The Emergency Service to the Rescue

CY EGAN

HARPER & ROW, PUBLISHERS
New York, Evanston, San Francisco, London

FIRST EDITION

Designed by C. Linda Dingler

Library of Congress Cataloging in Publication Data

Egan, Cy.
    Some very special men: the Emergency Service to the rescue.
    1. New York (City).   Police Dept.   Emergency Service
Division.   I. Title.
HV8148.N52E35   363.3'09747'1   73-14255
ISBN 0-06-011163-1

To Jean L. Giacomini

Contents ....

Illustrations follow page 150.

Foreword..

On the night of December 23, 1951, barely a year after I began my newspaper career, I was sent to a rooming house in downtown Brooklyn, where the New York City Police Department's Emergency Service was battling a hashish-crazed French Moroccan sailor who had run amok and terrorized fellow tenants with an eight-inch butcher knife.

Clad in the trench coat and slouch hat of an image-conscious cub reporter, I arrived on the scene with a veteran legman from *The New York Times*. As tear gas wafted from the building, I stood beside the *Times* stalwart in a nearby doorway, excited by the drama that was being played out but somewhat apprehensive that the mayhem might spread, with unfortunate consequences for both myself and my companion.

Not so the *Times* man. With conspicuous gallantry and characteristic poise, he was writing intently in his note pad, meticulously recording every facet of the event, which ended finally in a blaze of gunfire. "I hope you counted the shots," he advised sternly. "It's important we get the exact number. These cops never seem to get it right."

That was my first professional contact with the Emergency Service and one of my first with *The New York Times,* and I must say both impressed me—the *Times* for its assiduous attention to detail and the Emergency Service for its valor.

Unfortunately, the berserk sailor did not survive the ordeal. Fortunately, I did, and my next major encounter with the Emergency Service was in August, 1953, at a Brooklyn veterans hospital where a deranged young man was saved after threatening for more than thirteen hours to leap to his death from a ledge.

The rescue, which is recounted in this book, naturally provoked memories of a night only fifteen years before when John William Warde succeeded in plunging to oblivion from a ledge of the Hotel Gotham in midtown Manhattan despite a frantic eleven-hour effort to save him. Along with the fiery end of the cruise liner *Morro Castle* and the German dirigible *Hindenburg* and the spectacular rescue of the surviving crewmen aboard the sunken submarine *Squalus,* the Warde tragedy easily is among the most vivid of my childhood recollections.

I was not aware of the Emergency Service's role in the Warde case at the time, nor did I learn until much later of its work in the aftermath of the crash of an Army bomber into the Empire State Building, although I also remember the latter event quite well. After hearing the radio bulletin, I rode the next train to Manhattan from my home in suburban Pelham, arriving to find the top of the skyscraper still enveloped in fog and scattered remnants of the catastrophe littering the streets below.

As a result of these early experiences, the die was cast. My fascination grew when I was afforded a firsthand opportunity to witness the Emergency Service in action as a police reporter at the scenes of disasters and rescue operations. There once was a time when I, like many other people, I suppose, considered the sound of sirens frightening and depressing, a terrible wail mourning the utter futility and sad reality of life. Today I hear sirens quite differently. Perhaps, after reading these pages, you will agree that they really are a signal of hope, a sign that there still are people in the world who care when misfortunes strike, who are ready to do what they can to help, and who are unusually gifted with the competence and bravery to deal with disaster effectively.

Although I first thought of writing a book about the Emergency

Service in 1963 and started sporadic research, it was not until 1971 that the idea took hold in earnest. It was sparked in large part by the outpouring of negative publicity concerning the Police Department after disclosures of corruption among some of its members. While many of the charges were valid and certainly indefensible, all tended—unfairly, I believe—to obscure the fact that within the police ranks there are, and always have been, dedicated professionals to whom honor is traditional and whose acts of bravery and humanitarianism are chiefly responsible for earning New York City's police force a reputation as "The Finest." Foremost among them are the men of the Emergency Service, and it seemed to me a most appropriate and opportune time to tell their story.

In the process of chronicling the history and activities of an organization which, in the last half century, has answered nearly a million emergency calls, much material has had to be condensed or deleted, thereby unfortunately eliminating the names of many brave men who are justly deserving of public credit for their deeds. These include unidentified emergency men, detectives, uniformed policemen from other sections of the force, and firemen, all of whom perform heroic work at rescue scenes, in conjunction with the Emergency Service.

Given the faultiness of human memory and perceptions as well as the propensity of participants, witnesses and chroniclers to see and report events in varying ways—occasionally mixing fancy with fact—I devoutly hope that a reasonable degree of fidelity has been achieved in this material. Intentionally altered are the identities of would-be suicides, notably in the "Jumper" chapter, and these have been fictionalized to avoid stigmatizing those who may have been restored to normal and happy lives. No valid purpose could be served by sullying them with the past.

I am deeply indebted to scores of former and current members of the Emergency Service for their patient and painstaking help and interest in providing the official data and technical advice for this book. Special thanks are due Sergeant Joseph J. Emru, an Emergency Service enthusiast without peer, who was more than generous with his time and knowledge. Others include Assistant Chief Inspector Walter E. Klotzback (retired); Deputy Inspector Arthur A. Freeman (retired); Captain Robert P. Oberle; Lieutenants Anthony Fiore, Matthew L. Byrne, James P. Brady, Edward Meyers; Officers Frank J. Novak, Patrick Driskill, Harry Burker, George Sica and George Roscher.

I also wish to acknowledge many colleagues on New York City's newspapers, whose stories and personal recollections supplied the flesh and blood for the bare bones of official police reports. Some are anonymous, others too numerous to mention. Suffice it to say that their work appeared in the New York *Post*, the *Times*, the *News*, on the wires of the Associated Press, United Press International and the now defunct Standard News Association, and in the old *Journal-American*, *Herald Tribune*, *World-Telegram and Sun*, *Mirror*, *PM* and the *World*. Material from the official police magazine *Spring 3100* and the Federal Bureau of Investigation's Law Enforcement Bulletin also was most helpful.

No project is possible without the help and encouragement of advisers, loved ones and friends, and I have been especially graced. I wish to thank my editor, Joan Kahn, for her understanding and firm hand; my father, Cyril B. Egan, for his early nurturing and guidance of my writing interests; Joseph L. Hoey, a dear friend whose wise counsel and contagious enthusiasm were inspirational from the outset; Marion and Lynwood (Jack) Giacomini and many others who must remain nameless but who I trust are well aware of the important roles they played.

Lastly, but most importantly, no words can ever adequately express my deep affection and gratitude to the fairest of them all, Jean L. Giacomini, the lovely woman to whom this book is dedicated. Without her devotion, unstinting support and expertise both on editorial matters and in the preparation of the manuscript, it most certainly would never have become a reality.

C. E.

New York City
November, 1973

1. ESD

During the mid-1950s, a young U.S. Navy lieutenant gazed down from the railing of his ship moored off a tiny island in the Pacific Carolines—more than twelve thousand miles from his native New York City—and what he saw made him wonder for a moment if he was hallucinating in the intense tropical heat.

Natives of the island had clustered around the ship after paddling furiously from shore in outrigger canoes in a mad race to sell souvenirs to the newly arrived sailors. Such displays of brisk tradesmanship are as familiar as palm trees in the South Sea Islands, but what endowed this scene with a particularly exotic touch was the unusual attire of the hucksters. The wildly gesticulating men wore torn and threadbare blue shirts, some with shoulder insignia bearing the legend of the New York City Police Department's Emergency Service.

The lieutenant remained mystified by the incident for months until he returned home and by chance encountered Deputy Chief Inspector Walter Edward Klotzback, then commander of the city's police law-enforcement–rescue forces—the Emergency Service and its companion Aviation and Harbor Units. The meeting took place at Brooklyn's Floyd Bennett Field, where the lieutenant was serv-

1

ing as a pilot. Klotzback was visiting a hangar at the field, which is headquarters for the Aviation Unit's helicopter fleet.

"Boy, you guys sure get around," the lieutenant marveled as he told Klotzback about the strange equatorial episode.

Klotzback broke into laughter over the bizarre tale and then offered an explanation.

For nearly ten years, the Emergency Service, which usually copes with emergencies only within the confines of New York City, had been reaching out beyond its jurisdictional boundaries in an international rescue effort to save the entire population of the Pacific island of Ponape. The project had started in 1947 after the island's post-World War II plight came to the attention of the policemen while talking with a young Jesuit missionary, Reverend Hugh F. Costigan. The priest had befriended the crew of a Harbor Unit launch during a stroll one evening along the shore of Welfare Island in the East River where he had been assigned temporarily as chaplain at a home for cancer patients after returning from eight years' service in the Philippines.

Costigan confided that he was soon to be sent to Ponape and was concerned since he lacked knowledge of small boat handling and other skills and equipment that he knew would be essential if he was to be of genuine help to the people of the island. Word of his dilemma spread quickly to Klotzback, who was then commander of the Harbor Unit, and to the land-based squads of the Emergency Service as well as the Aviation Unit.

Adopting the island as a pet philanthropy, the policemen promised to help Costigan improve the conditions there. Before he departed for Ponape, members of the Harbor Unit trained him thoroughly in navigation and repair of small craft. He reciprocated by playing shortstop on the Harbor Unit team during its annual baseball game with the landlubbers of the Emergency Service, walloping four homeruns as a farewell present.

The policemen sent thousands of dollars, technical advice, a jeep, a cement mixer, a generator and scores of tools to the island, enabling the natives to turn acres of jungle timber and iron salvaged from an abandoned Japanese fort into a church, convent, school and five new boats.

Klotzback explained that old uniforms had been stuffed in the shipping cases to prevent the tools from rattling around. "I guess they salvaged the shirts, too," he said.

When Ponape's economy later was threatened with collapse during the mid-1950s by a sudden slackening in the demand for its chief product, coconut oil, the policemen rallied behind it again by raising funds to build a $20,000 agricultural and trade school so that it could attain self-sufficiency by cultivating a variety of farm products for its own population as well as for export.

For spearheading the rescue efforts, Klotzback was named Saum (Lord) of Metelanim, an ancient kingdom of Ponape, by Moses Hadley, the Isipano (paramount chief) then reigning on the island. He also was accorded hunting and fishing privileges.

Today, after nearly three decades, the Ponape rescue operation is still being carried on by the small army of more than six hundred specially trained policemen whose careers are devoted to acts of bravery and missions of mercy in one of the world's largest and most frenzied cities.

The venture exemplifies the kind of spirit and tradition that has prevailed for nearly half a century among the hand-picked members of the Emergency Service and the Aviation and Harbor Units, who are called upon at all hours of the day and night to cope with disasters and thousands of lesser calamities that arise daily in the city's fast-paced life.

In a typical year, the land, sea and air police answer as many as 46,000 messages of distress and tackle eighty-six separate categories of major and minor crises.

The land-based Emergency Service's assignments range from dragging adventurous youngsters from air-conditioning ducts, construction workers from under collapsed cranes and hapless bank employees from locked vaults, to helping overpower barricaded and defiant criminals.

A small sampling of its annual list of emergencies includes:

Nearly six hundred persons overcome by carbon monoxide or other deadly gases.

More than two score trapped and injured in elevator accidents —half in elevator-car mishaps and the rest in plunges down shafts.

Upward of thirteen hundred luckless souls imprisoned in stalled elevators.

Nearly three hundred human beings who fall, jump or threaten to leap from bridges and buildings. (The vast majority of the would-be suicides are foiled, but the others manage to hurtle to death or serious injury before rescue efforts can be initiated.)

Almost six hundred victims pinned in automobile wrecks or entombed in the smoking ruins at fires.

Other emergencies are seasonal in nature. In the spring, people fall from high places where they are working, from building windows that are opened with the warming trend in the weather, or from roofs of private homes they are repairing after a long, hard winter. Summer brings an upsurge in highway accidents, drownings, lightning victims and persons overcome by lack of oxygen while working in stifling heat. The hurricanes and storms of fall deluge the policemen with calls to clear away falling poles, trees and electric wires, pump out flooded basements and shore up dangerously leaning fences, walls and chimneys, torn signs and loosened traffic signals, cornices and store windows. In the winter, the headaches come from snow and ice and the menace of carbon monoxide asphyxiation and boiler and steam explosions from faulty heating systems.

The policemen respond to all fires of two alarms or more, help remove the sick and injured from apartments and other places with difficult access, recover the decomposed bodies of persons who have lain dead and unnoticed for weeks and even months, and retrieve automobiles that crash into excavations and ditches or hurtle off waterfront piers. The rescue crews can almost set their watches by the industrial accidents they handle, which reach peaks early in the morning or late in the day, when people are either too groggy from sleep or too tired, impatient or annoyed from working to be alert.

At major catastrophes such as airplane and train wrecks and explosions, the policemen coordinate rescue efforts with firemen, hospital disaster units and troubleshooting crews from gas and electric utilities.

The Aviation and Harbor Units, now operating under a separate but closely coordinated Air-Sea Section, work with the land-based units in annually fishing about 125 bodies out of the waters surrounding the city and rescuing a like number of persons who flounder while swimming in forbidden areas. Almost one hundred youthful mariners are plucked from drifting rafts, and more than nine hundred small-boat owners are assisted when their craft go aground or adrift, or start to sink.

The rescue work is not always life-and-death drama, but all the assignments are adventure-filled and many are touched with weird, whacky and whimsical aspects that make amusing cameos of everyday living. It is not unusual for the emergency policemen to be asked to help hapless citizens who drop keys, eyeglasses or even false teeth down sewers or subway gratings, and tradition demands that every genuine plea for help be answered.

One Bronx housewife called after a ring given to her to commemorate her twenty-fifth wedding anniversary broke apart as she stood at a bathroom sink and the band fell into the drain, although she had recovered the diamond with a quick grab.

"I'd read in the papers that the emergency police are called upon to do all kinds of work, so I thought I'd try them," she said. "The wonderful part to me is that not only did the policemen take the pipe apart and get my ring, but they put the pipes back together again. They were regular plumbers in tuxedos."

Asked to clarify the latter remark, she said the policemen had done their job in such a polite and efficient manner that instead of overalls they might as well have been wearing formal attire.

Paradoxically, the Emergency Service, which is primarily devoted to humanitarian work, was born of violence—the offshoot of old police reserve squads first organized in Civil War times to deal with riots. The reserves consisted mainly of policemen who were excused for four hours after either their second or fifth tour of regular duty each week and then brought back for eight extra hours to sleep overnight in station-house dormitories so that extra men would be available at all hours, especially at night, to rush in patrol wagons to the scenes of public disorders.

The concept assumed ominous overtones after World War I with the mustering of a 650-man unit of policemen, nearly all with military combat experience, who were equipped with machine guns and rifles and whose express goal was to combat political agitators.

The unit was headed by a police captain with specially designated military rank and was organized along the lines of a regular army battalion. Military drilling methods were followed in the training schedules and the members went on regular summer encampments for field maneuvers.

One of the ideas behind the project evidently was to keep a riot squad available at all times to enforce a sort of martial law without going through the formality—and taking the time—to turn out National Guardsmen. The exclusive focus of the reserves on riots and crowd control soon proved of little value in a city where the need for a unit to cope with a growing variety of emergencies became increasingly urgent. Steady population growth, a building boom and a flood of new devices—particularly in the home—created mounting problems that the ordinary policeman on the beat could not handle. Horses, still prevalent on the streets in those days, were tumbling into excavations. More and more people were jumping or falling under subway trains. There was a rise in the number of drownings along the waterfront and in park lakes. Cases of persons overcome by leaking gas were commonplace.

During the early 1920s, the reserve policemen started to answer the emergencies on a hit-or-miss basis when not engaged in riot or crowd control. The program was so effective that by 1925, Police Commissioner Richard E. Enright authorized the purchase of two custom-built fourteen-thousand-dollar trucks with equipment geared specifically to the handling of all kinds of emergencies. Both were manned by policemen from the riot battalion. The vehicles, capable of what was then considered an amazing speed of sixty miles an hour, each carried three sergeants and twenty-one officers. One truck was responsible for covering all of Manhattan and the Bronx, and the other the entire area of Brooklyn and Queens. Two lieutenants were in charge.

The service combined the duties of a rescue squad, Pulmotor truck, riot platoon, first-aid and motor-patrol squad. The equipment stowed on the trucks, which were enameled in dark blue with POLICE DEPARTMENT EMERGENCY SERVICE in gold letters on their bodies, brought their total cost to more than twenty thousand dollars.

The project was expanded over the next five years to include eight more trucks, all operated by the reserves, but the strain of the extra work and long hours of duty were exhausting and the reserves battled bitterly for changes in the system.

When Grover A. Whalen, a dynamic and far-sighted innovator,

took over as police commissioner in 1929, he was quick to grasp the need for a departmental unit devoted entirely to emergencies, with its own staff of expertly trained policemen working regular tours of duty. He took the bold steps necessary to make it a reality.

On March 8, 1930, Whalen commissioned ten more trucks, and two days later abolished the reserve system. The men began working on three regular eight-hour shifts around the clock. By now, a sergeant and six officers were assigned to each vehicle, and the jurisdiction had been expanded to include Staten Island.

"We must always remember that preparedness is our watchword," Whalen told the more than 450 men in the revamped unit. On April 10, 1930, in General Orders No. 20, Whalen amended the Police Department's Manual of Procedure to establish a separate departmental unit called the Emergency Service Division.

In the ever-changing process of official nomenclature, the unit has since been redesignated Emergency Service District and later Emergency Service Section, but it has been known throughout most of its history simply as the ESD.

The first commander and a prime mover in the initial organization was Inspector Daniel A. Kerr, a six-foot-tall, Irish-born former blacksmith who was known as "Iron Dan" for his incredible feats of physical strength.

Born in 1871 and appointed to the police force in 1895, Kerr achieved a reputation as the strongest man in the department after glorious victory in a legendary wrestling match with a fellow policeman named Selig ("Ajax") Whitman, who had been a professional weightlifter.

Whitman had amazed his friends by lifting 1,350-pound dumbbells with his teeth, pushing boxcars with 27,000-pound loads up steep grades, smashing stones with his fists and catching in his arms a steeplejack who had toppled from a scaffolding on the Queensboro Bridge.

Kerr wearied of hearing of Whitman's accomplishments and challenged him to a test of strength. It was a titanic bout, but when it was over Whitman was pinned to the mat and Kerr scarcely fatigued.

Kerr combined his physical prowess and talents for emergency work with a consummate knowledge of Shakespeare. He was not averse to quoting the Bard freely and at length to illustrate certain cogent points to his men. He proclaimed that it was the desire of the police department to correct certain misconceptions about the agency's functions and to establish it in the community under the motto "At Your Service."

The inspector was largely credited with streamlining the efficiency of the new unit, which in the first year of its operation answered more than two thousand calls for help.

After the branch had been permanently set up, a school of specialized training was created at the Police College, with a curriculum embracing all subjects allied with emergency work.

In the ensuing years, the Aviation and Harbor Units were absorbed into the new rescue service. Both were restored to autonomous status on June 20, 1973, but remain integrally linked with Emergency Service operations.

The brain center of the Emergency Service is located behind the West Fifty-fourth Street police station in Manhattan in a small two-story yellow brick building with a buzzer-operated green door, which opens into an incredible world of machinery and a workshop where expert technicians invent, repair and refine many of the tools of their trade. Upstairs, an entire floor is jammed with files and desks at which policemen sit busily monitoring calls for help and coolly channeling orders to dispatch men and equipment to the scenes of emergencies that occur at an average rate of one every twelve minutes.

To cope with routine cases, a round-the-clock vigil is maintained by an armada of radio motor patrol wagons packed with equipment selected through years of experience to cope with the gamut of basic emergencies.*

Two to five wagons are assigned to patrol duty in each of ten squads—three of which are located in Brooklyn, two each in Manhattan, the Bronx and Queens, and one in Richmond. Each squad's jurisdiction extends over an area encompassing from three to eight police precincts.

The citywide coverage enables some element of the fleet to speed to any point in New York's five boroughs within five to eight minutes. The emergency calls are transmitted over a specially assigned ultra-high-frequency radio band and are monitored and coordi-

---

* For the complete list of equipment, see Appendix A.

nated by a computerized system in the Police Department's Communications Division. Each wagon carries a two-man team drawn from a roster of twenty-five to fifty policemen distributed for a week's period among three eight-hour shifts daily at nearly every squad.

One of four sergeants in command supervises each shift, and while the wagons are out patrolling, the sergeant and a policeman chauffeur remain in squad headquarters with the big truck that is kept in reserve for disasters and other emergencies demanding heavier and more elaborate equipment.

The trucks, once open-air vehicles resembling fire engines and now ten-ton closed vans, answered all calls before the smaller wagons were introduced into the service in October, 1949, after two years of field testing. They are the pride of each squad. The newest cost more than $28,000 and carry over two hundred items of equipment, thus anticipating every conceivable kind of emergency. Many of the special appliances and tools are the inventions of individual policemen for accomplishing some particular purpose outside the scope of standard equipment that is bought from manufacturers. Most of the improvised devices were developed as the result of rescue cases that ended in failure. Some tools would prompt envy in the most expert burglar. Others meet tasks from saving the lives of tiny babies to subduing bands of desperadoes.

All the trucks have equipment stowed according to a standardized schedule, so that a man assigned in a hurry to go out on a truck from another unit can find anything he wants at once. Even in darkness or smoke, he knows instantly where he can lay his hands on a certain size ax or crowbar.*

The trucks are also equipped with two built-in 7.5-kilowatt alternating-current generators that can supply minimum electricity requirements for hospitals, prisons and other public buildings during power failures. The units can be used to power portable lights on each floor of a blacked-out institution, or can be plugged in directly to the darkened building's circuit. Kept in reserve are two generator trucks, each with a capacity of up to 55 kilowatts, and twenty portable 2.5-kilowatt generators on wheels that can be rolled into marshlands and other desolate areas to power illumi-

---

* The truck's inventory is listed in Appendix B.

nation for searching operations. While most hospitals now have auxiliary power supplies, a truck is sometimes called to help support essential medical services, such as incubators, in emergencies. On one occasion in the past when the lights failed while a patient was on the operating table in a Brooklyn hospital, a truck was on the scene within five minutes after the surgeons and nurses in the operating room were plunged into darkness and confusion. The squad set up four portable lights in the operating arena and kept them going for an hour and twenty-five minutes. The surgery—an appendectomy—was a success. When hospital ambulances are delayed or unable to respond to calls in time of blizzard, the vehicles transport sick and injured.

Good physique, quick reactions and ironclad stability are mandatory to get into the Emergency Service and especially to stay there. The job calls for men with the emotional tenacity to handle dead or mangled bodies and to work at dizzying heights without queasiness. Candidates preferred are those with training as machinists or artisans, who possess a natural bent for such skills as mechanics, carpentry, steam fitting, plumbing, welding, rigging, electrical work and first aid. Expert swimming ability is required along with knowledge of artificial respiration and resuscitator techniques.

There is no recruitment program for the ESD since all candidates are volunteers and there is a permanent waiting list of nearly two hundred. Applicants must have an unblemished record of at least two years' service on the police force before they are even considered for a job, and it generally takes up to a year more for an applicant to be picked. After careful screening of personal and professional qualifications, candidates are transferred into the service as vacancies occur or when their specialties are needed. Newly assigned men attend two weeks of basic instruction at the service's Specialized Training School, now located at Floyd Bennett Field, after which they are sent to the busier squads to learn the arts and crafts of the job.

"We can teach them the theory for an emergency they may run into," one veteran explains, "but in actual practice there is always something that is just a little bit different."

Training follows the preceptor method, veterans teaching the newcomers for the most part, and it never really ends. In-service training is conducted on a daily basis at each squad under the supervision of the sergeant in charge and patrol lieutenants, who serve as field supervisors to disseminate new information on rescue techniques among the squads. Once a year every member returns to the training school for a week-long refresher course so that he will be ready for any new emergency that may arise, and individual members attend sessions whenever requested by superiors to overcome shortcomings that show up in their work.

Morning and afternoon sessions, which are conducted five days a week (for both new and refresher students), include: care and maintenance of ropes; basic knots; block and fall techniques; use of the Morrissey life belt; gas and electric emergencies; elevator instruction; ice and water rescue; crowd control; firearms training; acetylene instruction; ground net techniques; radiation testing; tear-gas usage; use of jacks; bomb procedures; applications of the penal code; first aid; resuscitation techniques. In addition to the training school, instruction takes place at such sites as Rodman Neck, Breezy Point, Wards Island and the Coney Island subway yards.

When tricky new equipment is added to the trucks and wagons, engineers from the manufacturer's staff lecture at the training school and squads on its use, and all new devices are subjected to rigorous field testing and evaluation before being made part of the regular inventory.

After every major catastrophe, or any minor emergency in which unusual difficulties are encountered, "brainstorming" sessions are conducted among the men who participated with a view toward determining what went right and what went wrong with the operation. The data are painstakingly reviewed and a list of recommendations for improvements is drawn up and incorporated in daily training sessions at the individual squads as well as the specialized school. The brainstorming findings provide a means of constantly updating equipment and rescue procedures through an exchange of experience among the squads.

While technical expertise plays a significant part in the choice of candidates, the nature of the work invariably attracts men with deeply human qualities and fervent concern for the lives of others. Probably no emergency police officer better embodied these attributes than the late Patrick J. O'Connor, who earned twenty-two departmental medals for valorous duty in his ten years of service. A great bull of a man who stood six feet five and weighed at least 280 pounds, O'Connor combined tough-gentle attributes that served him equally well whether his job was to overpower a vicious gunman or to supply lifesaving solace and hope to some troubled soul threatening to end all by leaping from a building ledge. He was so huge that a favorite caper among his fellow officers was to slip into his empty shoes, which they could easily do without taking off their own, and clomp around to delighted laughter.

Fellow policemen recall the time when O'Connor and a partner, Mike McCrory, arrived at the apartment of a Chinese man who had gone berserk and was chasing his family and friends with a meat cleaver. McCrory took one look at the raving man and his weapon and announced to O'Connor, "Get out of the way. I think we'll have to shoot the guy." O'Connor shouted, "No! Let me talk to him."

O'Connor planted his huge bulk squarely in front of the shrieking man and outscreamed him with a barrage of words that sounded strangely Oriental. "What the hell are you doing?" McCrory demanded. "You don't speak Chinese."

(In O'Connor's case, his partner was right, but linguistic accomplishments are not uncommon among emergency policemen. Some speak as many as three languages, among them Spanish, Yiddish, Italian, German, French, Greek and a touch of Gaelic. When a language specialty is needed that is not available among the men, linguists in almost any tongue can be located through a computer in the personnel records unit at police headquarters, which will instantly select policemen in other branches of the force who have the skill.)

Unabashed by McCrory's discovery of his pidgin Chinese, O'Connor glanced around to explain, "Look, I'm just trying to make the guy feel at home."

O'Connor kept talking and gesturing, and the man was so baffled that he forgot about the cleaver, which hung limply in his hand. The ruse worked long enough for reinforcements to arrive. O'Connor then led a charge on the man. In the confusion, someone got tangled up in a light cord hanging from the ceiling and the room was plunged into darkness. Before the lights came on again, O'Connor had taken several blows on the head from his fellow officers, who struck out wildly in the melee. But he had his quarry firmly in hand and was shaking with laughter over what had happened.

As much as he could enjoy a good belly laugh even when facing danger, O'Connor displayed the kind of serious dedication that marks the attitude of the emergency policemen toward their work. Once while rushing a sick boy to a hospital, he gave the vomiting youth mouth-to-mouth resuscitation, taking his mouth from the boy's only long enough to shout to his partner to drive faster. When a man's leg was severed in a fall under a subway train, O'Connor crawled to the victim's side to hold pressure points above his thigh and stem the flow of blood. The action was responsible for saving the man's life. The train was moved, and the injured man hauled out and rushed to a hospital.

Of all of O'Connor's feats, none stood out more clearly as an example of the kind of personal qualities the ESD seeks in its men than the time he stood and let an irate old lady beat him furiously with her cane after he had inadvertently offended her with a thoughtless remark.

"He could sympathize with a woman like that," McCrory, a boyhood friend and one-time high school classmate of O'Connor's, explained. "He had a great feel for people; he could understand what was really going on in their heads."

Fellow officers saw O'Connor as almost compulsively driven in his love for life and desire to improve the human condition. Even when handling decomposed bodies, he exhibited no sign of disgust—only concern and dismay. He spent many of his off-duty hours aiding persons in distress, often traveling to the Bowery to befriend and help derelicts.

Ironically, it was O'Connor's deep sense of duty to his fellow men that led to his sudden death at the age of thirty-one. He was killed by a passing oil truck when he stopped one Thanksgiving eve on a Brooklyn parkway to help an old man change a flat tire.

Today, a plaque with his picture hangs on the wall of the office at Manhattan's Emergency Squad 1, and engraved below it are the words: "Greater love hath no man than he lay down his life for his friend."

Walter Klotzback, who was known as "Mr. Emergency," was another larger-than-life figure who epitomized the energetic spirit of the Emergency Service, which he joined at its inception. He served in all its branches before rising through the ranks to take full command for many years until his retirement as an assistant chief inspector in 1963, when he was succeeded by Deputy Chief Inspector James J. Morrissey.

The son of an engine-room worker on the Staten Island ferry, Klotzback came from a family that boasted generations of steam fitters and engineers—an ancestry that endowed him with a natural aptitude for what was to become his life's work. He was born in downtown Manhattan, and never went beyond the eighth grade in school.

A husky six-footer with massive hands, he was only sixteen when he passed himself off as twenty-one to work as a sandhog in compressed air in the Holland Tunnel, which was under construction beneath the Hudson River. While working at this job and other heavy building tasks on many skyscrapers and piers, he gained an unusual knowledge of how the city is constructed that later proved invaluable. He finally realized his dream of becoming a policeman in 1924 and was assigned at first to foot patrol in an area where a gang called the Pepper Robbers was operating. The thieves were known for throwing burning red pepper into the eyes of jewelry store owners before scooping up loot and fleeing. Klotzback caught two of them and won official approval. But instead of an appointment as detective, his reward was a recommendation to a departmental unit that was later incorporated into the Emergency Service.

Klotzback quickly drew official recognition and praise for his uncanny ability to size up rescue problems and devise unique methods to solve them. He early showed his command potential by perceptiveness in recognizing and utilizing the special skills of his fellow division members—those who could shinny up greasy cables, throw lassos, slither into narrow spaces between buildings. He was responsible for systematizing the stowing of equipment on trucks, and he spent many long hours in the service's machine shop, inventing and fashioning ingenious tools that later were adopted as models by rescue units around the world. He once studied spinal fractures for months in a hospital so that he could adapt for emergency use a "broken back or neck board" that is still carried as standard equipment on the trucks.

Never an armchair general, Klotzback, who was known by the nickname "Klutch," was in the thick of actual rescue operations throughout his career, personally working on the nuts-and-bolts jobs, even after he assumed full command in 1952. When one of his squads was reported at an impasse with the task of releasing a seaman trapped in a freak mishap aboard a freighter, he raced to the scene by car—and into what he once rated his toughest rescue problem. The accident had occurred after two seamen swung a lifeboat over the water side of the empty, high-riding freighter docked at a Hudson River pier, and climbed into the craft to lower it for an inspection test. When a davit supporting one of the cables broke off, the lifeboat crashed down the ship's side to a vertical position, hurling one of the seamen into the water, from which he was pulled to safety by fellow crewmen. The other seaman instinctively grabbed the cable supporting the other end of the boat, and was yanked upward until his hand was wedged inside the metal housing of a block-and-tackle pulley. The screaming sailor dangled in midair forty feet above the water and eight feet from the freighter's side, his hand imprisoned in the pulley and gripped there by the weight of the runaway lifeboat swinging below him.

When Klotzback arrived, he found that there was no boom amidships on the freighter that could be swung out to allow rescuers to reach the seaman, or to extend as a narrow platform on which the suspended man could rest the weight of his body. The location of the accident on the water side of the ship made the task of finding a way to approach him from below doubly difficult. Klotzback hailed a passing tugboat that was towing a derrick barge. The barge was maneuvered alongside the freighter and a line from the derrick's boom was hooked to the lifeboat to raise it and ease the pressure on the seaman's trapped hand. The squad members were ordered to heat the base of the davit holding the lifeboat with blowtorches to soften the metal so that pipe wrenches could be used to bend the davit back until the boat and the hanging seaman were within three feet of the freighter's hull. A hook-and-ladder fire truck had been summoned by Klotzback, who ordered that a sixty-foot ladder be carried aboard the freighter and let down over the ship's side to rest on the stern of a police launch, which had raced in from midstream and positioned itself directly beneath the seaman. With the ladder leaning against the freighter, and bobbing up and down crazily as the police launch rocked in heavy swells, Klotzback mounted to the top and balanced precariously to burn away the pulley housing with an acetylene torch. "It was difficult to hang on," he later recalled. "But the real danger was that I'd burn the guy. He was pleading with me not to hurt him. What I remember most vividly is wishing that he was unconscious." To keep the pulley housing cool while the torch's pinpoint flame ate through it, he directed the ship's crew to play a hose stream of water over the freighter's side. Miraculously, when the housing fell away, the seaman's hand was extricated with no irreparable damage. Klotzback, exhausted by the ordeal, left for home.

"The best thing about being an emergency policeman is the way you feel when you go home," he has said. "You go with a real feeling of having done something good. That's why the men like this work. You get to know how it is to feel real satisfaction."

When asked once how he felt after his dreams of becoming a detective were shattered by assignment to the Emergency Service, Klotzback smiled. "I thought it was just another job in overalls," he said. "But I found out it was being a cop—plus a lot of other things."

The feel for people and their problems that is considered so essential in emergency tasks is cautiously tempered by a restraint characteristic of men who care but recognize that they must hold emotions in check if they are to function calmly and efficiently. To assuage some of the barefaced reality that is part and parcel of their work, the policemen are not averse to peppering reports with a kind of defensive humor. The hard-bitten cynicism that is so often identified with police work is anathema in the Emergency Service. The humanizing aspect of rescue assignments sometimes inspires "official" reports such as these:

January 21, 1960—Person trapped in tank. Upon arrival was informed . . . that the victim . . . was in the process of making repairs to a 1,000 gallon oil tank in the basement of premises. The glass-lined tank was in the process of being cleaned of sludge which had about one quarter filled the tank. The method of cleaning the tank was to shovel out the sludge into a bucket, which was then hoisted out of the manhole in the top of the tank. After most of the sludge had been removed, the victim was in the process of wiping the inside of the glass-lined tank with paper to remove all traces of sludge. At about noontime the victim called to his helper to lower a ladder so he could get out and eat lunch. However, the helper had gone to the street and had taken their truck to obtain sandwiches and coffee, leaving the victim in the tank. The victim's calls were unheard at the location and he was unable to get out of the tank. At about this time, an oil tank truck arrived and deliverymen began to make the street connection for delivery of oil. The victim remained in the tank until a sufficient amount of oil was pumped in to float him within reach of the manhole, whereupon he climbed out. Victim was conscious and breathing and required no medical aid. He went home early. No services rendered by this squad.

October 30, 1958—Person fell in apple press in one-story Queens factory. Upon arrival was informed . . . that an employee at plant, while operating 55-ton hydraulic apple press machine, accidentally fell into machine which was loaded with apples and was pressed along with apples to be made into cider. Crew, using 10-ton Norton jack, crowbar and wire cutters, opened side of press, removed victim to large cardboard ($4' \times 8'$) and funneled him into 4 one-gallon cider bottles. Bottles became mixed with a shipment of cider loaded onto a trailer truck and after diligent search was not located at present. Present at scene, Lt. McIntosh, 106 Pct.

November 20, 1958—Ein Deuscherman Vis Das Handen in Mashinen Geshmashed in Vun-Shtory Breucklyn Butcher Shop: Ven das trucken ist here gecommen, ist vas gefounden dot ein Fritz Gompenmoller, gebornen in 1940 uf Strassbourg, Deustchlandt, vas mit das handen geshtucken in das livervurst mashinen. Offisier Von Brokken vis ein monkey wrench getvisten oudt das iron gebolten und maken das mashinen apart. Geplacen das krinder in ein shtrong geclampenholder, und vis ein sharp hackenzaw gecutten easy das krinder und nicht gecutten das handen. Das handen frum outten das krinder ist beputten ein blud tighten gestrappen on armen zo ist nicht blud gecommen oudt. Ist putten Fritz in ein shtretcher und in hospitalvagen. Ven das trucken ist gecommen in qvarters gebakken, Offisier Von Brokken ist das hackenzaw gesharpenen goodt. Oberlieutenandt Kransmeyer vast overzeerenen das chob.

The zest of the policemen for emergency work faces its severest test at disaster scenes where incredible carnage makes all their efforts at lifesaving seem inevitably haunted by death.

One of the most gruesome episodes in the Emergency Service's long history of coping with disaster began shortly before midnight on February 3, 1959, when American Airlines Flight No. 320 from Chicago wheeled in the night sky over suburban New Rochelle, New York, and nestled into a blanket of clouds for its final approach to New York's La Guardia Airport. Inside the cabin of the giant four-engine Electra turboprop, two stewardesses moved among sixty-eight men, women and children, helping fasten seat belts for the landing. The passengers were chatting and exchanging last-minute farewells, but a few peered out the plane's portholes in a futile attempt to catch through the dense overcast a brief glimpse of the ever-fascinating panorama of New York's lights.

Up in the cockpit of the $1.7 million airliner, Captain Albert H. DeWitt, fifty-nine, a thirty-year veteran pilot with 28,000 hours of commercial flying experience, concentrated on the glittering array of control-panel instruments showing the craft's course and rate of descent. DeWitt was using the automatic pilot to operate flight controls and guide the airliner down through the cloud cover and heavy weather below.

As far as DeWitt could tell from the instruments, the plane still was dead on course as it swept over a radio range station in the Clason Point section of the Bronx and dipped out over the East River on the final 2.8-mile letdown to the runway—a concrete ribbon stretching five thousand feet diagonally to the southwest. A voice from La Guardia's control tower crackled over the plane's radio: "American Three-twenty, cleared to land on Runway No. 22, wind southwest at six miles an hour." DeWitt acknowledged the call with a terse: "Three-twenty."

The last radio advisory to the airliner, twenty-two minutes earlier, had put the cloud ceiling at four hundred feet and the visibility at two miles in light rain and fog, and DeWitt expected to drop out of the murk momentarily and find the plane lined up squarely between the glowing border lights of the runway. He was unaware that in the intervening time the weather had closed in suddenly over the river below, with clumps of fog and solid sheets of rain swirling across the icy waters. Moments after roaring out of the clouds, the fifty-ton airliner thundered into the river a mile short of the runway.

About seven hundred feet east of the crash point, the red-and-white tugboat *H. Thomas Teti, Jr.,* with two barges in tow, was groping through the fog on its way from Seabrook, Connecticut, when the explosive sound of the crash rumbled across the water. Two skippers exchanging tours of duty in the tug's pilothouse switched on the vessel's powerful searchlight and swung the beam through the mists until it settled on the shattered plane, which was wallowing in the water and sinking fast.

A distress call was flashed over the tug's pilothouse radio and relayed by the Coast Guard to police borough communications centers, where the switchboards had already begun to light up with calls from anxious residents of shorefront homes on both sides of the river. Within minutes, police officials were mobilizing the men of the Emergency Service and Aviation and Harbor Units.

A crash boat patrolling out of the Harbor Unit station at College Point, Queens, just east of La Guardia, picked up the Mayday call and sped toward the scene. In the bow of the craft, laid out as a small hospital with room for ten patients, policemen checked first-aid equipment for use in the event that survivors were found. Canvas body bags for the dead were taken out of lockers. Other Harbor Unit launches, scattered on round-the-clock patrol at various points along the city's waterways, were alerted to the catastrophe and raced to the rescue.

At the Aviation Unit's headquarters in Hangar No. 4 at Floyd Bennett, a small truck dragged out a platform bearing one of the bureau's five Bell 47-J Ranger helicopters. Two police pilots scrambled aboard and seconds later the whirlybird lifted off into the overhanging mists and headed north for the crash scene to hover over the water in the hunt for survivors.

At the headquarters of two land-based squads in the Bronx and Queens, telephones rang simultaneously with the rush of radio messages alerting police throughout the city to the calamity. The shiny green-and-white rescue trucks roared into life as the chauffeurs assigned to them bounded aboard with squad commanders. Only seconds elapsed before the heavy garage doors slid back and the trucks were speeding out into the foggy night with sirens screaming. Other ESD vehicles on patrol converged on shore points along both sides of the river, shining searchlights into the fog-shrouded waters.

Out on the river, the tugboat maneuvered close to the plane. The gasoline-stained waters were strewn with passengers and crew members—some already dead, others waving and shouting hysterically for help. A rope ladder was tossed over the tug's side and several members of the vessel's crew scrambled into the water to save those still alive. Other crewmen wielded boat hooks from the deck to haul in floundering victims, one a man who was submerged under four feet of water but was discovered when the tug's searchlight reflected off his metal belt buckle.

Nine persons were yanked to safety before strong riptides carried the others out of sight in the darkness. The plane began to slide beneath the surface, and the tug's crew suddenly saw an arm with a striped sleeve waving from the remains of the crumpled cockpit. Captain DeWitt was trying to break out through the jammed door. The tug nosed up against the wreckage and crewmen attempted to tear the door open with boat hooks, but the battered hulk pulled away and the hand disappeared. The plane sank to the river bottom in twenty-nine feet of water until only three feet of the vertical tail section jutted above the surface like a tombstone amid the angry whitecaps.

When the police crash boat reached the scene at 12:10 A.M., the tugboat with the survivors aboard headed for College Point, where the Harbor Unit's normally comfortable two-room shelter was crowded with policemen in dripping slickers. Streets nearby were a nightmare of wailing ambulances and flashing lights. Most of the survivors aboard the tug were screaming or crying, and one crewman was shouting, "We need splints. Get the stretchers down here." Two men, one with cuts on his face and the other in shock, managed to walk ashore draped in blankets and assisted by ESD policemen, but six other adults had to be carried to ambulances on stretchers. An eight-year-old boy came ashore in a policeman's arms. His mother, who was among the survivors, later died at a hospital.

Out on the river, a second police launch arrived and the crash boat returned to the College Point dock with a body. "They're floating toward the Bronx-Whitestone Bridge," a police officer aboard the launch reported. Soon after, the second launch returned with five bodies secured in canvas bags. As the hours passed and the drizzle and fog continued, Coast Guard picket craft, fireboats and a flotilla of private vessels scoured the river with the police launches while a police helicopter clattered overhead. Before dawn, the bodies of twenty-two persons had been lifted from boats at College Point and carried through the mud past policemen, firemen, reporters and photographers to ambulances bound for the Queens County Morgue. What had begun as a rescue operation had turned into a grisly mission of recovering bodies and bits of wreckage. The search was based at College Point and across the river at a beach club in the Bronx, and teams of ESD policemen and airline personnel waded along the craggy shorelines in mud churned by driving rain, pulling in bits of bedding, pillows, and a cargo door with its metal twisted out of shape. The searchers were hopeful at first that many of the bodies would be found in the plane's sunken fuselage, but debris drifting to both sides of the river indicated that the passenger cabin of the aircraft had broken open in the crash. High tides washed much of the flotsam ashore at Clason Point and left it scattered on the rocks. Two of the plane's seats were pulled from the shallows off the Bronx with passengers still strapped to them—one a middle-aged man in slacks and sport shirt, the other a woman in her late thirties with long brown hair and a brown knitted suit with matching shawl still around her shoulders.

Within a few days, launches and helicopters had aided salvagers in dredging the plane's broken fuselage and wings from the riverbed so that the wreckage could be transported to a hangar at La Guardia and reassembled for minute examination by technical experts seeking the cause of the catastrophe. But the ordeal of recovering bodies, some as far as thirty miles from the accident scene, went on for months, while shifting currents kept yielding up grotesque souvenirs of the tragedy—trench coats, briefcases, electric razors, wrist watches, medicine vials, cuff links, wallets, hats and a pink satin packet containing an expensive strand of pearls.

With the recovery of the last of the victims four months after the crash, the ESD closed the files on one of the most challenging operations in its history.

Among the other disasters in which the ESD has played important rescue and technical roles:

July 28, 1945—A Mitchell B-25 Army bomber, lost in a blinding fog with three men aboard, rammed at two hundred miles an hour into the north side of the Empire State Building at the seventy-ninth floor—915 feet above street level. The plane tore a jagged eighteen-foot hole in the skyscraper's thick concrete skin and bent a huge I-beam girder in the interior back eighteen inches. Exploding wing tanks turned the seventy-ninth floor into a funeral pyre, and one of the craft's flaming engines skidded the width of the building and burst through the south wall, plunging like a dying comet to the roof of a nearby penthouse. The shock wave rocked the skyscraper and snapped elevator cables, sending a car with two women passengers plummeting one thousand feet into a subbasement. Although seriously injured, the women survived. ESD crews joined firemen in sifting the blackened ruins, which yielded the bodies of ten men and women office employees—all burned beyond recognition. Twenty-seven injured were rushed to hospitals and one later died. The charred bodies of two crewmen and a serviceman hitchhiker on the plane were found subsequently, one at the bottom of an elevator shaft.

May 29, 1947—A Cleveland-bound DC-4 commercial airliner, struck by a freak squall on takeoff from La Guardia, shot off the end of the runway and piled up in flames. Ten of the forty-eight aboard escaped from the blazing wreckage, but four eventually died in hospitals. After the fire was doused with foamite and the white-hot aluminum cooled, ESD policemen worked in mud and pelting rain under the glare of searchlights to recover the charred remains of the other thirty-eight victims, many with the clothes seared off their bodies.

November 22, 1950—The ESD teamed with other rescue forces to extricate seventy-nine dead and 340 injured from the worst train wreck in the city's modern history. The Thanksgiving eve tragedy occurred when a Long Island Rail Road commuter express, bound for Babylon, thundered into the rear of a stalled Hempstead-bound local a half mile east of the Kew Gardens station in Queens. The rescue crews spent hours tearing into the twisted wreckage of the telescoped cars to carry victims down a fifteen-foot embankment to ambulances and morgue wagons.

January 14, 1952—A radar-guided twin-engine Convair, inbound to La Guardia from Boston, roared out of the morning fog and dived into a mudbank in the East River only three hundred yards from where the ill-fated Electra turboprop was to crash seven years later. All thirty-six persons aboard survived by swimming free through emergency exits of the craft, which settled in only nine feet of water with its right wing and tail section remaining above the surface. ESD policemen aboard launches aided in picking up survivors and chopped holes in the fuselage of the sunken plane to search and make certain that all had escaped.

February 1, 1957—A Miami-bound four-engine DC-6A faltered on takeoff from La Guardia and plowed into a poultry farm on Rikers Island in the East River—only three hundred yards from the site of the 1952 crash. ESD crews helped save eighty-one persons aboard, but twenty others perished when three thousand gallons of gasoline in the plane's wing tanks exploded in flames.

December 16, 1960—The worst aviation disaster in ESD history occurred with lightninglike suddenness when a propeller-driven Super Constellation and a DC-8 jet, both circling under leaden skies while awaiting clearance for landings at the La Guardia and International airports, collided ten thousand feet over the northeastern tip of Staten Island. The Constellation plunged like a bird struck dead in flight into an empty playground bordering Staten Island's Miller Army Airport, killing all forty-four persons aboard but sparing the lives of hundreds of children in a nearby public school. The jet, leaving one of its engines embedded in the body of the stricken Constellation, zoomed through light rain and snow across New York's Upper Bay and spiraled into Brooklyn's densely populated Park Slope section. One of the jet's wings sliced through the roof of a four-story tenement and the plane cartwheeled with explosive force into a church known as the Pillar of Fire. The craft's fuel tanks detonated like bombs and flames swept eleven buildings in the neighborhood. The ESD went to the sites of both crashes to assist in recovering the bodies of 133 killed, including six persons on the ground. The sole survivor—an eleven-year-old boy thrown clear of the jet—died later.

December 19, 1960—Not more than seventy-two hours elapsed after the midair disaster before the ESD was summoned to help rescue scores of civilian workmen and U.S. Navy personnel overcome when a fierce fire raked the innards of the U.S.S. *Constellation* while the giant aircraft carrier was under construction in a dry dock at the Brooklyn Navy Yard. Fifty civilian workmen died in the inferno, but dozens of others survived due to massive resuscitation efforts by the ESD, which transported its entire oxygen tank refilling unit to the scene on a truck to recharge resuscitator cylinders as they were depleted.

March 1, 1962—The ESD engaged in one of its most macabre body-recovery operations after a Boeing 707 Astrojet, climbing into sunny skies from International Airport with ninety-five persons aboard, suddenly rolled on its back and fell straight down into Pumpkin Patch Channel, a tidal flat three miles southwest of the runaway. Biting cold weather quickly covered the crash area with ice, and a bulldozer with oversize wheels was called in to break through to the entombed passengers. The water was not deep enough for divers and was too shallow for launches to come in close to the wreckage, so the ESD crews were forced to wade through the broken ice floes with shovels and clam hooks to reclaim bits and pieces of bodies, most with severed arms and legs, some of the fragments not much bigger than a hand. Among the property recovered was an attaché case containing $75,000, whose origin and destination were never explained.

October 3, 1962—A one-ton boiler, with three malfunctioning safety devices that officials later said caused a deadly buildup of steam, burst from its moorings in the basement of a telephone company building at the northern tip of Manhattan and roared like a rocket through a cinder-block wall into an adjoining cafeteria that was alive with the soprano chatter of dozens of women employees at lunch. Surging upward, the boiler stabbed a hole in the ceiling that swallowed up office workers, desks and filing cabinets on the floor above and sent them showering down into the bedlam of screaming women running for their lives. The giant tank deflected downward and rumbled 180 feet through the cafeteria, leaving a trail of mangled bodies and rubble in its wake. The biggest outpouring of ESD equipment and men since the 1960 airplane collision helped dig out twenty-one dead buried in the wreckage and aided ninety-five injured who escaped, some when the blast blew them out through windows into the street. Two of the injured later died.

2. Shootout..

While its work now encompasses all kinds of emergencies, the Emergency Service still shares the responsibilities of the old-time reserve policemen for supplying manpower and equipment to quell riots on the streets and in the city's prisons and for performing other vital law-enforcement functions.

Under provisions of police rules and procedures, the commanding officer is empowered to maintain a Firearms Battalion, with rifles, shotguns, machine guns and tear-gas devices for use against criminals, or to provide security escorts for visiting heads of state or for money and gold shipments between various banks throughout the city.

When not engaged in rescue work, the patrolling wagons answer regular radio calls of signal 30, for crimes of violence, and respond to bombings, holdups and sieges with barricaded gunmen. The vehicles also answer signal 32s, for a variety of other police actions, including searches for burglars and prowlers and dispersal of disorderly gatherings. Nearly one hundred arrests are made and more than thirty thousand summonses issued yearly in the course of routine patrol work.

In murder and assault and robbery cases, magnetic detectors

are employed to retrieve guns, knives and other weapons and items of evidence from sewers, catch basins, lakes and riverfronts for use in tracing killers and other lawbreakers and in prosecuting them for crimes.

When federal revenue agents stage raids on illegal still operations in the city, ESD mechanics often are recruited to destroy the confiscated equipment or to dismantle it so that it can be removed as evidence.

More than once, the service's picks, shovels and heavy equipment have been used to recover the bodies of gangland victims entombed in cement blocks or buried under tons of earth in desolate underworld graveyards.

The ESD has a long record of tactical successes in public and prison riot control over the years, but its history is not without controversy in terms of the kinds of causes it has found itself allied with or opposed to in the line of duty. The record shows, however, that whatever the merit of the cause, technical know-how and professionalism have resulted in keeping loss of life and injuries to a minimum. As a first principle in preventing the kind of disorganized and spontaneous police reaction that can turn a merely unruly crowd into a raving mob bent on death and destruction, the ESD constantly reviews the trends in public disorders and updates a number of well-rehearsed contingency plans for dealing with every possible type of crowd situation. Its files are loaded with maps, charts and lengthy reports on the makeup of every community in the city, along with precise directives on how to cope with various kinds of trouble in each area. Besides outlining exactly what personnel and weaponry are available and when and how they should be utilized, the files list residents of the communities who are considered influential among their neighbors and can be recruited as peacemakers in times of stress to calm tensions. All the plans advocate the massing of manpower as a deterrent to violence, but stress that actual force should be employed only when absolutely necessary.

As a result of preparedness, the ESD never has had to use tear gas to disperse a public disorder and has rarely used gunfire, except in retaliation against snipers and attacks by armed rioters.

During World War II, a riot in Harlem produced widespread violence and great carnage, but the ESD won official praise for its role in helping to curb the toll. The trouble, which for a time threatened to parallel a previous blood bath in Detroit that had cost thirty-five lives and left hundreds injured, was spawned on the hot Sunday evening of August 1, 1943, when a white police officer arrested a black woman for creating a disturbance in the lobby of a Harlem hotel. The woman resisted and a black soldier came to her aid, grabbing the officer's night stick and knocking him down. The officer drew his revolver and fired a bullet that tore a minor flesh wound in the soldier's shoulder. After the woman was subdued and the soldier taken to a hospital for treatment, a rumor spread throughout the ghetto area that the soldier had been shot and killed by a drunken white policeman. An angry crowd of three hundred persons, mostly teen-agers and young men in their twenties, besieged the hospital. Rocks and bottles were thrown and the mob fanned out in a rampage of store-looting and vandalism. More than 2,500 policemen, including ESD contingents, were mobilized and rushed into Harlem. The police were supported by hundreds of members of the City Patrol Corps and the Air Warden Service and more than one thousand black civilians who were deputized on the orders of Mayor Fiorello H. La Guardia. The blacks, three hundred of them women, were equipped with night sticks and armbands and authorized to make arrests.

As the antiriot forces moved through Harlem's streets, the crisis seemed headed for a reenactment of the fiasco only two months before in Detroit, where policemen had shot at everything that moved, and shot to kill. A danger of random slaughter lurked in the shadowy darkness that blanketed the Harlem area due to a wartime dimout imposed on the city by the military to prevent the glare of New York's skyline from profiling offshore U.S. troop and supply ships as targets for marauding German U-boats. Uncertain city and police officials hesitated at ordering an immediate lifting of the dimout edict without authorization from the military. The ESD's brilliant searchlights were a crucial weapon in pinpointing the rioters and saving innocent persons from death and injury. The blinding beams poked into hallways and store entrances to give flying squads of policemen a clear view of what activity was in progress and what steps were necessary to combat it. At the height of the riot, an ESD truck, rushed into action as a surrogate tank, backed through the mobs to rescue four policemen under siege by seven hundred persons outside a store where the officers had cornered a band of five looters. Bulletproof vests, rifles, shotguns and other equipment were supplied by the ESD to help break up violence and to seal off the riot zone against invasion by outsiders bent on racist violence. The latter tactic marked a complete reversal of the action in Detroit, where policemen made no effort to bar intruders and laughed and looked the other way while white hoodlums armed with lead pipes, knives and guns stole into the riot area and roamed at will, attacking lone blacks. The Harlem crisis was managed so effectively from the outset that when Mayor La Guardia visited the community in person to speak to the residents and appeal for their cooperation to stem the violence, he was cheered by the crowds. By the time the trouble was over, six blacks were dead in looting incidents, 543 injured and 484 arrested—a tragic toll, but considerably less horrendous than in Detroit.

While the job of quelling riots in the city's prisons rests primarily with the Department of Corrections, the ESD responds with technical assistance in the form of acetylene torches, searchlights or weaponry, and as a backup force to thwart escapes and to search for missing prisoners.

Among the first major prison riots the ESD helped suppress were two fatal uprisings at the old New York County Penitentiary on Welfare Island in the East River. The century-old institution, later replaced by the current prison facility on Rikers Island, was a notorious breeding ground for prisoner melees and inmate grievances of a strikingly contemporary nature—unsafe and unhealthful conditions, bad food, overcrowding and inmate-operated narcotics rings.

On August 6, 1930, four ESD trucks and three launches were sent to the prison after a fifteen-minute flare-up among four hundred white and black inmates over which group had the right to use the recreation-area baseball diamond. Knives, baseball bats and other makeshift weapons were wielded in the battle, which left twenty-seven inmates injured, seven critically, but the guards had the situation in hand by the time the ESD arrived. One of the injured, a black man serving a short sentence for a minor offense, died twenty-two days later of a dozen knife wounds suffered as he tried to escape the violence of the howling mob, in which the whites outnumbered the blacks four to one.

During the late months of 1932, friction developed between Irish and Italian inmates when a trusted crony of the Irish clique, named Joseph Bendix, defected to the Italians, who were led by Harlem gangster Joe Rao, a close associate of prohibition "beer baron" Arthur ("Dutch Schultz") Flegenheimer. A few days before the riot, a vengeance squad of Irish convicts, organized by an inmate named George Holshoe, caught up with Bendix in an isolated part of the prison and gave him a savage beating that sent him to the prison hospital. True to prisoner code, Bendix claimed he had suffered the injuries in a fall down a flight of stairs.

With unrest and ominous tension seething in the wake of the attack, Warden Joseph A. McCann investigated and discovered through the prison grapevine the real cause of Bendix's injuries. McCann also learned that a reprisal was planned against Holshoe and other Irish convicts. He summoned a small group of leaders from both factions to his office for a peace conference. The session opened amicably enough but suddenly exploded in violence when Holshoe took a swing at a member of the Italian group after the latter denied that Bendix was an ally of, and an informer for, the Italians. In no time, the fight swirled into the hallway outside the warden's office, where fifty inmates who were filing past were swept up in the melee. Holshoe crumpled to the corridor floor with fatal stab wounds in his back and chest as the prisoners whipped out homemade knives and razor blades and ripped brass hose nozzles off the walls for weapons. The uproar resounded down the prison corridors and the unarmed guards were powerless to halt the rebellion. A call was put in for armed guards from outside the prison walls as prisoners in the mess hall and the west wing shouted and milled about and crockery and chairs flew through the air, crashing on the concrete floors. In other wings of the prison, convicts outside their cells seized fire buckets to hammer against the iron bars and refused to return to the cellblocks. Garbage cans were banged on walls and the din created by the shrieking prisoners spread throughout the prison.

McCann telephoned for help, and eight ESD trucks from Manhattan, the Bronx and Queens responded. Four Harbor Unit launches sped to the island and circled in the surrounding waters as policemen stood on the decks with machine guns at the ready to thwart any inmates who might try to escape by swimming to the Manhattan or Queens shores. Two high-winged, open-cockpit amphibian planes from the fledgling Air Service Division went aloft and flew over the prison, prepared to drop tear-gas bombs. The first policemen arriving at the prison found the armed guards still outside struggling to get through the prison gates to help their outnumbered comrades, who were being struck and shoved by the rioting prisoners. The crews surrounded the administration building and policemen rushed inside the walls to rescue the embattled guards. The rampaging inmates were rounded up with rifles and pistols that were fired—on strict orders—only over their heads as a nonviolent tactic to cow them back into their cells. The operation was executed so deftly that only two inmates were hurt, and within a half hour after the alarm was sounded, the revolt had been successfully ended.

Under current procedures, the ESD rarely enters a riot-torn prison, except when specifically requested to do so by the warden, who must give his prior approval to all actions taken against defiant prisoners. When five uprisings erupted within the space of two months at the Manhattan House of Detention (known as the Tombs) and correctional facilities in Brooklyn and Queens in the latter part of 1970, the ESD helped only to the extent of supplying weaponry and equipment and serving the prison guards in an advisory capacity. After those outbreaks, a program was instituted to train Corrections Department personnel to combat internal disturbances entirely without outside help, when possible.

The rash of prison revolts was a spin-off of the general upsurge of militant activism during the late 1960s that kept the unit increasingly busy with law-enforcement duties at the scenes of bombings, bomb scares and violent protest demonstrations. The bomb assignments were hardly new to the crews, who were seasoned veterans at the work, especially from their experiences with the trail of explosives left by the so-called Mad Bomber, who waged a campaign of terror throughout the city for over sixteen years, during the 1940s and '50s. The first of the Mad Bomber's devices was found stashed in a wall alcove of a West Side Consolidated Edison powerhouse on November 18, 1940, and neither the ESD nor the Bomb Squad had reason to suspect at the time that it was more than just the isolated work of a crank. But a deadly pattern unfolded in ensuing years during which thirty-two similar contrivances were planted in telephone booths, theater seats, public toilets and bus- and train-terminal safety lockers. The ESD aided in recovering ten of the bombs intact and helped gather evidence in the shattered wreckage after twenty-two others blew up with terrifying effectiveness and wounded fifteen persons. The bombs, fashioned from plugged sections of pipe stuffed with black powder, were primitive and inefficient at first, but gradually grew in sophistication. The detonators consisted of a watch with a tiny terminal soldered on the face so that the hand moving around the dial would make contact, close a wire circuit and send a triggering electrical charge into the explosive powder from a cartridge of dry-cell batteries.

Fearing almost from the outset that publicity might invite imitation by others and encourage the bomber to even greater destructiveness if his activities prompted widespread panic and concern, police officials clamped a tight lid of secrecy on the case and the related work of the ESD and Bomb Squad. By late 1956, it was apparent that only a remote chance remained that the fugitive could be traced either through the sources of his material or the cryptic notes that were found occasionally at locations where his bombs failed to explode or were mailed to the police and the utility. A decision was made to lift the curtain of secrecy, and police announced that a psychopath was believed responsible for the terrorism and asked for the public's help in capturing him.

Lured by the limelight, the bomber exchanged a series of letters with the *New York Journal-American,* in which he hinted at the motive behind the bombings and little by little divulged other information about himself that enabled detectives to track him to his Waterbury, Connecticut, home on the foggy night of January 21, 1957. Expecting a wild-eyed maniac, the police discovered instead a rather meek and grandfatherly-looking bachelor named George Peter Metesky, who matter-of-factly confessed that he had manufactured the "units"—as he termed the bombs—in the garage adjoining the gray frame house where he lived with two spinster sisters. In the garage detectives found the parts for a bomb larger than any Metesky had made before, which he said he had intended to explode in the newly completed Coliseum in midtown Manhattan. Metesky, a self-trained electrician and machinist of Lithuanian descent, confided that he had planted bombs on lonely trips into the city in the warped hope that he could draw public attention to an expanding bitterness he had nurtured over nearly three decades against Consolidated Edison's predecessor firm. He complained that he had been gassed in a 1931 accident while working at one of the company's power stations and had been unjustly denied compensation when he was laid off from his job after contracting tuberculosis as a result of the mishap. Metesky also said he had planted fifteen additional bombs, but police could never find a trace of them and were unsure whether they were figments of his imagination or had been found by porters or other building maintenance people and thrown away. Psychiatrists pronounced him unfit to stand trial and he was committed to a state hospital for the criminal insane. When he was found to be no longer a threat to society in December, 1973, he was released and all pending charges against him were dropped.

Ironically, Metesky had begun his bomb rampage only two months after the Police Department completed work on the prototype of a bomb-carrying truck that later was used extensively to remove his unexploded devices and is now part of the ESD's fleet of emergency vehicles. The development of the truck stemmed from an entirely separate bomb case at the 1939–40 World's Fair in Flushing Meadows, Queens, which claimed the lives of Bomb Squad Detectives Joseph J. Lynch and Ferdinand A. Socha. The pair had been summoned to the fairgrounds on July 4, 1940, when a small overnight bag emitting a strange ticking sound was discovered in a fan room at the British Pavilion. The bag was gently carried to an open area some two hundred yards away and the detectives attempted to cut it open to examine its contents. It blew up with shattering fury, killing both outright and wounding five policemen who were standing guard nearby. Crime-laboratory analysis later determined that the satchel had been packed with sixteen to twenty-four sticks of dynamite wired to a time fuse, but the motive for the bombing and the identity of the perpetrators are cloaked in mystery to this day. A review of the tragedy showed it was due not so much to lack of professional skill as to a woeful lack of technical equipment, including a means of transporting explosives safely from congested areas to a demolition range where they could be dismantled or detonated under conditions of minimal danger.

Stunned by the deaths of the detectives—the first and only fatalities in the entire history of the Bomb Squad—Mayor La Guardia personally ordered and supervised a crash program to build a bomb-removal truck with a special chamber that would effectively contain the flying fragments of an exploding bomb and at the same time permit the controlled escape of the rapidly expanding gases from the blast. Experiments were conducted in a desolate Brooklyn shorefront area known as a dumping ground for the bodies of victims of gangland's Murder Inc. and resulted in the development of an unearthly-looking tractor-trailer with a hutlike structure mounted on the rear. The enclosed structure resembled a huge inverted wicker basket, and was made of a double layer of steel webbing woven from cable five-eighths of an inch thick. A ten-inch space separated the two layers to act as an air cushion against the shock of a bomb burst inside the chamber and simultaneously allow dispersal of the ballooning gases through the mesh screen. Each strand in the mesh was pretested to withstand a strain of up to eighteen tons, which might be expected from a blast of up to one hundred sticks of dynamite. Within ten months after the World's Fair tragedy, the truck was assigned to active service with the ESD, which now operates two of the vehicles, from garages in Manhattan and Brooklyn.

When a bomb or bomb scare is reported, the alert is flashed simultaneously to the ESD and the Bomb Squad. The ESD usually is the first to reach the scene, and confines its work to clearing out the affected building or area and cordoning off a security zone at least one hundred yards in radius from the suspected explosive. While ESD crews are cautioned not to handle bombs or suspicious packages and to leave this task for the Bomb Squad, the policemen are trained to defuse, remove or detonate all kinds of explosives when necessary in extreme emergencies. Lectures and field sessions are given by Bomb Squad members at the ESD's training school in the use of every piece of equipment in the Bomb Squad's inventory. The tools include an electric stethoscope for detecting hidden clocks and other time-fuse devices; special tongs that can be manipulated by remote control from the end of a two-hundred-foot cable to tear apart a suspected container; and a glass knife for slicing through the electrical wiring of a bomb without sparking circuitry and setting off an explosion. Each ESD truck carries a heavy steel-mesh bomb blanket for smothering blasts and a tank in which a bomb can be immersed in thick lubricating oil to clog and jam the whirring parts of clock mechanisms. Besides knowledge in handling such modern explosives as plastic and letter bombs, ESD instruction includes up-to-date information on various incendiary devices, ranging from Molotov cocktails to more recent innovations by various militant groups, including gasoline-loaded Ping-Pong balls and intricate fire bombs made of hard-top cigarette boxes packed with combustible powder that is ignited by the heat of a battery-powered flashlight bulb.

One unusual case involved a five-hundred-cubic-centimeter bottle of explosive chlorosulfonic acid that developed a crack while sitting unused on a shelf in a laboratory in one of the buildings that make up the Bellevue Hospital complex on Manhattan's East Side. The highly volatile chemical, which is used in research but had lain untouched for thirteen years, threatened to blow up with exposure to the air, and the ESD helped evacuate two hundred patients from the building on stretchers and in wheelchairs before the Bomb Squad removed the bottle for disposal.

Traffic was halted in front of the hospital while the bottle of acid was carried to the bomb carrier, which transported it to a nearby East River pier where it was loaded aboard a Harbor Unit launch. Then, in accordance with telephoned instructions obtained from Eastman Kodak Company in Rochester, New York, which manufactured the acid, the launch sped with the bottle to Ambrose Channel outside the harbor, where the contents were slowly dumped overboard. The company had advised that the acid could be neutralized by introducing it, a little at a time, into a large body of water.

Explosives and incendiary bombs that cannot be deactivated on the spot are nudged into a steel mesh envelope that is toted to the bomb truck on a long pole by armor-suited detectives. The envelope is perched on a pulley-operated platform at the bomb chamber's rear door and, when the door is closed, the pulleys automatically haul the platform to the chamber's center. To avoid transporting the explosive through traffic-clogged streets during the day, the bomb carrier is sometimes driven to the nearest waterfront or other deserted area, where it remains until after nightfall. The trip is then resumed, through sparsely populated sections, to the Bomb Squad's demolition range at Rodman Neck, a desolate marshland area in the Bronx, overlooking the East River.

The time-tested procedures now make bomb-disposal work a surprisingly safe operation when compared to some other law-enforcement tasks.

For nearly six years up until June, 1973, twenty two-man teams of ESD policemen served in a special Stakeout Unit to deal with a mounting wave of armed robberies at stores and other business establishments. The men were assigned to keep hidden armed vigils for up to thirty days at a time in stores repeatedly victimized by holdup men.

Characteristically, the operations were conducted with extreme precautions, which included equipping the men with bulletproof vests marked POLICE in three-inch-high yellow letters across the front and back to ensure that their identity was unmistakable in any confrontation with gunmen. Intercom systems of FM radio receivers were linked to ultrasensitive microphones secreted near cash registers to alert the hidden policemen instantly to any holdup attempt. Before the so-called plant was set up, careful study was given to the proper placement of the policemen in an area that afforded the best vantage point for surveillance of the store through peepholes and at the same time assured that no innocent bystanders would be caught in the line of fire when the staked-out officers emerged.

Trained in defensive and offensive tactics, the laws of arrest, lawful use of force, search and frisk methods and the handling of prisoners with due regard to their legal rights, the men were able to maintain an unblemished record in which no bystanders or policemen were killed or injured. Numerous stakeouts ended in death for the bandits, however, since many were hardened criminals with lengthy records who preferred to shoot it out rather than face long prison sentences.

Nevertheless, the unit, which made about four arrests for every bandit slain, was disbanded. The reason given 'was "efficiency," and the men were reassigned to other duties within the ESD.

The pursuit and capture of psychopaths, who display vexing

unpredictability and an eerie potential for violence, can be especially menacing for emergency policemen. Many have been injured over the years answering calls to help subdue ex-mental patients and other disturbed persons who go suddenly and inexplicably berserk and threaten harm to themselves or others. The lack of conscious criminal intent in most "psycho" cases is small consolation when the crazed individuals are tough and burly and brandish weapons. But humane considerations take precedence and policemen shun the use of weapons, to engage in less lethal hand-to-hand combat, often risking serious injury to themselves. In one incident, a policeman was stabbed in the back, a second knifed in the shoulder and a third kicked in the groin after responding to a predawn call one summer morning that a "man was going wild" inside a Bronx home. An attempt was made for two and a half hours to argue the thirty-four-year-old ex-mental patient from a narrow second-floor hallway in the home, where he was lurking with a hunting knife and threatening to "kill any cop" who approached. A tear-gas canister was lobbed into the hallway to flush him out. The fumes drove the man out of a window and he plunged through a canopy onto the patio of an adjoining home, where the policemen were injured battling him into submission. The man suffered only minor bruises. He was returned to a mental hospital.

Known criminal psychopaths fall into an entirely different category, and the ESD plays a major role in helping to seize desperadoes who defy surrender and barricade themselves in apartments and other hideouts to shoot it out with police.

Of all the desperadoes the ESD has fought in blazing gun duels, few have ever matched the legendary Francis ("Two Gun") Crowley, who was captured in one of the longest and most violent shootouts in the city's history. The Brooklyn-born Crowley, who had been a foster child, worked sporadically as a fifty-dollar-a-week lather and already had begun by age nineteen to build an image very much like the character made famous by actor James Cagney in the 1931 film *Public Enemy*. A gum-chewing semi-illiterate with a great fondness for taxi dancers—although he once stubbornly insisted that he "never smoked, drank or swore"—Crowley boasted a dapper appearance and flaunted a reputation as a cold-blooded bandit, cop-hater and gun-worshiper. He reveled in the alias "Two Gun" and was moved to fits of uncontrolled rage when anyone but intimates addressed him as Francis or "Shorty," a nickname he inherited because he was only five feet three and weighed little more than one hundred pounds. He preferred to be called Frank by those who knew him only casually. His obsessive hatred of the law stemmed from the "shellackings" he claimed he received at its hands in his troubled childhood and from having seen a boyhood friend shot to death by a policeman.

Crowley nevertheless managed to avoid any major entanglements with the police until February 21, 1931, when an alarm was broadcast for him after he and three other youths climaxed an argument with two men at an American Legion dance in the Bronx by shooting and wounding both. Detective Ferdinand Schaedel quickly seized the other three suspects, but it was not until three weeks later that he overtook Crowley at the headquarters of a plastering firm in a midtown Manhattan office building. Schaedel relieved Crowley of his gun and was placing him under arrest when the fugitive whipped out a second, hidden weapon and opened fire, wounding the detective in the abdomen and the leg. As Schaedel fell, he fired several shots after the fleeing youth. Two ESD squads were called to search the building but could turn up no trace of the fugitive.

Crowley surfaced briefly two weeks later to rob a plastering boss, for whom he once had worked, of an eleven-hundred-dollar payroll at gunpoint aboard a crowded subway train in Manhattan. When the train halted three stops north of Times Square, he vanished with the money into the crowds. The fugitive's fortunes took a fateful turn for the worse within a few days, however, when he went out for a night on the town with Rudolph ("Fats") Duringer, a ponderous truckdriver who also was known by the nickname "Tough Red." The genesis of their friendship was never quite clear, but Duringer worked for a trucking company in Ossining, where he lived with an aunt, and made frequent trips into the city. He often spent his nights at the Primrose Dance Hall in Harlem, a favorite hangout of Crowley's. Crowley claimed that he had known Duringer only a few days when both found themselves in the Primrose on the night of April 25, 1931. A dance hostess— twenty-three-year-old, henna-haired Virginia Brannen—caught Duringer's eye, and Crowley obliged with an introduction. Two other dancers joined the party—Robert St. Claire, a twenty-three-year-old lather, and Mrs. Mildred Moore Armstrong, nineteen. The night wound up with a predawn tour of Harlem speakeasies in a car Duringer had stolen. When it came time for breakfast, Crowley's entourage consumed two fifths of whiskey instead of the traditional ham and eggs. Determined to keep the party going, the group piled back into the car and headed for Westchester County. What happened as the car crossed the county line was a subject for much legal controversy later, but police charged that Duringer, in a wild flight of alcoholic fantasy, pleaded with Miss Brannen to marry him and shot her once in the chest below the heart after she spurned the proposal and said she was going to marry a sailor. Duringer insisted he was insanely drunk and had pulled the revolver to fire shots through the floor of the car because the party was dull and needed a touch of excitement. He claimed Miss Brannen panicked at seeing the weapon and was killed accidentally when she attempted to wrest it from him. Duringer disposed of Miss Brannen's body by dumping it behind a low wall surrounding a seminary just outside the city limits. Then— as if nothing had happened—Crowley drove Mrs. Armstrong and St. Claire to the Bronx, where he left them off.

Within a few hours, two passers-by discovered Miss Brannen's body after spotting her limp upraised arm, which had been snagged in some bushes and was still visible above the seminary wall. Through cabaret cards found in her purse, detectives traced the victim to the Primrose, where they learned she had been in the company of Mrs. Armstrong and St. Claire as well as two other men. Mrs. Armstrong and St. Claire were located, and reluctantly gave details of the shooting. Less than two days later, two detectives intercepted Crowley and Duringer in the car speeding along a Bronx street. A three-mile chase ensued, but the fugitives shook off the pursuers in heavy traffic. The bullet-riddled car was found abandoned a few hours later. For the next several days, a series of robberies were credited to the pair, and Duringer then holed up in an apartment on Manhattan's West Side with one of Crowley's dance-hall girl friends, a twenty-one-year-old blonde named Irene ("Billie") Dunne. Crowley went off to see Helen Walsh, a six-teen-year-old Brooklyn redhead whom he had known for two years and to whom he had been intermittently engaged.

In the predawn hours of May 6, 1931, Crowley and Helen were sitting in a car in Nassau County when a police officer approached to ask to see Crowley's driver's license. Fearing he had been recognized, Crowley pulled a gun and shot the officer dead. He then fled back to Manhattan with Helen, and one report was that he forecast their arrival at Billie Dunne's apartment by telephoning to tell her: "You better clear out. I'm bringing a real girl home with me. You can go with Duringer." Although Billie already had become enamored of Duringer, her reaction was violent. Sometime that night she reportedly confided her feelings to friends at the Primrose, one of whom passed the information on Crowley's whereabouts to the police. On the afternoon of May 7, detectives arrived at the door of Billie's two-room apartment on the top floor of a five-story graystone building on West Ninetieth Street. Billie had gone out. Finding the door locked, the detectives ordered Crowley and Duringer to surrender. Crowley answered the demand by firing blasts through the door from two automatic pistols and the detectives made a tactical retreat to summon reinforcements. Eight ESD units were called out to aid a small army of policemen in laying siege to the building. As word spread, a crowd that eventually grew to ten thousand persons converged on the site.

The policemen attempted at first to flush Crowley from the apartment by firing tear-gas canisters through the rear windows, but as fast as the gas bombs were propelled into the apartment Crowley lobbed them back out again. The policemen then went to the roof of the building and used axes and sledge hammers to chop through the ceiling of the apartment and dump tear-gas grenades. Helen fled into a closet, and the pudgy Duringer tried to get in with her, but had to content himself with what cover the half-open closet door afforded. He had thrown three weapons out the window in a gesture of surrender, but the bombardment had little effect, if any, on Crowley's bravado. Out in the open, and braving the police fire, he kept blazing away at his would-be captors with two .38 pistols and a gun he had taken from the police officer he had killed. Barrage after barrage of pistol, rifle and submachine fire was poured into the apartment by policemen, who were forced by the unusual layout to direct the attack in such a way as to avoid the possibility that ricocheting bullets might deflect toward neighboring apartment buildings, where tenants were leaning from windows to watch the battle. The siege lasted for two full hours, during which Crowley incredibly managed to dash off a brief summation of his thoughts in a note that was later found in the apartment. Addressed to whom it might concern, it read in part: "When I die put a lily in my hand, let the boys know how they'll look. Underneath my coat will lay a weary kind heart that wouldn't harm anything. I hadn't nothing else to do. That's why I went around bumping off cops. It's the new sensation of the films."

Police finally unleashed a cataclysmic salvo and made a charge on the apartment, splintering the door with axes and crowbars. They found Crowley still on his feet and defiant. Out of ammunition and grazed by bullets three times in the thigh and once in the right wrist, he fired a stream of insults at his captors. "Well, at least you couldn't kill me," he snarled. His girl friend, Helen, who had fled the closet sometime during the shootout, perhaps because of an accumulation of tear-gas fumes there, cowered in one corner of the bullet-pocked bedroom, where she had been forced to take refuge because the hefty Duringer had appropriated all the room under the bed. Both bore cuts from flying bits of plaster and glass.

En route to the hospital in an ambulance, Crowley was found to have secreted two guns in his socks, the butts held tightly to his legs by his garters. He had some choice words for Billie Dunne. "She ratted on me," he said, "and I was darn good to her. I bought her everything she wanted. Her right name ain't Billie, anyway, it's Vera. I never was a squealer and I never will be."

Both Crowley and Duringer were swiftly tried and convicted, respectively, of the murders of the Nassau County police officer and the Brannen woman. Duringer went to the electric chair eight months later, complaining because the prison warden had chosen his twenty-sixth birthday as the date for the execution. On January 21, 1932, Crowley downed a hearty meal of T-bone steak, mashed potatoes, salad, rye bread, rhubarb, jello, bananas, chocolate, almonds, tea, milk and soda, and walked unflinchingly to the death chair, handing out cigars to death-house keepers on the way. Turning down a last-minute plea for a visit from Helen

Walsh—who had been the star state witness against Crowley at his trial—he explained, "I hear she's going with a cop."

Crowley's crazy flamboyance made him an almost warm and sympathetic character alongside professional killer August Robles, whom Walter Klotzback—one of the policemen cited for meritorious work in the Crowley shootout—once rated as the toughest barricaded criminal his men had ever faced. The forty-one-year-old Robles, whose maroon eyes were narrowed by a perpetual squint, more than compensated for his lack of flair with sheer deadliness. He outshone his two-gun predecessor in two respects: he was a four-gun man, and he made good his boast that the police would never take him alive.

Robles staged his last stand in February, 1955, while he was being sought in the Brooklyn ride slaying of a man who had been about to turn state's witness in the trial involving an attempted robbery of a policy banker in Baltimore—a case that bore overtones of police protection. Every policeman in the city, detective and officer alike, was part of the manhunt for the five-foot-six, 140-pound bespectacled fugitive, who had boasted to a barroom companion, "Any cop who tries to get me, I'll shoot. The only way they'll take me is dead."

The search, which included the random stopping of subway trains, emptying of movie theaters and the following up of numerous tips, was intensified even further, with the image of the Police Department at stake, after Robles managed to outwit would-be captors in two encounters by cunningly disarming three detectives and shooting his way to freedom in a battle with four others. The end for the fugitive came on the afternoon of February 20, after police received a tip that he was holed up in the apartment of two cousins in an East Harlem tenement. Not about to let Robles elude them again, six policemen, five of them detectives, went to the building and entered while ten others were deployed outside to cut off any escape attempt. The detectives, including Vincent J. Heffernan, who had been among the trio embarrassingly disarmed by Robles only three days before, took up positions outside the flat where Robles was reported to be hiding. When they pushed open the door, a burst of gunfire rang out, and Heffernan and another detective were wounded. The other detectives returned the fire, then retreated to carry the wounded men to safety. A call was sent out for reinforcements.

ESD trucks arrived with submachine guns and tear-gas bombs, and the Fire Department responded with hook-and-ladder and emergency equipment. Hundreds of police were rushed into the area and ambulances raced from nearby hospitals, attracting a crowd that numbered about 100,000 persons. Suited up in bullet-proof vests and helmets, the policemen took up positions on the roofs of buildings surrounding the tenement, weapons held at the ready. A squad of detectives entered the tenement and went to the corridor outside the Robles flat, where they assumed protected positions in the doorways of nearby apartments and commanded Robles to come out. Robles shouted, "Wait till I finish a letter." The police waited, but there was no move on Robles' part to surrender. Detectives fired a salvo through the door, and a volley of answering shots roared from the apartment. The siege was on. While Robles was kept occupied with gunfire from vantage posts in the corridor, the policemen fired rifles, machine guns and revolvers through the rear windows of the apartment from the rooftops of adjoining buildings. An ESD officer crouching low at the window of a fourth-floor apartment blasted a series of tear-gas bombs across a twenty-foot areaway into the window of Robles' apartment. Time and time again, police shouted through loudspeakers ordering Robles to give up, but the fugitive dashed defiantly through the apartment to return gunfire coming at him from all sides. More than an hour after the battle had begun, the explosion of a tear-gas bomb set fire to the flat. The flames spread quickly. Firemen moved in to pour water on the blaze, and Robles was driven toward the rear bedroom windows by smoke and flames and the hail of bullets pouring down from nearby rooftops. He tried a final ruse by shouting for a priest, but the police answer was another shouted order for him to surrender, which he ignored. Suddenly, shots from the besieged fugitive ceased.

A team of police burst into the apartment, which was charred by fire, soaked by water, splintered by bullets—and stained with Robles' blood. Robles, barefoot and clad in a blood-soaked undershirt and brown trousers, lay sprawled on the floor of the back bedroom, a gaping hole in his chest. His head, resting on a pair of woman's slippers, was partially under the lower of two bunk beds built against the wall. His eyeglasses still were on. Above the dresser was a religious calendar with a picture of Christ. A diamond ring glittered on his left hand, and toppled on its side on the floor near the body lay a toy ambulance.

The confusion of all-out gun battles sometimes mercifully blurs individual responsibility for the act of taking a human life. Vastly more soul-searing are man-to-man encounters such as the one in Brooklyn's Coney Island on the night of August 31, 1962, when ESD Officer Herbert Nolan, thirty-five years old and the father of two young girls, strode slowly down a dimly lighted street for a showdown with death.

The small but wiry policeman looked for all the world like a miniature war tank on legs. His head was completely encased in a turretlike helmet of steel armor plate with a narrow slit in front to give him forward vision. Girding his torso was a bulletproof vest—a crinkly canvas shield not unlike a baseball catcher's chest protector but loaded with bullet-stopping material. As Nolan lumbered out of the darkness, a group of late-working young girls in blue-and-white uniforms peered cautiously from the windows of a nearby factory building standing amid wooden bathhouses lining the street. They recoiled at the sight of his monsterlike figure.

It was 11:08 P.M. Behind Nolan the necklaces of lights silhouetting the rides at Coney Island's amusement park glistened against the night sky. Hurly-burly sounds of the midway echoed faintly in the distance above the roar of Atlantic Ocean surf pounding on the nearby beach. Ahead, crouched in the shadows behind a fire hydrant, was a madman firing two guns. Nolan could hear the whine of bullets ricocheting off the pavement around him and the fire his fellow officers were directing against the gunman. His pace was unbroken, even though, in his seven years of service on New York City's police force, Nolan had never killed a man.

Only forty minutes earlier, the goateed gunman, John ("Puck") Clark, twenty-seven, an itinerant guitarist with a reputation as a troublemaker, had stormed into the neighborhood in a fit of rage. He was bent on avenging a beating he had suffered at the hands of local residents after he had reportedly assaulted and robbed the landlady of a nearby boardinghouse where he had been living for a time. The landlady's leg was fractured in the attack, and Clark had vacated his room and disappeared. When he returned a short time later, he was set upon by an angry mob.

Crazed by desires for revenge, Clark approached a young woman outside the boardinghouse and apparently recognized for a split second that she had once provided him with food and money when he was penniless. He threw his arms around her in a momentary gesture of affection and then, inexplicably, drew a gun from his pocket and fired a single shot into the back of her head. As she fell, Clark, a polio victim who wore a brace on one leg, hobbled into the boardinghouse and fired a bullet into the shoulder of the landlady's husband as he lay sleeping in a ground-floor room. When the landlady went to her husband's side, Clark attempted to shoot her but the gun misfired twice. He then, with amazing agility, climbed out a bathroom window to the street and fired two random shots at a young couple, wounding both. He ducked into an alleyway alongside the boardinghouse and limped through the darkness to the boardwalk, where he saw two uniformed police officers standing together talking before setting out on their final rounds of the night. Both men had their backs to Clark and neither saw him as he crept up from behind and fired two shots in rapid succession into the backs of their heads. One fell dead, the other was mortally wounded. Clark bent down and slipped two .38-caliber service revolvers from the officers' holsters, tucking his own gun into his belt. When he straightened up, he saw that a crowd had been attracted by the shooting and was rushing toward him. Clark began firing wildly, and the crowd veered and ran for safety. An off-duty rookie policeman fought his way through the stampeding mob and drew his gun to start after the killer. Clark pegged a shot that knocked the revolver from the man's hand, and the officer dived for cover. The reports of shots brought other police swarming into the neighborhood as mounted officers assigned to the area shielded panicked passers-by with their horses and herded them out of the line of fire. Clark hobbled along the boardwalk toward the amusement park, wheeling at times to fire on policemen closing in on him. In an attempt to escape, the guitarist dragged himself over the boardwalk railing and tumbled into the sand. Struggling to his feet, he doubled back under the wooden planking and headed inland. When he came out from

under the boardwalk, police radio cars pinned him in their spotlights. Clark realized that he was trapped and hurled himself behind the fire hydrant to shoot it out with his would-be captors.

Now Officer Nolan was stalking toward a final confrontation
with the killer, tracing the flashes from the two guns in the darkness. It took Nolan two minutes to walk nearly 150 feet through
a hail of bullets to within twenty feet of his target, close enough
to see the killer's trigger fingers frantically squeezing off one shot
after another. Nolan raised his .38-caliber Smith & Wesson revolver and took aim. One bullet crashed into Clark's face and four
tore into his chest. Clark toppled forward into a mud puddle. The
siege was over. Nolan walked slowly back to the truck where he
had suited up for the battle. When he pulled off his helmet, his red
hair was matted to his forehead with sweat.

"I often wondered what it would feel like to kill a man," he
whispered to fellow officers gathered around him.

Then someone showed Nolan the hat that had belonged to the
policeman who was killed. There was a bullet hole in the sweat-
band and blood on the crown. Nolan passed his hand across his
mouth, turned his back and walked away. He was later awarded
one of the department's highest decorations for heroism.

A new and traumatic element was injected into shootouts during the late 1960s when embattled gunmen turned increasingly to
the use of hostages as pawns in showdowns with police. The phenomenon, rare in the ESD's early days, first gained currency with
the airplane hijackings that began in 1961.

"Hostage-taking is one of the toughest problems," explains Deputy Inspector Arthur A. Freeman, who devoted five years of his
twenty-one-year police career almost exclusively to an in-depth
study of the problem for the ESD (before his retirement in late
1973, to become a roving consultant on hostage incidents). "But
it is manageable. It can be handled successfully when the plans
for combating it are carefully and thoroughly thought out in advance."

Freeman, a large, husky man whose quiet, easy manner and
all-pervasive calm belie his role as the nemesis of desperate gunmen, breaks down hostage-takers into four general categories:
the psychopath, who views the hostages as tools to bolster his
helpless state and as a weapon of reprisal against a world he feels

has treated him unfairly; the militant, who employs human pawns to dramatize his social and political grievances in hopes of enforcing changes; the terrorist, who seizes hostages to barter for ransom and other demands; and the trapped criminal, who uses them to aid escape.

"Sometimes the lines are not quite that clear-cut," Freeman says. "Motives overlap, and ways of dealing with these incidents must be tailored in some respects to the needs of each individual situation."

Understandably reluctant to reveal the specifics of the various contingency plans worked out with psychologists and police personnel since intensive exploration of the hostage problem started in 1969, Freeman says the hallmarks of all are patience, restraint, a tightly disciplined and highly trained containment force of policemen and flexibility in negotiations to win release of the hostages.

"The one thing to avoid is creating a sense of hopelessness in the perpetrators," Freeman says. "Where there is a sense of futility, a feeling that there is no way out, desperate men are driven to desperate acts. You can turn a man into a paranoid schizophrenic in an instant if the pressure is too great. And a man in this situation will do one of two things. Either he will express his frustration inwardly by commiting suicide, or worse still, express it outwardly by commiting homicide against the hostages or the police.

"We know their goals, and we also know their frustrations. In any siege, we naturally are their chief frustration. The police are the immediate barrier that stands between the perpetrators and their goals. The outcome therefore depends a great deal on how that barrier is presented, whether it is too tight, too loose, and above all whether it is firmly and uniformly coordinated. We strive for unity and command control.

"To maintain that control, all units remain in radio contact with each other, hold their fire until ordered, and non-ESD units are in on this too, so that there is absolutely no individual action. No ESD policeman fires unless he is directed to do so by the supervising officer. The firing is controlled to prevent dangerous cross fire and ricochets, which might jeopardize civilians or the men involved in the operation itself. Any order to fire at will is given only in sniper cases, and then solely to those units that have a clear view of the gunman or his hiding place."

The politics or ideology of barricaded gunmen plays no part in the ESD's thinking. "No matter who the perpetrators are or what they are," Freeman says, "the response is the same—contain the perpetrators, evacuate civilians and control the fire power."

The strategies have met with unqualified success. In all calls involving defiant criminals and psychopaths, armed shooters and snipers in one recent year, the perpetrators were extricated, removed and disarmed by the ESD without a single shot being fired. The statistics show that the ferocity of more widely publicized shootouts is hardly typical of most, which end peacefully with the policemen talking crazed gunmen into surrender even while facing them at point-blank range.

The most brilliant accomplishment along these lines began on the rainy evening of Friday, January 19, 1973, after four men invaded a sporting goods store in Brooklyn's Williamsburg section. The men took thirteen persons hostage after their planned holdup was aborted when an employee pressed a silent alarm button, bringing police radio cars from three surrounding precincts racing to the store.

By the time Freeman reached the scene, a forty-minute gun battle already had transpired between the police and the trapped gunmen, who had armed themselves with high-powered rifles from the store's shelves. One policeman was dead, two others wounded and six pinned down by gunfire on the rain-soaked street in front of the store. The dead policeman was ESD Officer Stephen R. Gilroy, a seven-year veteran of the force, who had been scheduled for promotion to sergeant within a few weeks as a reward for excellence. He was killed by a single bullet in the head as he crouched behind an elevated-train pillar outside the store, awaiting a chance to get a clear shot at the gunmen.

Gilroy and Officer Brian A. Tuohy had arrived in the first ESD vehicle within ten minutes after the holdup alarm was transmitted. Five minutes later, ESD Lieutenant Edward P. Haddican arrived with Officer Gilbert C. Grape and ordered Gilroy, Tuohy, Grape and other policemen to don bulletproof vests and move into containment positions across the street from the store. Gilroy was killed and the other officers wounded when the gunmen attempted to shoot their way to freedom.

ESD marksmen then unleashed a withering barrage of fire at the store entrance while fellow policemen scrambled into the street to retrieve Gilroy's body and drag the injured men to safety. The shots were the last to be fired by the ESD for the remainder of the episode, which lasted forty-seven hours and held the city and the entire nation in the grip of suspense.

Freeman's carefully drawn plans were immediately executed on his arrival and the goals were threefold—to contain the premises, to control the fire power and to rescue the policemen still pinned down in the street as well as fifty persons trapped in nearby stores and exposed to the line of fire.

Teams of sharpshooters, clad in bulletproof vests and armed with high-powered telescopic rifles, ringed the store at ten containment posts. Orders were barked over a bullhorn directing all non-ESD policemen out of the immediate area. The policemen under fire in the street were assured that help was on the way. While isolated bursts of gunfire roared repeatedly from the store in angry response to police pleas that the gunmen surrender, there was no answering fire.

To evacuate the stranded policemen and civilians, the ESD called for an emergency rescue ambulance—a twenty-one-ton Army personnel carrier that had been purchased in the fall of 1968 at the height of antiwar street demonstrations but never used. The vehicle was rushed into the area on a flatbed trailer. With ESD Officers Oswaldo Damiani and Raymond Bordonaro at the controls and Joseph Manzo and Leo Griffin crouching on the protected side, the armor-plated vehicle entered the line of fire and all six policemen under siege in the street were walked to safety. The fifty persons trapped in nearby stores were similarly rescued. The carrier was hit forty times by bullets but no one was injured.

The rescue ambulance then moved to block the store's front entrance, but could not be maneuvered into position because an abandoned police car obstructed its path. To remove the obstacle, ESD Officer Joseph Cochran darted twenty-five feet in direct view of the store while fellow officers covered him with guns. Crawling into the passenger side of the car, Cochran lay on his stomach with his head down near the driver's door and reached up to turn on the ignition. With one hand pressing the accelerator and the other clutching the steering wheel, he blindly drove the vehicle clear before leaping out and running back to cover behind a brick wall. The rescue ambulance then rumbled to within a few feet of the store entrance to block the escape route.

When asked later if the ordeal had frightened him, Cochran said, "To be perfectly frank, I didn't think about it. Believe me, I'm not trying to make light of it; it's my job. But what I really was worried about was that I would have an accident and block the street worse."

Up to this point there had been no communication with the gunmen, although police had learned there were four of them from one hostage who had managed to escape during the initial exchange of gunfire. It was not until a bullhorn was thrown to the sidewalk in front of the store and retrieved by a hostage that police discovered the gunmen were militant blacks and that one of them had been critically wounded.

Inside an insurance agency across the street that had been set up as a temporary police command post, Freeman stood amid the paper-littered desks conferring with Police Commissioner Patrick V. Murphy, and Chief Inspector Michael J. Codd and Chief of Patrol Donald F. Cawley, both of whom were later to succeed Murphy as police commissioner. Deputy Chief Inspector Simon Eisdorfer joined in lengthy discussions about possible use of several "game plans" that had been developed by the ESD and other departmental units to rescue hostages. The project had been under way since the previous summer as the result of a Brooklyn bank robbery in which two men held eight persons hostage for fifteen hours and demanded safe conduct to Kennedy International Airport and a plane to fly them to Algeria. One of the men, it later turned out, was an admitted homosexual who had planned the holdup to obtain money for a sex-change operation for his boyfriend. The policemen withheld their fire during that siege rather than risk lives, and the gunmen had succeeded in forcing authorities to transport them with the hostages to Kennedy in a small van driven by an FBI agent. The incident ended dramatically as the car approached the waiting jetliner at Kennedy and the FBI agent, pulling out a gun hidden in his sock, whirled and shot one of the gunmen as other agents rushed the vehicle and captured the second bandit. All the hostages escaped unharmed.

Since that time, the "game plans" had been practiced for months in a bare, run-down room at the Floyd Bennett training school, where specially chosen policemen playacted armed robberies, seizing hostages and getting trapped while other officers watched and studied the proceedings for future use.

ESD commanders also had painstakingly reviewed the grim lessons, only two weeks before, of a wild two-day gun battle with a sniper atop an eighteen-story motel in New Orleans that ended in death for five civilians and four policemen and injury for at least fifteen persons. Six of the wounded were policemen struck by ricocheting bullets fired by fellow officers.

"We learned a lot from their mistakes," one ESD policeman said.

Rather than endanger the lives of the hostages and police personnel, Freeman and his superiors decided to shelve the "game plan" indefinitely in favor of a longer and more arduous attempt to persuade the gunmen to surrender peacefully. As Freeman was to comment later: "The public sometimes gets the impression that we're at a standstill in these situations. But we're not. The point is we take everything very easily, one small step after another. We often don't look like we're making any progress when we're actually going ahead by leaps and bounds."

For a time, it appeared that the agonizing decision might backfire and encourage the gunmen, bolstered by the huge supply of guns and ammunition and the prize bartering point of the hostages, to turn the siege into an almost endless standoff.

Throughout the night, two black Moslem ministers, a black clergyman and a civil-rights lawyer summoned to establish better rapport addressed surrender appeals to the gunmen from the rescue ambulance as it rumbled back and forth in front of the store entrance. One Moslem priest eventually was permitted inside the store by the gunmen, but their determination was unwavering. All vowed that they would "go to Paradise" rather than give up.

The first break in the stalemate came when the cornered men asked for food and for medical attention for their wounded comrade. Although reluctant to supply food, which could nourish the gunmen's resistance and prolong the impasse, police nevertheless relented out of consideration for the hostages, and even passed in cigarettes. The request for a doctor was considered far more significant since it provided an important clue that the policy of nonviolence was correct.

"They insisted that they were willing to die and go to Paradise," Freeman remarked later. "But the demand for a physician was the tip-off that they weren't really all that willing. That's why they wanted a doctor—to save the wounded man from going to Paradise."

Medical help was promised at first only on the condition that two of the hostages carry the wounded man out to the sidewalk. The ploy failed, but over the next few hours the gunmen freed two hostages in a conciliatory move, convincing Freeman and others that they actually were not the fanatics they professed to be. Police psychologists were called in to confirm the theory and the hastily gathered "think tank" consulted on all subsequent tactics. When the despairing gunmen severed all communications at one point by tossing the bullhorn and a walkie-talkie from the store in disgust, a black doctor was allowed to enter and minister to the wounded man.

Hopes that the gesture would soften the gunmen's stand were soon dashed when the nerve-racking test of wills was renewed and gunfire was the only reply to further surrender appeals, prompting one policeman to conclude, "Guns may be the answer that will finally prevail."

There was some discussion of the feasibility of routing the men from the store with tear gas, but the idea was discarded in fear that the projectiles might ignite and detonate gunpowder and other explosive chemicals, with disastrous consequences. Tear-gas grenades currently used by the ESD are designed to generate heat on impact to prevent besieged criminals from tossing them away or back at police.

Meanwhile, the two released hostages as well as the co-owner of the store, who had escaped during the initial gunfire, were questioned intensively about conditions inside the store—the physical layout and the position of the hostages and the gunmen—and a decision was made to assemble equipment for an assault on the structure in the event that the gunmen started shooting the hostages or attempted to break for freedom by using them as shields.

Tentative plans called for encircling the building with a barbed-wire barrier and then storming it from four different directions so that the gunmen could not possibly cover all the areas of attack. A bulldozer was to crash through a side entrance while the rescue ambulance rammed into the front and a fire department cherry picker dropped policemen to the roof. For additional shock effect, a crane was to swing a heavy demolition ball against the walls of the building.

Still another approach considered was a fast breakthrough to the hostages through the wall of an adjoining furniture warehouse. By a strange fluke, this was the idea that led to a resolution of the impasse.

ESD Lieutenant Stanley Carris began deploying the barbed-wire barrier while Captain Dennis Healy and two other policemen, who were experienced in construction and demolition, slipped into a building two doors away from the sporting goods store to chop through the far wall of the furniture warehouse in a dress-rehearsal test to determine how much time would be required to make an actual passage through the wall nearest the store. The far wall was chosen for the test so as not to panic the gunmen. As Healy and his companions smashed through the wall with drills, sledge hammers, crowbars and wire cutters, the puzzled criminals, hearing the strange but distant noises, ran to investigate their origin, leaving the hostages unguarded. One of the captives—the other co-owner of the store—grasped the opportunity to uncover an escape route. With the gunmen gone and their wounded accomplice powerless to interfere, the store owner ripped away plasterboard covering a hidden and long-abandoned stairway in the ninety-year-old building and led the other hostages up to the roof. A ladder was lowered from the top of a nearby building, enabling the hostages to complete their escape. It was fully five minutes before the gunmen discovered to their dismay that the balance of power in the battle had tipped against them. Within less than two hours, after they were assured that no reprisals would be taken against them, the trapped men surrendered without a single shot being fired.

When asked later about the bizarre turn of events that had provided the long-awaited solution to the crisis, Freeman said, "Undoubtedly we were lucky, but it was more than luck. We created the conditions to be lucky. After taking all the necessary steps, when the break developed we were in a position to take instant advantage of it."

Three days after the siege, Eisdorfer, then chief of the Bureau of Special Operations, met with the officers involved to conduct a critique of the operation in the presence of Dr. Harvey Schlossberg, a police officer who is a consulting psychologist and had acted as a key adviser on the shootout strategy. The session produced many recommendations. One called for the training by department psychologists of a certain number of detectives and high-caliber police personnel to carry out negotiations with hostage-takers. Another suggested the formation of think tanks in each precinct to devise ways of dealing with similar situations. A third advised improvements in assembling and servicing the special equipment used during the siege, including cutting down the time needed to fuel the rescue ambulance.

After the policemen finished criticizing the shortcomings of the operation, Schlossberg was asked to render his opinion. The psychologist said that the siege had been discussed the night before at a seminar he had attended at the Psychoanalytic Institute.

"They came up with unanimous approbation of the operation and an expression that it was the most professional operation they had ever seen," Schlossberg said. "There was no shooting by the police; nobody was injured after the initial operation, and the police acted under great restraint even though one of their members was killed and two were wounded."

Wholeheartedly agreeing with his colleagues that police had followed the wisest course in deferring an all-out attack, Schlossberg observed, "It gives you an opportunity to come up with strange things like the owner leading the hostages to the roof while the gunmen were being distracted by the digging and tunneling."

The psychologist summed up his evaluation by saying, "It worked excellently. I personally feel it was an excellent job."

3. Jumpers..

Combating the bombs and bullets of overt violence is a harrowing task for Emergency Service policemen but no more hair-raising than the job of calming the inner mayhem of desperate human beings who scale bridge superstructures and mount building ledges determined to kill themselves.

In a sense, armed criminals are far more manageable than the suicidal, whose tortured aberrations are born in an emotional no man's land of conflict and uncertainty. The dangers are particularly acute when neurotic jumpers develop macabre desires to drag would-be rescuers along with them to death.

Apartment houses, hotels, hospitals and office skyscrapers throughout the city provide innumerable staging platforms for persons intent on self-destruction, and many of the structures are relics of bygone eras, with richly ornate façades and labyrinthine architectural designs that create all kinds of obstacles to rescue attempts.

In the early days, the ESD relied on saving would-be jumpers by talking them back to safety, by lassoing them or by sending a policeman down in a bos'n's chair, rope harness or Morrissey belt to overpower them. While talk succeeded on some occasions, the entrapment techniques were less effective because all demanded an accuracy and split-second timing that allowed for no margin of error. A jumper seeing a lariat or a harnessed policeman spinning toward him had ample opportunity to carry out his death threat.

The problems were tragically illustrated by the ESD's failure to prevent a sensational suicide plunge by John William Warde, an obscure twenty-five-year-old bank clerk who staged a lonely eleven-hour death vigil on a seventeenth-floor ledge of the Hotel Gotham in midtown Manhattan.

The Warde case, which attracted worldwide attention and later was recounted in a classic *New Yorker* magazine series and a motion picture, began at eleven-forty on the morning of July 26, 1938, when the clerk, who had a history of mental illness and two suicide attempts, stepped onto the ledge outside his room at the hotel, where he was staying with his married sister and her husband after returning with them to the city from Chicago. The slender, dark-haired man stood rooted to the eighteen-inch ledge, 160 feet above the street, rejecting frantic pleas by his relatives, police and a priest from nearby Saint Patrick's Cathedral. Newspapers and radio stations put out the story casually at first, then in increasing volume, and within a few hours, ten thousand persons jammed the streets around the hotel as the ESD mapped rescue strategies.

Warde's peculiarly sheltered position on the ledge made any attempt at the rescue methods then in use hopeless. He was shielded from approach on either side by huge architectural colonnades running up the building's face. The ornamental ledge just above his head ruled out any chance of dropping ropes around him, and the hotel's heavy cornice, four stories above, overhung too far for anyone in a bos'n's chair or Morrissey belt to swing close enough without being visible long before.

Hours dragged by as a steady effort was kept up to coax Warde to come in, but toward late afternoon, the ESD began implementing plans for a desperate gamble to save him. A twenty-by-forty-foot cargo-salvage net was borrowed from the U.S. Coast Guard station on Staten Island and rushed to the hotel. Darkness was setting in by the time it arrived, and the scene was garishly illuminated by police searchlights and the brilliant magnesium flares of newsreel camera crews. The net was hauled up to the hotel's sixteenth floor on ropes lowered from windows on either side of Warde and from buildings across the street, and an ESD officer and a fireman donned life belts to prepare for a descent from above. A police sergeant was stationed with a field telephone in the steeple of nearby Fifth Avenue Presbyterian Church to watch Warde through binoculars and signal the appropriate moment for the net to be stretched out and the rescuers to drop on the youth in tandem. All seemed to be proceeding smoothly when a ghastly hitch developed in the elaborate rescue plan. The cumbersome net sagged against a chunk of masonry jutting from the hotel's façade twenty-five feet below Warde, and efforts to spread it failed. Warde suddenly sensed what was happening and turned to a policeman leaning from a window near him. "I've made up my mind," he said. He took a final puff on the last of innumerable cigarettes he had smoked during the day, and instead of crushing it underfoot on the ledge as he invariably had done before, he tossed the butt down into the street. Seconds later, at exactly 10:38 P.M., Warde summoned up his courage and leaped from the ledge. His body sailed past the net, which still hung limply and only partially open, and hurtled downward, grazed a ledge at the eighth-floor level and spun over to crash through the hotel's marquee. When he struck the sidewalk, he was killed instantly.

Stunned by the tragedy, Inspector Henry Malley, then the ESD's commander, the very next day issued orders to his men to suggest ideas for a device that would avert a recurrence of the rescue failure. The response was a raft of diagrams from ESD members. After an intensive study of such factors as the velocity and impacting force of falling bodies, the physical properties of various kinds of rope and the best possible rigging methods, a suicide net was designed incorporating the best features of many plans submitted. The net was woven by a group of men from the Harbor Unit, all former seamen with an expert knowledge of ropework. The work was considered a cooperative effort, and no individual was given credit.

The net consisted of 3,200 feet of three-strand, quarter-inch manila rope woven into a webbing of four-inch-square mesh, and bordered on all four sides by one hundred feet of three-quarter-inch rope. The length was kept to thirty feet to provide the maximum coverage of area without making the net too unwieldy to be maneuvered quickly into position, and the width of twenty-five feet was arrived at on the theory that no one could broad-jump far enough from a standing start to clear it.

The net underwent strenuous experiments, which were conducted at first at a downtown Manhattan police station—a three-story structure that was tailor made for the operation because of its numerous windows. Policemen spent long, bruising hours leaping from the station-house windows into the outstretched net, and staged drills in rigging it to meet every conceivable jumper situation. The net was next taken for a strength test to Randalls Island, in the East River off Manhattan, where a two-hundred-pound sand dummy was dropped into it from the overpass of the Triborough Bridge—a height of one hundred feet. The dummy impacted at a force of twenty thousand pounds, but the net withstood the strain nicely.

For rigging purposes, a number of accessories were invented to set the net up at ground level or extend it from a building wall beneath a ledge or window. After further tests, two other nets were constructed and all were deployed to strategic points in the city. The nets quickly proved their worth by saving the lives of two persons leaping from low levels, but the crowning achievement came six years later, on August 22, 1944.

In a tenth-floor apartment at the El Dorado—a fashionable twenty-nine-story apartment house on upper Central Park West—Mrs. Samuel Guttner, a housewife, awoke that day troubled over the strange and brooding behavior of her maid.

The maid, Denise Thomas, thirty-five, a black woman from Harlem, had come to her five weeks earlier to help with the household chores four days a week, and three weeks later Mrs. Guttner had given her a live-in job after hearing her complain repeatedly of loneliness and of having no one with whom to talk over her troubles. The first few days had gone well, but then eerie things began happening. Denise confided to Mrs. Guttner that evil people were chasing her and shadowing her in the streets and that she suspected a plot was afoot to put her in prison. The maid's moods grew more and more morose, and she spent long periods brooding alone and staring down into a pebbled courtyard from the window of a small bedroom Mrs. Guttner had assigned her. For several days, she had not eaten.

Mrs. Guttner went to the maid's bedroom to check on her and found her still in a depressed state. "Denise, if you aren't feeling well, I'll clean house," she said cheerfully, and set about straightening up the apartment. The maid sulked in silence. Toward midmorning, Mrs. Guttner suggested that Denise go with her to see a physician, and she left the apartment to get her car. Minutes later, she returned to discover that the maid had locked herself in her bedroom. Mrs. Guttner rattled the locked door and begged Denise to come out, but the maid refused, crying out that she would rather die and that she was going to jump from the window. "I just can't get myself together," the maid whimpered. "I feel miserable."

After more attempts to soothe Denise and to persuade her to open the door, Mrs. Guttner ran to the telephone and called the police. She blurted out hurried answers to a police communications bureau operator's questions about the sex and age of the threatened jumper, her location and the type and height of the building involved. The information was relayed instantly to the ESD.

Within minutes, ESD vehicles, with sirens deliberately silenced as part of a now carefully rehearsed plan to deal with such emergencies, arrived quietly in front of the massive yellow brick apartment house. More than thirty policemen fanned out through the building, lugging rescue equipment and keeping out of view as much as possible to avoid arousing alarm.

In the Guttner apartment, policemen surveyed the situation and ruled out forcing the maid's bedroom door in fear that she might jump. Mrs. Guttner was encouraged to keep up her conversation with the distraught woman, and police coached her in what to say.

"I have to go out," Mrs. Guttner pleaded at one point. "I have an appointment. Please don't let me miss it."

The maid did not answer.

"Denise, you've been in there hours now. Stop this nonsense," Mrs. Guttner demanded. "What are you doing in there?"

"Nothing," Denise said in an almost inaudible whisper.

"If you're not doing anything, why don't you let me in? I want to make you happy; let me hold your hand. Come on out and I'll fix some tea for you."

"I'm trying to get myself together," the maid replied.

"Then get yourself together," Mrs. Guttner said. "You can't do it with the door locked. Now, Denise, I won't stand for this. I'm going to call the police."

Throughout the conversation, policemen were busy rigging rescue equipment in apartments above and below Mrs. Guttner's as neighbors, attracted by the commotion, hung out of windows surrounding the courtyard to watch. The maid was observed through her bedroom window combing her hair, powdering her nose and slipping into a good dress. The rescuers worked in smoothly coordinated teams, out of sight of each other but linked by communications through field telephone lines strung between the various apartments. Each team heard the others' voices but would not see them until after the rescue operation was complete. The work proceeded quietly, with the men taking elaborate care not to shout or bang equipment against walls or floors to create a clamor that might alert the maid.

In an apartment above Mrs. Guttner's, ESD Officer Maurice J. Barrett was chosen for his lightness of weight and muscular build to descend to the window of the maid's bedroom by rope. Barrett donned a Morrissey life belt, a heavy leather-and-canvas girdle with steel snap hooks attached to its sides. A sergeant measured the distance between the floor and ceiling inside the apartment to determine how far Barrett would have to drop, and marked off equal lengths on two three-quarter-inch manila ropes that were attached to the snap hooks on Barrett's belt. The other ends of the lowering lines, one a reserve to rescue Barrett in case the other broke, were anchored to pipes inside the apartment. Metal guards were attached to the windowsill to prevent chafing of the ropes. While Barrett checked out a built-in rope-braking mechanism on his belt that would help him control the rate of his descent, ESD Officer Harry Hammond was rigged in similar equipment in a ninth-floor room overlooking the courtyard.

Meanwhile, the rolled-up eighty-pound net was lifted from a canvas bag and positioned on a windowsill. Guy lines of three-quarter-inch manila rope were passed by policemen in adjoining windows and affixed with snap hooks to fifteen-inch-long loops protruding from both sides of the net roll. In another apartment, below Mrs. Guttner's, teams of policemen finished the task of screwing together sections of one-and-a-half-inch steel pipes.

Across the courtyard, crouched near the window of an apartment, a police sergeant observed the operation and was kept abreast of its progress through a field telephone on the floor beside him. When all was ready, the sergeant gave a signal and the net burst outward from the window, spreading rapidly as the guy lines attached to it pulled taut. Simultaneously, from the dining room and kitchen windows below, two twenty-foot steel pipes emerged like giant javelins and speared through the three-inch metal rings that bordered both sides of the net at five-foot intervals. The net was then lowered to a horizontal position, forming a wide hammock below the maid's window.

The net was no sooner spread than Barrett mounted the windowsill above, and shrieks went up from neighbors watching from nearby windows and from spectators in the courtyard below. Inside the Guttner apartment, policemen had crashed through the maid's bedroom door to overpower her, but the hysterical woman had fled into a small bathroom, slammed and locked its steel door and climbed out onto the narrow windowsill.

The scene suddenly took on the atmosphere of a psychopathic ward, with the maid crying hysterically, policemen leaning from nearby windows and shouting, and the screams of spectators echoing and reechoing through the courtyard. Denise sat down on the windowsill, dangling her legs 100 feet above the ground, with the net swinging crazily below her like a gallows rope.

"Everybody thinks I'm crazy, but I'm not," she cried to the crowd. Then, surveying the scene around her with wild eyes, she pleaded, "What I need is a doctor. Get me a doctor."

When policemen outside the bathroom door shouted back to assure her that a doctor had arrived and was waiting inside the apartment, the maid screamed angrily, "Doctors all say I'm a freak. I tell them all I need is a little kindness. I'm not crazy."

As the frenzied and disjointed exchange continued, Barrett started his descent, but Hammond waited behind the curtained window directly overlooking the net. The maid, hearing noises, gazed up to see Barrett swinging in midair above her. She stood up on the windowsill, frantically looking for a way to escape. Finding none, she leaped into space as a great gasp went up from the crowd.

Her body arched slightly backward, bouncing into the net with a muffled, straining thud, and the crowd roared with relief when it realized the net had held. Hammond sprang from the window where he had been waiting and vaulted into the net to confront the flailing woman. Barrett plummeted to join in the rescue, and a wild battle broke out before the hysterical maid was wrestled across the undulating net and lifted through a window into a room where other policemen were waiting to grab her. After the woman ceased struggling and was calmed by police, she was allowed to sip a glass of water and to smoke a cigarette with trembling fingers before she was driven in a radio car to a nearby hospital for a physical examination. She later was transferred to the psychiatric ward at Bellevue Hospital for observation.

Back at the apartment house, scattered remnants of the crowd that had witnessed the rescue watched as ESD policemen dismantled the net and other equipment in a mood of quiet jubilation. The events of the day had marked the first time in the city's history that a person leaping from such a height had been saved by the suicide net and proved that the device could be used to prevent a death plunge such as Warde's.

Several improvements were made in the nets and the techniques of using them. Primary consideration was given to assembling a net on the ground, and nowadays this net always is set up first as a precautionary measure. When both nets are up, the ground webbing acts as a reserve in case the wall net fails to do the job.*

When erected at ground level, the net is suspended from U-shaped prongs atop four twenty-foot-high poles by means of thick loops woven into its corners. The bases of the poles fit over upright fifteen-inch-long tapered bronze shafts that are embedded in heavy metal traffic stanchions to provide secure footing. The undersides of the stanchions are especially cut for traction and all rest on small rope mats for further nonskid stability. The poles are raised to a vertical position with the net by teams of policemen tugging on guy lines attached to the net's corners with snap hooks. The hooks eliminate the necessity for time-consuming tying of knots and the danger of fashioning unsafe knots in darkness, and the guy lines prevent the net's collapse if the loops should work off the U-shaped prongs.

* Diagrams of wall net and ground net appear in Appendix C and Appendix D.

Under current procedures, a team of sixteen policemen can rig the ground net within five to ten minutes, but fewer men can do the job if necessary by raising half the net at a time. Four guy lines usually are tied down to steady the poles while other pulling lines are left free so they can be manipulated to regulate the tension and sway in the net as the poles bend inward with the weight of a falling body when it strikes the mesh.

When experience showed that considerable strength and leverage were required to shove the wall-net poles outward with the weight of the net on them, handles in the form of L-shaped bars were devised to insert into the ends of the shafts. Each handle is manned by two policemen and locks into the windowsill as an anchor once the pole is fully extended.

To avoid the risk of the jumper's slipping through the space between the inner edge of the net and the building façade, four-foot sections of one-and-a-quarter-inch pipes are rigged with hooks that snap onto the net's border. The bars hold the net trim to the wall when lashed to moorings inside. When no suitable anchorages are available, ladders are jammed between ceiling and floor inside the apartment for the purpose of lashing down the bars and holding main and guy lines. To prevent snarling and to leave its corner loops accessible for opening the net, a special procedure was established for folding the webbing in four sections with both ends rolled toward the middle. Signals by whistle, or by blinking flashlight after dark, were devised to alert rigging crews on when to extend the wall net, and walkie-talkies later were added to the communications system.

When necessary, the net can be dropped down a building façade and pulled in by policemen at windows with boat hooks to enmesh a jumper against the wall. In narrow courtyards, it can be folded in half or quarter sections and strung from windows or fire escapes. Teams of thirty to fifty policemen also are trained to hold the net by hand to catch jumpers in the event that there is no time to complete standard rigging procedures.

The most spectacular test for the nets did not occur until after the ESD began experimenting in 1965 with nylon construction instead of the traditional rope, which was found to deteriorate with use. The first nylon nets were reduced in size to twenty by twenty-five feet to make them easier and faster to handle, and were designed and manufactured by ESD Officer Blaise Sciame. Sciame took on the job himself to save on labor costs when commercial contractors insisted on charging eight hundred dollars for each net, though the price of materials was only two hundred dollars. While nylon greatly increased the strength of the nets and made them lighter and more durable, it also gave them more bounce—a factor that posed hazards to persons hurtling from great heights. The nightmarish vision of a jumper striking the net only to be catapulted upward and dashed to the ground gave police technicians some anxious moments, but the problem more or less solved itself.

Since the net was pretested to safely catch a two-hundred-pound person plunging from a height of only six floors, the ESD was understandably concerned about how well it would work when it was called out on April 10, 1967, to save a twenty-year-old youth threatening to leap from nearly three times that height.

Shortly after ten o'clock on that morning, two New York City Housing Authority policemen were sent to change the lock on the door of an apartment occupied by a young man named John Wilkins, in the John Adams Houses, a low-income complex in the southeast Bronx. Wilkins had been holed up in the three-room apartment for several weeks since the death of his mother and had been told that he was not a legal tenant and must get out voluntarily or face eviction. The bereaved youth argued in vain with housing officials to have the ruling changed, then stubbornly refused to leave and ignored several eviction warnings sent to him by mail. When the policemen rang the doorbell of the seventeenth-floor apartment, footsteps sounded inside and an anguished voice cried out, "Who is it? What do you want?" The policemen identified themselves and Wilkins shouted angrily, "Go away. Leave me alone." One of the officers reached for the doorknob, but his hand froze when the youth shouted through the door that he would shoot the policemen or jump from the window, or both. The startled policeman backed off to call for reinforcements. Police radio cars converged on the towering red brick building and a crowd began to gather in the courtyard outside. By this time, Wilkins was prowling restlessly through the apartment, pausing occasionally to stare down into the courtyard from an open living room window. A call was put in for an ESD squad quartered a half mile away.

Up on the seventeenth floor, a neighbor who had known Wilkins' mother pleaded with him through the locked door to give himself up and police stood by, advising her on what to say. Wilkins clung stubbornly to his threats and announced to police outside the door the precise time he would jump—11:30 A.M. He then retreated to the living room window and leaned out to gaze down at the crowd. The neighbor hurried into an adjoining apartment with a plainclothes policeman and hung out the window in a desperate attempt to talk Wilkins into surrendering.

Down in the grass-covered courtyard, ESD police were wary of the prospect of setting up a net directly beneath the window where the youth was standing. The assumption was that he might not be lying when he intimated he had a gun. The ghetto neighborhood was well known for heavy traffic in so-called Saturday-night specials and other illicit firearms, and sending a policeman into the net to trap the youth seemed risky enough without the further hazard of exposing the rescuer to the possibility of a mid-air shootout. The rigging of a high-level net would be difficult if not dangerous in the strong southwest winds that were whipping through the project with occasional gusts up to eighteen miles an hour. The best chance of saving the youth appeared to be in spreading a net at ground level even though his 190-pound body, hurtling 160 feet downward, would smack into the nylon web at an estimated ninety miles an hour and strain the net to nearly three times its pretested strength. It was a calculated risk that the net would do its job properly and give way slowly enough to break his plunge.

The ESD crew swung into action, unscrambling the net on a grassy patch between the building wall and a row of wooden benches along a pathway winding through the apartment complex. The net was raised atop two poles, and the other side secured to the building wall. The poles stood free in the heavy metal stanchions, and police could find a solid anchorage for the guy line attached to only one of them. Wilkins, clad in undershirt and black slacks, watched the progress of the work from his vantage point in the window, resting his elbows on the sill and nonchalantly smoking a cigarette as his woman neighbor kept talking to him from the nearby window. Wilkins paid little attention to her pleas and kept his eyes fixed on the policemen scurrying on the ground below and the constantly growing crowd of tenants gazing up at him in awed silence. It was almost eleven-thirty when the job of rigging the net was completed, and the police backed away while preparations were made to deploy the wall net if necessary. Wilkins finished another cigarette and flipped it out into space, watching with morbid interest as it glided downward with the wind, sailing beyond the net's edge and landing in the grass.

Hysterical screams of "Don't do it" rose as the crowd sensed that Wilkins had come to a decision. The youth clutched the windowsill with both hands and heaved himself forward. His body cleared the window frame and plummeted headfirst toward the ground, with arms and legs flung out in a grotesque froglike posture. He soared outward, and for a split second it seemed that he would miss the net and crash headlong to the ground, but his body landed with shuddering impact at one of the net's outer corners, just short of the tip of the pole with the guy line that had not been tied down. The net trembled violently and one corner collapsed as the pole buckled under the tremendous blow. Wilkins was wrapped in the folds of the net and tumbled gently to the ground.

Placed on a stretcher and carried to an ambulance under police guard, Wilkins was in the hospital emergency room within minutes. Extensive x-rays showed that he had miraculously come through without a scratch. He was kept under observation at the hospital for several hours, then transferred to Bellevue for psychiatric examination. Detectives, meanwhile, carefully searched his apartment and failed to turn up any trace of a gun. Wilkins' survival not only recorded a milestone in police rescue work; it also marked the highest point from which anyone had fallen or jumped from a land-based structure in the city—and lived.

While the rescue still stands as the masterpiece among those made with the suicide nets, the ESD reluctantly concedes the life-saving device has limited usefulness. The courtyard of an upper East Side apartment house was too narrow to permit spreading of a net to save a thirty-two-year-old window washer who plunged five floors from a roof parapet one night in July, 1954. Disappointed by his wife's refusal to leave their two children alone and take a walk with him, the window washer had spent some time in a neighborhood tavern drowning his sorrows. On leaving, he told the bartender, "You'll see no more of me." His wife was awakened shortly after by a faint voice from outside her bedroom window crying, "I love you. I love you. Come and help me." Horrified, the woman ran to the window and saw her husband perched on the parapet. She screamed and pleaded with him not to jump. Neighbors already had called police. An ESD squad arrived and struggled to set up a net, but the configuration of the air shaft foiled all efforts to hang the net. Policemen and two priests—one of whom had officiated at the man's wedding in a neighborhood church only three years before—spent an hour talking to him as hundreds of onlookers gathered in the darkness to watch. When the man suddenly turned at one point to talk to one of the priests, he lost his balance and toppled into the courtyard.

The more modern skyscrapers, with their sheer towering heights and windows sealed for air conditioning, make wall-net rescues a practical impossibility. The ESD has never been able to use a net successfully even at some of the older giants like the Empire State Building, which became a magnet for jumpers after it was completed in 1931, the world's tallest skyscraper. The sudden and unexpected way in which suicides and attempts took place at the Empire State made it impossible in most instances for police to reach the building in time to take any effective deterrent action. On two occasions, rescues had appeared possible after jumpers stepped off the eighty-sixth-floor observation deck and landed on a narrow ledge one floor below. But both men overcame whatever crippling injuries they had suffered and crawled off the ledge to complete their suicidal plunges before the ESD arrived. In the summer of 1947, alarmed over the rising carnage, which then totaled sixteen deaths, the Empire State's security force consulted with the ESD and set up a suicide patrol, pending construction of a barrier around the parapet of the observation deck to thwart jumpers. The patrol was patterned along much the same lines as today's system for detecting airplane hijackers. Empire State guards and other personnel were trained in keen observation and application of psychological profiles to single out suicidal persons from run-of-the-mill visitors and tourists. The program had only limited success. By the end of 1947, work was completed on a suicide barrier—a seven-and-a-half-foot-high fence of diamond-shaped steel latticework topped by vicious-looking scimitar hooks bent inward and capable of inflicting painful gashes on anyone attempting to climb over them. The jumper craze became a thing of the past for many years after the fence was installed, but suicides and attempts at the building were not entirely over.

One man who reached the observation deck only to find his plan for a death leap foiled pulled a revolver out of his pocket and shot himself. On May 3, 1956, a red-haired woman whose identity was a mystery gained entrance to a fire-exit stairwell on the eighty-fourth floor and jumped into the interior space between the stairway railings. Her body plummeted to the fifty-fourth-floor level, where an iron crossbar sliced off both her legs. The rest of her torso hurtled downward, crashing to a landing on the forty-third floor. ESD policemen who removed the dismembered remains in a body bag later found the woman's topcoat and a small purse containing $1.20 in change on the eighty-fourth-floor landing.

The only successful suicide plunge from the observation deck after the fence was erected occurred early on the morning of July 22, 1963. A seaman, who was among the first sightseers to visit the observation deck that day, rushed from the elevator right to the wall. He mounted the parapet and grasped the hooks atop the fence, hoisting himself up and over with acrobatic ease. Then he lowered his feet to the outside edge of the parapet, clutching the fence top with bloodstained hands.

A tourist ran to the elevator to alert a guard, who rushed out and thrust his hand through the fence to grab the man's left foot. The man kicked violently and stomped the guard's hand. As tourists shrieked at him to come back to safety, the seaman shouted to the guard, "Let me go," and edged along the parapet. He then leaped backward with so much force that he cleared all the setbacks on the way down. His body struck the pavement just in front of the office that sells tickets for the observation deck, narrowly missing crowds of shoppers and office workers.

"He only was mad when I tried to stop him," the guard later

told the reporters and police. "As he flipped over, he had the serenest look I ever saw in my life. He looked relieved, like he was glad it was all over."

In confrontations with jumpers over the years, ESD policemen have weathered many dangers. Every rescue attempt holds a potential for violence that threatens their own lives and poses dilemmas of calculated risk-taking that could end in total disaster.

Sergeant James J. McGuire crawled along a narrow coping of a midtown office building, thirteen floors above the street, to reach a nineteen-year-old AWOL sailor threatening to leap to death on May 13, 1943. The distraught man had turned his back to the parapet to talk to ESD Officer Frank Deedy, who distracted him while McGuire inched along the coping. A great hush fell over the crowd in the street below. As the sailor bent down to pick up matches tossed to him by Deedy to light a cigarette, McGuire sprang and shoved him to safety.

"A lot of it is luck," said McGuire, who more than twenty-one years later took full command of the ESD for nearly three years as one of Klotzback's successors. "You don't have time to think. You do your thinking afterwards, and sometimes it scares you."

ESD Officer William Faulkner swung in a Morrissey life belt from an eleventh-floor window of Brooklyn's Hotel Saint George on July 7, 1951, and crashed through the plate glass of a half-open window one floor below to block the path of a woman who was about to jump.

The first lesson all ESD men learn is not to show nervousness, not even when dangling from a high bridge without a life belt on. "When we get to them, if we do, they're usually unstrung, if not completely hysterical," one veteran explains. "A nervous cop can make a nervous jumper nervous enough to jump." The second lesson is to make sure the jumper does not take a policeman with him if he plunges. The third is the element of surprise, the waiting like a cat for that split second when the jumper is off guard enough to be corralled.

The violence quotient in rescues was dramatically illustrated on a balmy spring night in 1965, when an ESD crew rushed to a building in Greenwich Village where a twenty-seven-year-old man named Albert Baker was threatening to jump. Clad only in blue jeans and boots and carrying a bayonet and knives in his belt,

Baker had climbed onto the ledge outside his fourth-floor loft and warned his girl friend, with whom he had been arguing, that he was going to leap off. A net was strung at street level, and a group of policemen went to the hallway outside Baker's apartment. On the ledge, Baker drew one of the knives from his belt and sent it flashing through the darkness into the street crowded with policemen and onlookers. "Everybody get out of here or I'll start throwing knives all over the place," he roared as the knife dug into the asphalt. When the policemen in the hallway crashed through the apartment door, the berserk man flung the bayonet, narrowly missing Officer George Heinz, who was rushing toward him. Baker was about to hurl another knife when Robert De Stefano, a local precinct officer who had joined the rescuers, drew his service revolver and fired one shot. The bullet went wild and struck Heinz in the right thigh, felling him. De Stefano lunged for Baker and subdued him with the help of a swarm of other policemen.

Besides guns and knives, makeshift weapons are often employed against police rescuers. A six-foot wooden pole was used to hold eighteen policemen at bay for more than two hours by a thirty-year-old patient who fled Manhattan State Hospital on Wards Island in the East River on the morning of February 14, 1956. The husky patient, who had been listed in the medical records as "quiet and cooperative" during his year's stay in the hospital, suddenly bolted for freedom while being taken back to his ward from a clinic. After leading a nurse and attendants on a half-mile chase, he disrobed and plunged into the icy waters of the river. He swam to another point on the island, found the discarded pole when he came ashore and climbed to a platform underneath a forty-foot-high archway supporting a steel bridge linking the island to nearby Randalls Island. While a Harbor Unit launch and two rowboats filled with policemen circled in the river below, an attempt was made to lasso the patient from the bridge roadway, but he warded off the noose with the pole. Officer John Penny then mounted the other side of the archway with a long boat hook and jousted with the patient in gladiator style as spectators viewed the weird scene from the shore. The pole turned out to be no match for the well-manipulated boat hook and the man finally was forced back down to the base of the arch, where Sergeant Charles Robinson and Officer Kenneth Weiss closed in and lashed him to a girder with ropes.

Fists, feet and teeth serve jumpers equally well in their battles to elude the police, who realize that the authority they symbolize is often infuriating to suicidal persons. Teeth and feet are favorite weapons of females, and experience has shown that the gentle qualities generally associated with femininity can never be relied on. A furious fight erupted one August day in 1962 when police confronted a twenty-nine-year-old divorcee as she was about to hurl her four-year-old daughter from a window of her tenth-floor apartment on the upper East Side and to jump after her. After frantic friends and a psychiatrist tried to reason with the hysterical woman, a police officer used a straightened coat hanger to pick the lock on the door of the bedroom where the woman was barricaded with the child. A life net already had been stretched beneath the window, and policemen burst into the room to find the divorcee hovering near the door and her daughter crying on the bed. The woman bit Sergeant James O'Hara on the forearm before she was wrestled into submission. Officer Thomas Mullen was punched in the ear and mouth and had his shirt torn by a woman bystander who protested police plans to remove the divorcee to Bellevue.

The swift and decisive action required to prevent jumpers from going through with their plans produces highly innovative rescue schemes, including clever use of props, psychological tricks, ruses and disguises. One officer halted a suicide by waving a broom out of a window below the man, who stood transfixed by the object until other policemen broke into his room and seized him.

A young man from Chattanooga, Tennessee, threatening to jump from a horizontal overhead girder to the roadway of a Harlem River bridge, was saved when a passing truck was flagged down and the driver ordered to park the vehicle directly beneath the jumper. As two ESD officers climbed after the man, he jumped, but his fall was broken by the truck's roof. In a similar case, a truck piled high with coffee bags was driven beneath a longshoreman, who was poised to leap after climbing over the guardrail of the elevated highway on Manhattan's West Side and dropping to a small exterior ledge a short distance below. The longshoreman was thwarted from jumping long enough for two ESD officers to be lowered by ropes from the guardrail to trap him.

When two hours of persuasive talk failed to budge a lovesick ex-sailor from the railing of the George Washington Bridge, ESD Officers Martin Stiastny and John Parchen improvised a motorized Trojan horse to get close enough to trap him. The officers drove to the New Jersey end of the span, stopped an open vegetable truck and explained the situation to the driver. Both hid in the back of the vehicle and sprang out to overpower the youth as the truck passed the spot where he was standing staring down into the water.

Casual offers of cigarettes and other items have worked on many occasions to entice jumpers from inaccessible spots. "You never know what you can use," says ESD Officer Mike McCrory, who holds numerous citations along with his colleague Officer J. Daniel Buckley for scores of successes in thwarting jumpers. "It may be a bottle of whiskey, a cigarette, a picture in a magazine, things like that. You can't tell what will work, the same way you never know what can send the person over."

A plumber teetering on the roof of a four-story Brooklyn dwelling because his wife had deserted with their five children was rescued after Officer Herbert Nolan put a pack of cigarettes on a nearby ledge and grabbed the man's arm when he reached for them. An icy can of beer requisitioned from the famed Rainbow Room atop the RCA Building in Rockefeller Center lured a forty-one-year-old actor from a seventieth-floor ledge, where he was dangling his feet in space and mumbling about his mother's illness and his own loss of a job. The actor walked twenty feet to retrieve the brew and was taken in tow by ESD Officers Henry Baker, Michael Calvin and Richard Muller.

Officer Christopher Russo surreptitiously set his wrist watch back one hour and handed it over to a twenty-eight-year-old factory worker who had announced the exact time when he would plunge from a sixth-floor ledge of a Bronx tenement. Removing his uniform cap and coat and even his life belt when it appeared to make the jumper nervous, Russo used the borrowed time to move along the narrow ledge to within thirty feet of the man while talking to him reassuringly in Italian, Spanish and English. The policeman confided that he had a wife and three children and hoped the man would not jump because he would then have to try to save him and might lose his life and leave his family uncared for. Softening under the appeal, the factory worker asked for a cigarette to smoke while he thought things over, and Russo tossed him a pack. The man then asked for a match, and Russo deliberately threw his lighter beyond reach. When the man turned to see where the lighter had landed, Russo was on top of him in a split second. Both tussled precariously on the ledge until Russo yanked the man back to the roof.

One of the most renowned strokes of psychological genius in the ESD's history occurred during the era when life nets had not yet come into use. A lovelorn twenty-year-old youth sat on the windowsill of his fourth-floor East Side apartment, turning a deaf ear to the pleas of his family and veteran ESD policemen, until one rookie officer got an inspiration. He seized the young man's sister and slammed her against a wall in the apartment. As the girl screamed in shock, her enraged brother started back inside to defend her and was subdued.

Still another gimmick saved ESD Officer Robert Byrne from certain death as he attempted to dissuade a man threatening to jump from the top of a swaying 115-foot crane at dawn on October 14, 1961. Byrne, with Officer Stanley Atkinson close behind, climbed the crane's boom to a point directly beneath the feet of the gaunt, unshaven man, who sobbed, "I'm better off dead. Leave me alone."

"Hey, fellow," Byrne said, "what's wrong? Life can't be that bad."

When Byrne got no answer, only sobs, he clutched at the man's foot. A kick nearly knocked the officer from his narrow perch, but he managed to hang on with one hand to a steel crosspiece that was slick with morning dampness. Atkinson shouted, "Hey, that cop has eight kids. If you knock him off, you know what will happen—those kids won't have a father." The man suddenly was gripped by remorse and stopped struggling. He agreed to follow the two policemen down, but all three came close to plunging to their deaths as the crane swung violently in strong winds and the man slipped down on his rescuers four times. A fire truck finally was called and an eighty-five-foot aerial ladder was raised alongside the crane. The three transferred to it for the rest of the trip to the ground. The man was taken to Bellevue for observation.

Disguises play an important part in rescues, and ESD men have masqueraded as everything from doctors to repairmen to Western Union messengers delivering bogus telegrams from sweethearts or public officials whom jumpers sometimes demand to see. Rescuers are advised to mask their identities as policemen and adopt disguises when the tactic will help them to get closer to jumpers or to establish a better rapport for talking victims to safety.

One detective borrowed a bartender's white jacket to pose as a doctor and calm a distraught widow with pseudo-medical talk as she sat on the fifth-floor windowsill of a West Side hotel.

"I'm a doctor from Bellevue Hospital," he told the woman, who kept yelling, "The gangsters are after me. They're going to get me if I go back inside." The hotel's deskman had been instructed to keep ringing the telephone in the woman's locked room on the off chance that curiosity would drive her back inside to answer it, but she refused to fall for the trick. The entreaties of the policeman turned "doctor," however, were enough to coax the widow to return into the room, and at a prearranged whistle, four police officers smashed open the door. The woman was floored by a flying tackle as she headed back toward the window, below which a net had already been spread.

Ironically, a similar disguise assumed by another detective nearly backfired during the rescue of a frail Nicaraguan woman from the summit of a midtown hotel.

"If you're a psychiatrist, I want nothing to do with you," the woman shouted angrily as she balanced on a twelve-inch ledge seventeen floors above the street. The policeman did some fast thinking. "No, I'm not that kind of doctor," he assured her as he inched forward. Two of his associates crept out of a window behind the woman and seized her.

All the mechanical devices, feats of derring-do and ruses employed over the years cannot begin to match the stunning successes that individual policemen have achieved through plain and simple talk. The ESD has an adage to the effect that if a man will talk, he can probably be talked out of destroying himself, but that those who really want to commit suicide are gone before help can arrive. The records overflow with tales of police officers engaging in persuasive small talk—sometimes for hours—to win the confidence of victims and to draw them back to safety.

"The worst thing is silence," McCrory says. "I'll talk to them about anything—women, racing cars, jobs. Sometimes I'll pretend to be someone who can give a guy a job. I try to get their point of interest. I mean, you don't go up there and say, 'Hi, I'm just passing by.'"

In learning to apply the correct psychology at precisely the right moment, most ESD men become unofficial psychologists in time, though none are given formal training in the subject. No instructions are issued on what to say to people seemingly on the verge of suicide; the approach is left strictly up to the men's personal discretion, and all their skill is acquired through on-the-job experience.

One of the champion talkers in the ESD's history was Officer Harold Christensen, who over the space of nearly two decades saved the lives of scores of men and women intent on suicide. During the same period, he watched helplessly while others succeeded in their purpose. Christensen, a cigar-smoking, 230-pound six-footer who was one of the persons who tried in vain to talk John Warde out of his leap, reached the peak of his skill in July, 1951, when he rescued a thirty-seven-year-old man from the top of the Queensboro Bridge, three hundred feet over Welfare Island. The man had thrown away his wallet at one point, and Christensen discovered that it contained a faded clipping of a poem entitled "Dark Ocean." The policeman, an avid reader of verse, took turns with his partner, Officer Daniel J. Mangan, reciting the poignant ode to the man, who burst into tears at one point. Christensen eventually was able to lunge and grasp the man's leg, and Mangan threw a safety belt around him to complete the rescue.

In another case, Christensen talked a garment manufacturer out of jumping from an eighteenth-floor window of the old Hotel Pennsylvania, only to learn a few weeks later that the executive had leaped to his death from another building. The policeman succeeded with little trouble in still another rescue by offering to buy the victim a beer and take him to see a baseball game.

"He's a pill at home," Christensen's wife once commented. "You can't leave anything around without him telling you it's dangerous. He spends two weeks fixing up the Christmas tree and on New Year's Day he's got the whole thing debulbed."

In their day-to-day encounters with jumpers, ESD men learn to read the face of hopelessness. The agonies, genuine or fanciful, that goad human beings to seek death by jumping are as broad and varied as life itself, covering the gamut from deep mental derangement to physical illness and infirmity of age, marital and family trouble, job failure in the middle-aged, school and parental problems of the young, failed love affairs, business and gambling losses, and hundreds of personal setbacks and tragedies that may seem petty to the outsider but are of enormous import to those experiencing them. Most of the time, the jumper thinks that no one cares about him or his problems, and the holding out of a helping hand, just the simple act of friendly and interested conversation, can provide the depressed with "instant therapy" and restore self-confidence. Someone really does care—that is the key.

"Some of our men are artists," one ESD veteran explains. "They can improvise both the physical and the psychological demands of the moment."

Many policemen on such assignments depend on a kindly and sympathetic manner, a calm in contrast to the emotionally charged situation, but approaches vary. For some, the main objective is to find out what is tormenting the victim and to propose a temporary solution. Others favor a tough, no-nonsense attitude. Spiritual solace in many cases is an effective antidote to the sickness of despair, and the ESD has found that a talk with a clergyman can often bolster the will to live.

"Whatever you talk about, the talk has to be calm and soothing" is the view of one ESD policeman. "And you've got to get them talking about anything—their family, friends, church, books, anything that eases their minds. That's three-fourths of the battle. When they reach a point where they're set to leap off a building or a bridge, they're cowards. Cowards who won't pay off old debts. They're all exhibitionists. It would appear they all want a little attention. Those who intend to die don't climb up on buildings and bridges. They always do it fast. One guy we took off the Manhattan Bridge was so scared that all he wanted to do was to come down as soon as he got up. Soon as we got him down he fainted dead away."

Another ESD veteran told of rushing to a midtown hotel one night to rescue a girl dancer who had called the switchboard and announced she was going to jump from her ninth-floor window. "We spread the nets all over the place," he recalled. "Nothing happened. I chopped down her door with an ax. And with all that chopping, she didn't even go near the window. Then I finally broke in and she was lying on the bed, crying. The way I figure it, nine out of ten aren't going to jump. The tenth? Maybe he will or maybe he won't, but all ten want the headlines."

Many ESD members share puzzlement over why anyone is so impatient for oblivion that he would want to hasten it himself. "Who knows why?" one veteran muses. "Any human ailment or affliction of the body or the mind. Real or imagined. Trouble. Trouble mostly with themselves."

Fear of failure at school drove one fourteen-year-old Puerto Rican girl to desperation. Expecting that she would not graduate with her ninth-grade class in a lower East Side school, the girl went home one June afternoon to her tenement apartment, said a brief hello to her father and locked herself in her bedroom. Turning up the radio loud, she sat down and wrote a note which read: "Dear mommie and daddy—I'm sorry for putting you to so much trouble, but I can't go on living." She carefully ironed the gown she had made for her graduation, put it on and climbed onto the window ledge. Two ESD trucks were en route to the scene when her mother managed to drag her back to safety. The next day, while the girl was undergoing psychiatric examination at Bellevue, the principal of her school disclosed that her fears of not graduating had been groundless and that she apparently had conjured them up after being scolded by a teacher for laughing and chattering during a play rehearsal.

The confusions and uncertainties of coping with a new life in New York were the breaking point for a twenty-year-old girl from Puerto Rico who was plucked from a Bronx rooftop in July of 1957. The girl had arrived in the city to live with a Puerto Rican factory foreman and his wife in a Bronx tenement apartment and care for the couple's five-year-old son while both parents were out working. If Puerto Rico had meant poverty and filth to the girl, New York meant loneliness. Unable to speak English, she found little understanding, never went anywhere alone, never dated and had no close girl friends. For months, she was torn between a desire for the more hospitable atmosphere of her Caribbean homeland and a feeling that she must stay in New York and earn money to send back to her impoverished family. The gift of a gay wardrobe of dresses and other kindnesses shown by her employer failed to erase her longing for home, but every time she made up her mind to return, more letters arrived telling of her family's pressing need for money. One summer night she vanished, returning several hours later to explain that she had gone to a movie and had wanted to stay out all night. Impatient with her behavior, her employer told her the next morning at breakfast that he was buying her a ticket to fly back to Puerto Rico. The girl received the news with seeming passivity, but after she had left the table, she went directly to the roof of the six-story tenement and began pacing back and forth along the parapet. Passers-by on their way to work saw her and called the police. The ESD spread a net at street level as a crowd of some three thousand persons collected to watch half a dozen Spanish-speaking police officers try to talk the girl back.

Several priests joined the effort, and it soon became apparent that the girl was listening to only one of them. He was a cleric who had come to the United States only a week before from Spain and had been a tutor to members of the Spanish royal family. The priest's gentle voice seemed to calm the girl, and ESD policemen withdrew while he talked to her. After giving the girl a handkerchief to wipe her brow, the priest stepped back in a maneuver to reassure her. He then urged her to pray and convinced her that she should be holding rosary beads. When he handed her the beads, he again refrained from making any moves that might upset her. She consequently suspected nothing untoward when he extended a crucifix for her to kiss. The act of devotion diverted her eyes just long enough for the priest to grab her and for other rescuers to move in. The girl struggled furiously to break free, and handcuffs had to be snapped on her wrists before she could be taken down to an ambulance.

Religiosity of a warped and childishly egocentric variety was behind the torment of an eighteen-year-old student who perched one cold December morning in 1963 on the seventh-floor ledge of a Rockefeller Center office building diagonally across the street from Saint Patrick's Cathedral. The hulking youth, who had a pair of rosary beads wrapped around one hand, somehow looked small and wispy, in the icy twenty-six-mile-an-hour winds, to the hundreds of passers-by who stopped to gaze up and to beg him not to jump. After ESD police arrived and stretched a net, Sergeant Peter Wardle ran upstairs and crawled through a window to get close to the youth.

"What's the trouble, kid?" Wardle began in a fatherly tone. "Tell me about it—what's troubling you?"

"My life is ruined," the young man answered, tears welling in his eyes.

"What happened? What's so terrible?" Wardle asked.

Sobbing openly, the boy explained that he had been studying at a Roman Catholic preparatory school in upstate New York with a view toward entering a seminary, and had been called in and told that he was not suited for a religious vocation. He was ashamed to tell his father, he said, and had decided to end it all instead.

"That's not the end of the world," Wardle assured him. "You can find other religious work to do for the church. Nothing's impossible as long as you're alive."

"I don't care," he cried. "There's no sense in living. I have nothing to live for. I'm going to jump."

Wardle, a Catholic himself, strained for other arguments and bargained for time as ESD Officers Ray Cariello and Robert O'Connell crept up behind the student from the other side of the ledge.

"You know if you jump—as a Catholic you must realize the consequences of suicide," Wardle cautioned.

The youth gave the sergeant a shocked stare, then looked away. By the time he turned back to answer, Cariello and O'Connell were pulling him, kicking, thrashing and weeping, to safety.

Alcohol, a significant factor in many jumper cases, often helps the mentally unbalanced and timorous to gather Dutch courage for their acts, and it is not unusual for otherwise normal people who consume too much liquor to scale bridges and buildings on barroom dares. One man who took several drinks too many one rainy spring day evidently saw himself reflected in the depths of the bottle as a circus aerialist. He strode to the East River's Queensboro Bridge and soon began to perform death-defying capers. Traffic clogged the span and thousands of spectators massed along both banks of the river as the man scampered with amazing agility along the suspension cables and zigzagged through other acrobatic feats. While a police helicopter hovered overhead, rescue vehicles raced along the bridge roadway and a Harbor Unit launch circled more than two hundred feet below, ESD policemen tried to overtake the elusive daredevil. To every plea to come down, the man shouted angrily, "I've got my rights." Frustrated, the police enlisted three ironworkers whose surefootedness on the bridge superstructure more than outmatched the inebriated acrobat's. He was quickly overpowered and lowered to the bridge deck by rope. They brought his bottle down too.

Another character who attained dizzying heights while high was a two-hundred-pound truckdriver from Texas, who staged a jazz dance late one summer evening in 1961 on a one-foot-wide ledge atop a seventy-five-foot sheer cliff overlooking a Brooklyn promenade. A life net was strung under the bellowing man, but he merely moved farther along the ledge out of range. He eventually was cornered and subdued after four ESD policemen walked out on the ledge to badger him back to where the net was located.

Not all intoxicated would-be jumpers fit the happy-go-lucky image, since the depressant impact of alcohol submerges some in a swamp of melancholy and resignation that all but smothers any small zest for life police rescuers can count on to talk them out of killing themselves. Alcoholics, despairing of problems in which their drinking has enmeshed them, make up a goodly percentage of those who contemplate jumping perhaps to win back the affection of a world that has spurned them.

In some cases the trouble—whatever it is—never seems to be dealt with successfully, even after the jumper has been rescued and committed for psychiatric care. A Long Island lithographer named William Sikes bedeviled the ESD with three successive suicide attempts in a little over six years. The first took place on the wind-swept Brooklyn Bridge one night in August of 1959 when police, alerted by a telephone call from Sikes's brother, drove to the span and spotted the lithographer standing on a cable ten feet from the top of the Manhattan tower. Wearing a white shirt and brown trousers, he was barely visible in the darkness.

When Sikes ignored all pleas to come down, ESD Officers Michael Chadwick and Robert Byrne started up the cable—a tube two feet in diameter with three-foot-high guide wires to grip for balance. The men got to within twenty feet of Sikes, who warned, "Come another step and I'm jumping off. I got troubles."

"*You* got troubles," Chadwick chided. "My pal here has six kids."

"Well, I've got one coming. But I lost my job and I'm no good to anybody," Sikes muttered.

"Well, what about your wife? What's she going to do with no one to look after her?" Chadwick argued.

"I'm going to jump for the insurance," Sikes said. "I've got ten thousand dollars insurance. With that kind of money, my wife will be able to get a new and better father for the kid."

After nearly an hour of talk, Chadwick wrung an agreement from Sikes to quit his perch if no searchlights were focused on him from the bridge roadway and news photographers were barred from taking pictures. But after he had trailed the policemen down the long curving arc of the cable to a point near the roadway, someone in the crowd below spat out, "Show-off." Furious, Sikes whirled and raced back up the cable with the policemen in pursuit. More talk and pleas followed, while the wisecracking bystander was hustled off beyond shouting distance. Sikes relented a second time and descended to the roadway, to be taken in a police car to Bellevue.

The ESD thought it had seen the last of the lithographer, but six years later, on October 27, 1965, Sikes—then twenty-nine and the father of two—was back in the limelight above an elevator tower on the roof of a twenty-six-story midtown Manhattan hotel. Straddling a ledge on either side of him, with life belts fastened securely to rooftop stanchions, were ESD Officers Matthew Mastronicola and Raymond Cariello, who patiently heard out Sikes's newest litany of sorrows over separation from his wife and sons. "Come near me and I'll jump," he shouted. "I've had it." Mastronicola and Cariello tried several times to close in, but had to freeze when Sikes, seeing them moving toward him, arose from a sitting position to let himself over the ledge and dangle by his hands. Each time the officers retreated, then Sikes scrambled back onto the ledge, almost falling on two occasions. The duel of wills dragged on agonizingly for an hour and a half in the glare of floodlights that illuminated the three figures as crowds watched from the street. Cariello got Sikes to chatting about fishing and boats and his estranged family, but the lithographer refused to allow the policemen to talk him to safety. As the conversation droned on, the officers, realizing that time for decisive action was running out, rechecked their safety belts. Then, exchanging a pre-arranged signal, both suddenly leaped to their feet and plunged out from the ledge. Ropes tugging at their life belts swung them around in two converging arcs and they landed directly on either side of Sikes. Before he could resist, the lithographer was grabbed firmly by the wrists and under the armpits, and within an hour he was back in Bellevue.

Not long after, however, Sikes somehow regained his freedom. On New Year's Eve—a little more than two months later—a watchman guarding a construction site almost in the shadow of Bellevue looked up and saw a man clinging about twenty-five feet from the top of a hundred-foot-high crane. An ESD squad was summoned and set up a ground net while two officers climbed the boom. One of the men was Robert Byrne, who experienced a strange feeling that he was reliving the past as he neared the man. "You look familiar. Didn't I help you out down there about six years ago?" Byrne asked, nodding to the lights of the Brooklyn Bridge twinkling against the night sky a mile and a half to the south. "Don't tell me you're going to do something silly again. This is no way to start the new year."

Sikes was too disoriented to remember his old rescuer, and re-hashed his troubles with his wife for a half hour before he was brought down without a struggle. He was returned to Bellevue and has not been seen or heard from by the ESD since.

ESD policemen seldom follow up on victims after they are taken away for psychiatric confinement. "I did once," one admits. "But not anymore. It's too painful. All you can do is pray somebody is giving them a hand and you don't meet them on a roof a month later."

One of the more spectacular talkathons in ESD annals occurred on the balmy spring evening of June 1, 1961, when a twenty-six-year-old unemployed father galvanized crowds in Manhattan's theater district by staging an unscheduled thriller on the catwalks of a huge electric sign on the roof of the Hotel Manhattan. At seven-thirty, as twilight was settling over the city, Joseph Clarkin, a hotel employee, glanced up as he was strolling on Eighth Avenue near Times Square. Silhouetted against the darkening sky he saw the figure of a man almost obscured by the white, blue and orange lights of the horizontal sign—a huge *M* rising above smaller letters spelling out "Hotel Manhattan." The man was on the upper-right-hand corner of the fifty-foot high letter *M,* four hundred feet above the street. Clarkin could not distinguish from that distance who the man was, although it later turned out that he had once worked with him at the Hotel Astor and had met and talked with him on the street only an hour before. All Clarkin knew was that someone was in trouble, and he ran out into the street to flag down a police radio car. Officers Francis J. Miles and Kenneth J. Walters took one look and sent a radio message: "Possible jumper at the Hotel Manhattan." The alert was transmitted to ESD headquarters, ten blocks to the north, and eight men under the command of Lieutenant John Dillon and Sergeant Anthony Ferrara headed for the scene. Miles and Walters rushed through the hotel's crowded lobby and took the elevator twenty-nine floors to the roof. Miles led the way up a shaky metal ladder to the top of the sign and across a girder to within twenty feet of the man, a slender figure dressed in faded tan trousers, a white shirt and a black-and-white cardigan sweater. "Don't come any closer or I'll jump," the man warned. Miles was startled when he recognized the man as a former hotel employee named Harry Jensen, who had worked briefly in a nearby fruit and vegetable market after losing his hotel job. "Harry, what the hell are you doing up here?" Miles shouted.

"Who's that?" Jensen asked.

"It's Frank Miles, the cop. I used to stop and get fruit from you, remember?"

Down in traffic-clogged Eighth Avenue, ESD trucks arrived in front of the hotel as hundreds of persons hurrying to nearby theaters stopped to gape at the drama being played out high above them. No time was lost carting safety belts, a net and other gear to the hotel roof, which was plunged into darkness minutes later when the lights of the sign were switched off to eliminate the danger that Jensen or those trying to rescue him might be burned or shocked. The sign was recessed over a skeletal structure of steelwork supporting it, and a roof-level net could not be set up effectively under Jensen. ESD policemen climbed the darkened catwalks of the sign to surround him. As Miles kept up a steady conversation, the policemen kept their distance, adhering to strict ESD policy of never interfering when someone else already has established rapport.

"What's wrong?" Miles asked. "Do you want a priest or rabbi? What can we do for you?"

Jensen buried his head in his hands and cried, "I need work. I need a job."

He rambled incoherently about lies he had been told and said that he had been unable to support his five children after losing his job as a houseman at the Astor. His wife had walked out on him a year before and he had been struggling to support the children on unemployment checks, which had recently been cut off. The money he had saved for rent had been spent on food, which in turn had brought an eviction threat from his landlord. On top of all this, Jensen said, he had been rejected for welfare aid because he failed to meet the necessary residency requirements, and the whole ordeal had so shattered him that he had spent time receiving psychiatric help at Bellevue. Miles shouted to him through the darkness, "We'll get you a job. That's a promise. Now come on down or we'll all be killed."

Jensen pondered the officer's words in silence for a few moments, as the other policemen waited out of view on the girders, ready to spring into action if the ploy failed. It was eight-thirty when Jensen, without a word, walked slowly along the girders toward Miles, who gently reached out to embrace him. From the brightly lit streets below, a cheer went up from the crowds. Jensen was still in tears when he reached the roof. He was handcuffed as a precaution, but the manacles were removed when police saw he was completely resigned. Widespread publicity given Jensen's story later brought help for his family from both government officials and the general public.

To convince jumpers that they are not alone in their troubles, and that there is still hope in life, the ESD sometimes allows persons who are coping with similar or even more horrendous problems to talk to them. A strong sense of identification with another man's heartache was a potent weapon in saving a twenty-eight-year-old railroad worker who was sitting astride a girder on the George Washington Bridge in August, 1958. After a priest failed to talk the man down, an electrician who was working on the span offered to climb up and make an appeal. The electrician had just that morning put his seven-year-old son aboard a plane to fly to the Mayo Clinic in Rochester, Minnesota, for a delicate heart operation. The two men talked quietly for about a half hour, the laborer grumbling that he had been separated for a year from his wife, had no place to live and "nothing to live for."

"Look, mister," the electrician said, "I know what trouble is. My boy has had an open heart since he was a baby. He can't play with other kids. He can't do what they do. Do you know what that means to a father?"

The laborer grew sheepish as the electrician told him, "I know what you're thinking now; I've thought of jumping off a bridge myself. And now I think we're going to save my son. Maybe the operation will work. Things get better. You've got to have hope."

When the electrician finished, ESD rescuers were no longer needed. The laborer slowly followed the electrician down.

Officer Herbert Nolan used himself to arouse sympathy and protectiveness when he met his former delivery boy one night—640 feet above the murky waters of the Narrows—on a cable of the Verrazano-Narrows Bridge between Brooklyn and Staten Island.

"Gee, what are you doing here?" the youth gasped as Nolan advanced toward him in the glare of spotlights shooting up from the bridge roadway. The ESD man, who had not seen the youth in the six years since he had made deliveries to the Nolan home, listened to the young man's story of domestic trouble. "My wife left me and took our child," he said. "I have no reason to live. Please leave me alone."

At a loss for a moment to say something that would console the youth, Nolan blurted, "Look, you'll feel much better once we get down. Remember, you can't change your mind once you've jumped."

The minutes flew by as Nolan groped for other arguments. Then he got an idea.

"You know something?" he said. "I'm afraid of heights. I'm getting dizzy. Please do me a favor and help me down."

Touched by Nolan's plight, the youth began moving toward the officer to help him. Nolan caught him with the assistance of three other policemen on the cable.

Where girls are concerned, ESD policemen know that there is nothing like flattery when all else fails. On May 11, 1959, a sixteen-year-old girl on the parapet of a twelve-story Bronx hospital was sweet-talked by a policeman with a wife and four children, who dredged up some experience from his bachelor days. Shedding his shirt and gun so he would not be recognized, Officer Theodore Weise offered the girl a cigarette, which she at first refused, and then told her, "You're too lovely a girl to do anything like this. You have beauty and youth. You have a nice shape. Don't be foolish. You're one of the nicest-looking girls I've ever seen."

Surly and suspicious at first, the girl melted under the barrage of compliments and reached out to take a cigarette from Weise. He gripped her hand and hauled her back onto the roof. "By the time I got through, she thought she was Jayne Mansfield," he commented later.

An appeal to manly vanity turned the trick when a fifteen-year-old high school student, who had been spurned by his thirteen-year-old girl friend, kept hundreds of spectators in suspense as he balanced on the parapet of a Bronx building on April 24, 1954. The girl friend was located and rushed to the building, where she begged the boy, "Please don't jump. I'll go out with you again; just come on back."

When the young man shook his head, turned away and moved toward the edge of the roof, ESD Sergeant Joseph Boller stepped forward with a new tack.

"Look, don't be a dope," Boller advised. "No girl is worth it. Women aren't worth a dime. You're no baby. You're a man, so come on back here with us and take your medicine like a man. You are a man—aren't you?"

The point struck home and the boy walked proudly off the parapet into Boller's waiting arms.

A similar challenge to the ego worked on a twenty-seven-year-old Atlanta steelworker who was all set to leap from the fourth-floor ledge of a Manhattan office building on September 7, 1965.

"I'm not going to grab you," ESD Officer Robert Hill told the man, who said he wanted to die because his wife had left with their children. "You'll have to come in on your own. You'd be more of a man if you walked back in off that ledge rather than jumping. How would you like your two kids to read about your jumping in tomorrow's papers? You wouldn't be much of a hero to them."

The man took a life belt offered by Hill and strapped it around himself. "I'm getting nervous out here," he said. Without a further word, he climbed back inside.

Though somewhat riskier than other psychological techniques, anger, threats and the shock of the unexpected also are effective rescue gimmicks.

A threat of punishment prevented a nineteen-year-old sailor from plunging one hundred feet from an approach ramp to the Manhattan Bridge on February 27, 1957. After trying for several minutes to cajole the sailor into giving up, ESD Officer Walter Lynch, Jr., demanded, "Do you have your leave papers? If you do, hand them over or you'll be in real trouble."

The sailor automatically fumbled for his papers and that was all the distraction the policeman and his partner, Officer John Lanigan, needed to pounce on him.

A priest, called by the ESD to talk with a former mental patient on the roof of a six-story upper East Side building, flew into a display of mock rage when the man scoffed at an invitation to pray. "Stand up," the priest boomed. The man scrambled to his feet and backed away in fright, into the arms of ESD Sergeant Joseph Anderson and a local precinct officer.

Taunts of "Coward!" and "You're afraid to fight!" from a free-lance photographer induced an unemployed Air Force veteran to leave a ledge near the top of a Bronx church steeple in April, 1952. The ex-airman had spent Saturday night drinking and had attended an early mass in the church before dashing up three flights of stairs to the steeple and mounting a twenty-five-foot ladder to the belfry. Several hundred rain-drenched spectators watched him defy ESD policemen, a priest and his mother. The photographer, deciding that derision might work, shouted, "You're a chicken-livered yellow phony, giving us all this trouble. If you have any guts, come on down and fight." The outburst infuriated the veteran, who yelled, "I'll knock your block off if it's the last thing I do. Stand back, you guys, I'm coming down." He did— right into a swarm of policemen.

Complete cynicism and unconcern seldom succeed in rescues, and are shunned by the ESD on the grounds that the dangerous strategy might backfire and supply the victim with a final justification for suicide. Most indifference or outright hostility shown in jumper cases occurs among bystanders, and generally stems from envy over the attention being paid the jumper or a sick desire for the morbid satisfaction of watching a death plunge. In the spring of 1964, when the issue of public apathy was making headlines across the country, the ESD twice contended with crowds thirsting for the malicious thrill of seeing a jumper die. On May 10 of that year, a carnival-like mob of over one hundred persons, including teen-agers and smaller children as well as adults out for a Sunday-afternoon sightseeing stroll, harassed an unemployed Puerto Rican laborer standing on a suspension cable of the Brooklyn Bridge. The man gazed down in confusion and terror when the adults and children chanted, "Jump, jump, hurry up and jump." Horrified and angry, ESD policemen charged into the crowd, prodding the protesting thrill-seekers back to the bridge approaches. Traffic was ordered off the span after motorists out for a Sunday drive jammed the roadway to gape and gawk. Sensing that the man already had been stirred up by the crowd's outcries, the rescuers canceled any attempt to go up after him in fear that further panic would trigger him into leaping. Deputy Chief Inspector William McCarthy, then commander of the ESD, joined with a priest in addressing the stranded laborer in Spanish through a bullhorn for forty-five minutes before he walked down the cable on his own. As the shaken man was driven away to Bellevue in an ambulance, McCarthy commented bitterly, "Some of those people who wanted him to jump should be in for observation with him."

A month later, on June 7, another quiet Sunday, a drama of even greater savagery unfolded in Manhattan's Morningside Heights section on upper Broadway when a thirty-two-year-old handyman climbed out on the tenth-floor roof ledge of the apartment building where he worked. Two police officers heard faint shouts of "jump" and *"brinca"*—the Spanish word for jump—as they passed nearby in a radio car, and traced the shouts to a crowd that was jeering the man. The officers raced to the roof of the building and tried to calm him as ESD trucks arrived and a ground net was spread. Two priests from nearby parish rectories talked in Spanish to the man, who said their pleas were of no use—he was going to jump. At this point, a policeman, stepping forward and holding out his hand, casually said he wanted to wish the man farewell. The handyman, caught off guard by the unexpected gesture, extended his own hand, and the officer held on to it with an iron grip, while other policemen clutched the victim by the shoulders and pulled him back to the roof. A chorus of boos, catcalls and hisses exploded from the crowd. After the man had been removed to the hospital, a few people in the neighborhood acknowledged shouting to him to jump, one saying, "I don't know why I shouted 'jump.' Maybe because I had a couple of extra beers." Others defended their action, one insisting, "That's a good way to stop him."

In one rare instance, a bystander's bizarre display of animosity may have helped to save a twenty-three-year-old salesman, who outdid Warde's record by defying rescuers for a little more than thirteen hours on August 22–23, 1953. The salesman, Frederick George, a Navy veteran who had checked into a Brooklyn veterans hospital with a peptic ulcer and "anxiety neurosis," had spent most of five days restlessly wandering the corridors of the eighth-floor ambulatory ward and avidly reading Arthur Miller's play *Death of a Salesman* before he slipped up to the fourteenth floor and out a window onto the three-foot-wide ledge. A motorist on a nearby parkway saw him and telephoned police. As the salesman, clad in pajamas and bathrobe, forlornly complained that "my family doesn't care for me," the ESD tried to rig a ground net, but George kept shifting his position on the ledge, which ran one hundred feet along the building's façade. A net was dropped from above in one attempt to trap him, but George, scooting past as the webbing whipped downward, shouted, "Don't try any more dirty tricks like that."

Meanwhile, a newspaper reporter contacted George's mother by telephone at her home in Queens and asked her to come to talk to her son, but she was too distraught. Instead, the salesman's brother arrived and was permitted to talk to George, even though the ESD is wary of appeals by family members and other intimates, who may have had some real or imagined part in the jumper's troubles. Domineering mothers in particular create scenes that can precipitate the very tragedy that police are trying to prevent, and the sight of a rejecting girl friend begging for reconciliation out of guilt is frequently enough to thrust a jumper into a final act of self-pity and self-contempt.

The inherent dangers were quickly apparent in George's case when his brother, after talking reassuringly for five minutes, switched to what he described as a "different approach," deriding George, daring him to jump and confidently telling onlookers, "He won't jump. He's bluffing. He just can't stand discipline. That's how he got an ulcer in the Navy." When the salesman flailed his arms in anger and moved ever closer to falling, the brother was asked to leave. Soon after, George's mother, who had changed her mind, came to the hospital trembling and crying. The short, gray-haired woman was led into a room overlooking the ledge, where she turned away and sobbed.

A rabbi, who had been summoned to the scene, recalled that another patient in the hospital was a young man he had successfully talked out of jumping from a clothes pole at a nearby apartment building only the day before. The man, a veteran, had been admitted to the hospital for observation. Hoping that the patient might talk George from the ledge, the rabbi went to see the man in the observation ward in an attempt to enlist his help. The patient refused, saying, "I only wish I were out there myself."

The pleading was taken up by a parade of psychiatrists, rabbis, priests, ministers and even a voluptuous blond nurse, who later offered her ample favors to George for the night and got a blank cold stare in response.

As word spread by newspapers, TV and radio, the ESD was flooded with offers of outside help from hypnotists, spiritualists, telepathists and a trick ropester with a rodeo at Madison Square Garden who wanted to lasso the salesman. All were turned down, especially the lasso artist, who the ESD feared, among other risks, might garrote George. ESD officers donned the green jackets worn by the hospital's patients and waited at windows along the ledge for an opportunity to capture George, whose every movement was broadcast by walkie-talkie from the ground. But one policeman who leaned out was warned by the salesman, "If you make a move, we'll both go together."

The passage of hours heightened fears that exposure or ulcer pains might cause George to faint and topple to his death accidentally, and containers of milk were nudged onto the ledge, where the salesman cagily fetched them and sipped the liquid. His strength restored, he pointed at several hundred spectators below and told a priest in a nearby window, "You name the hour you want me to jump, and I'll do it. Think of the money you can win on bets." Then, ecstatic over all the attention, he yelled, "Well, I finally amounted to something. I'm a success now."

After nightfall, when stiff winds threatened to sweep George off the ledge and his legs and feet began to turn blue, he accepted a pair of slippers, but rejected an extra bathrobe. Not long after, however, he took off the slippers, placed them beside him and announced, "I don't believe I'll be needing these much longer." As he sat down with legs dangling and his head nodding from sleepiness, a war of nerves built to a fever pitch between police and a hospital psychiatrist, who firmly opposed any moves to take George by force and insisted on further efforts to get him to leave the ledge voluntarily. After several angry exchanges, the psychiatrist withdrew in disgust when a decision was made by police to gamble on a rescue plan. For the ticklish assignment the ESD deferred to two city firemen, who had worked together for years as an expert team in swinging down façades of blazing buildings to rescue trapped victims. As the firemen eased into harnesses in a fifteenth-floor corridor, an unusually nervous newspaper reporter, who had covered the story from the start, was prowling the corridor one floor below, alternately eying a wall clock, which read 2:30 A.M., and poking his head out a window to scowl at George. The firemen crept onto the ledge above the salesman, facing each other at a short distance in the darkness. At a given signal, both leaped downward, and a powerful searchlight flooded the hospital wall with brilliant light designed to blind the salesman to their approach. Despite the dazzling light, George instantly saw what was happening, leaped to his feet and skirted the entrapment as the firemen swung down on either side of him and a net dropped from above in a vain try to contain him. Furious, the firemen stalked after the fleeing salesman, shouting curses, but the newspaper reporter, who had witnessed the thwarted rescue, was even more indignant. "Jump, you bastard; the bars close at three," he shouted. The stunned salesman whirled to confront the reporter, and the firemen moved closer to him while firemen and police entered rooms at both ends of the ledge and stood at windows to shorten the area to which he had unhampered access. At this point, the psychiatrist, who had returned to watch the operation, yelled, "Get out, Fred. I can help you and you know it." The salesman asked for five minutes to think it over. He was offered the keys to a car to use for a getaway. Then, shivering and sobbing, he turned his back to the ocean wind and allowed rescuers to pull him through a window to safety.

While most victims rescued from heights by the ESD are suicidal, scores are window washers, painters, roofers and others stranded in broken safety belts or on inoperative or collapsed scaffolds while working on tall buildings. The problems range from repairing machinery on stalled power-driven platforms to performing death-defying acrobatics. ESD Officers Jack Leonard and Edward Cavanagh once dangled nine stories above the ground in life belts to save two painters hanging helplessly from the end of a scaffold that had snapped a supporting line in Stuyvesant Town, a huge apartment development on the lower East Side. Lines were girded around the victims, who were lifted through a window, frightened but otherwise uninjured. The ESD faced a more complex mission when a forty-year-old steeplejack was left suspended upside down by one leg two hundred feet in the air, after witnessing the death plunge of his seventeen-year-old son from a scaffold that collapsed while they were painting and cleaning the wall of a midtown Manhattan office building. The platform fell to a vertical position, pitching the youth off and leaving the father with his leg entangled in its steel frame outside a nineteenth-floor window of one of the building's elevator shafts. ESD rescuers rode the elevator to a point below the floor, climbed through the car's roof hatch and broke through the shaft window. A rope was looped under the steeplejack's arms, and he was towed in, moaning, "Why couldn't it have been me instead of the boy?"

Despite its more terrifying aspects, the business of rescuing jumpers is not without moments of irony and high comedy, and ESD files are filled with zany episodes. When two policemen knocked at the door of a Riverside Drive apartment where a man was about to leap from a window, he greeted them with two shots from a .32-caliber pistol. Then, seemingly oblivious that his act had strained relations with his rescuers, he went to the window, where police had set up a net, and asked plaintively, "Is it secure?" Assured the net was safe, the man jumped into it.

Another jumper obliged police by telephoning back with better information on his whereabouts after giving them the wrong name of the bridge from which he intended to plunge.

"I've got to get my wife and kids back," the jumper announced in the first call, warning that he was on the Brooklyn Bridge and was going to dive off, "unless I get them to come home."

"We have a woman in the station house who says she's your wife," the police operator replied. "If you want her, come here."

"What's her first name?" the caller asked craftily.

"This woman is with a police matron in another part of the building," the policeman parried. "If you'll hold on, I'll find out."

The jumper hung up, and police were rushed to the Brooklyn Bridge, but reported back that no suicide was in sight there. Then the jumper called back.

"Hey, you were supposed to be on the Brooklyn Bridge," a policeman scolded. "Where are you?"

"I thought it was the Brooklyn Bridge," the jumper apologized. "I don't know where I am, but there's a lot of construction going on."

That was the tipoff needed. Remembering that roadway work was in progress on the Manhattan Bridge, just north of the Brooklyn Bridge, the police went to that span, located the man and took him in custody. A call for an ESD truck with a net was canceled.

Innocent citizens are at times mistaken for jumpers when they stand at windows to get a breath of air or do some sightseeing. A curvaceous redhead in a bikini created pandemonium at the famed Delmonico Hotel on Park Avenue one March day when a passer-by thought she was about to step off a ledge outside her sixteenth-floor room. ESD policemen and members of the hotel staff crashed into the room and swarmed all over the woman, who breathlessly explained that she was only "leaning out the window to sunbathe."

A mad dash to save a man supposedly about to dive off the top of the celebrated Parachute Jump in Coney Island's Steeplechase Park one night ended as police arrived and a bedraggled figure stumbled out of a tiny wooden shack at the base of the huge skeletal structure. An excited bystander shouted, "That's him! That's the guy!" The man, locally noted as a connoisseur of the more inexpensive and inelegant wines of the region, sheepishly admitted that he was indeed the person seen reeling on the 250-foot tower. He explained that after the amusement ride had been closed down in the late 1960s for lack of patronage, he had been commissioned to maintain the beacon at the top so that planes approaching Kennedy and La Guardia Airports from the south would not crash into the structure. In return for replacing the beacon's burned out light bulbs, he said, he had been accorded rights to sleep in the shack, plus ten dollars' drinking money for each spine-chilling climb.

An art student at the New School for Social Research in Greenwich Village stirred a jumper scare one day when he grew restless while sculpting a nude model and quit his kneaded clay to saunter up to the roof and sit with his legs over the parapet. In true artistic fashion, the student was wearing neither shoes nor socks, and someone concluded he was going to jump. The art student had returned to his sculpting by the time ESD police arrived. A half-hour search turned up no sign of anyone bent on suicide, but Officer Michael Chadwick spied some tracks of bare feet in the roof's tar. He trailed the footprints down the stairway to a classroom, where students were leaving for the day, including the barefoot Rodin. A few probing questions solved the mystery, and also sniffed out the information that the student sculptor had been working under the inspiration of several drinks.

During a traumatic visit by the Beatles in the summer of 1966, the ESD was called to corral two teen-age blondes—one seventeen and the other eighteen—who squatted on a five-foot-wide ledge on the twenty-second floor of the Americana Hotel and vowed to stay until they personally saw Paul McCartney. "Paul! Paul! We want Paul," the girls screamed as nets were strung from an adjoining hotel ledge ten floors down. ESD Officers Richard Powers and Patrick O'Connor padded across the gravel roof toward the girls, and Powers fell to his knees, pleading, "I have a daughter your age. I understand how you feel. It would break my heart if my daughter was out here like this." One of the girls dissolved in tears, and the policemen sprang and swept both to safety. At a hospital, a doctor found the girls were suffering from "acute situation reaction." The ESD diagnosed the case differently and charged both with disorderly conduct.

Acute situation reaction applied more aptly to a father stricken by a severe headache while visiting in a midtown hospital with his wife, who had just borne their sixth child. The dazed husband shuffled from his wife's bedside and through a window onto a ledge four floors above the street. ESD Officer Kenneth Kafka, a man of few words, especially in situations where words fail, arrived and sneaked up on the harried father to yank him back, thus ending what was later to be unofficially known as "The Case of the Justified Jumper."

4. Trapped ....

The Emergency Service draws great attention for heroism and professional excellence at the scenes of sensational cases such as those involving jumpers, but the bulk of its rescue work is played out in obscure day-to-day vignettes of personal drama that rarely, if ever, make headlines.

Every year, the ESD saves hundreds of persons entrapped in accidents ranging from impalement on picket fences and other sharp objects to entanglement in industrial and household machinery, and imprisonment in automobile crashes. Its meticulously kept logbooks read like a truth-is-stranger-than-fiction compendium of human frailty, travail and courage, with entries such as these:

A thirty-two-year-old pregnant woman, who was opening a window in her Brooklyn tenement apartment one March evening in 1966, toppled out and fell two floors onto an automobile jack that had been left standing upright on the sidewalk by a motorist. The jack pierced her abdomen but left her unborn child untouched. Since the prime consideration in all impalements is to minimize the danger of shock and of aggravating fatal hemorrhaging by wrenching or removing the embedded material, an ESD crew concentrated on steadying the jack so that both it and the woman could be removed to a hospital and the case turned over to surgeons. The woman was eased into a body bag, and a team of policemen, working with precision under the direction of Sergeant Robert Kirchmeier, lifted her into an ambulance, which was then driven along streets that offered the smoothest ride and the least danger of jolting in potholes or quick stops. After seven hours of surgery, doctors reported that the jack had been excised and all the woman's vital organs repaired. Both she and her child survived.

A fifty-year-old bachelor advertising executive, fearing the embarrassment of waking up neighbors by shouting for help, spent all night clinging to a drainpipe outside a window of his apartment on Manhattan's East Side, where he was stranded while attempting to gain entrance. The executive, who had broken off his key in the apartment's locked front door after returning from a party, went to the building's roof and clambered down the pipe to within a few feet of the third-floor bedroom window, where his leg became snared in a loose bracket holding the pipe to the wall. His neighbors discovered him in the morning, and an ESD crew trussed him in a supporting rope, cut away the bracket and hoisted him back up to the roof of the four-story building. The executive told police that he had spent the night "writing a book of philosophy in my head." He said he had finished "about three chapters" and intended to call the volume "Modern Matter of Fact."

A seventy-four-year-old woman insurance broker suffered through twelve hours of lonely agony until she was rescued after she fell during a fainting spell and wedged her right foot between the bathtub and an old marble washstand in the bathroom of her Greenwich Village home one morning in the spring of 1957. Grasping the shower curtain, she tried to raise herself and twist free, but the pain was too great, and she lay back with the telephone tantalizingly beyond her reach in the next room. Since she usually was out on business calls during the day, she was not missed at her office until closing time, when two of her employees came and asked the building superintendent to climb into her apartment through the fire-escape window. The ESD was summoned and extricated her by standard procedures. Entrapment between bathroom walls and fixtures is extremely common, especially among the young and the elderly, and the solution calls for unscrewing or sawing the anchoring bolts so the fixtures can be moved.

The technical expertise of ESD Officer Otto Weid helped save a shipping clerk who was struck in the head by a plummeting metal rod while chatting with a fellow employee outside an East Side appliance firm on May 9, 1947. The slender three-foot rod, whose origin was never determined, speared into the clerk's forehead, penetrating down through the roof of his mouth to the level of his upper teeth. He collapsed on his back on the sidewalk with the rust- and paint-speckled shaft still quivering in his skull. When an ambulance arrived, medical attendants were reluctant to lift the clerk, fearing that jostling the thirty-two inches of rod protruding from his head might cause further—and possibly fatal—injury. To handle the patient safely, the rod's external portion had to be sliced off near the skull without damaging vibrations such as might be caused by sawing. Weid produced the perfect tool for the job—a bolt-cutter normally used for snipping through heavy chains. Wielding the pliers-like tool with the utmost delicacy, Weid lopped off all but two inches of the rod. The clerk was rushed to Bellevue Hospital, where doctors performed four and a half hours of surgery to extract the embedded six-inch portion and repair damage to the frontal lobe of his brain. The patient made a complete recovery.

Other cases encountered by the ESD cover a wide variety of mishaps, including persons who lock themselves in bathrooms, prisoners in handcuffs whose guards have lost the keys, fat people stuck in bathtubs, bartenders with hands caught in cash registers, bakers snarled in dough mixers, and victims trapped in elevator cars and subway turnstiles.

When a Brooklyn brewery worker was knocked unconscious after toppling into a sixteen-foot-deep vat on July 25, 1973, ESD Officers Walter Hickey and Francis Clifford risked drowning at worst and inebriation at best by swimming through the foaming beer to save him.

Removing tight finger rings that resist the traditional soap and water treatment is another major task, with most victims married women whose wedding bands pinch when their fingers grow pudgy from overeating or swell during pregnancy or after banging against walls and furniture during vigorous housework. Others catch rings in household appliances such as electric washers, mixers and blenders. One technique for removing rings intact consists of slipping a strong, thin cord under the band and winding the cord several times around the finger between the ring and the knuckle to depress the swollen skin. The lower part of the cord is gently unwound so that the ring works slowly over the spiraled portion and off. Tougher cases once required filing and sawing with jeweler's tools over a metal guard placed beneath the band to protect the finger from cuts. But the process was long and tedious, and the ESD now has a special clipping device with a slender lower jaw that fits under the ring and an upper jaw that squeezes down to snap it. When the metal is too hard to snip, the victim is taken to a hospital, where a dentist's drill is used to sever the band on two sides so that it falls off in semicircular sections.

ESD vehicles contain an assortment of special tools for extricating the hundreds of persons who are imprisoned each year in the twisted steel of automobiles and buses that smash into stanchions and retaining walls, overturn or collide with other vehicles on the city's highways. One is a giant can opener that is jabbed into the roof of the crumpled auto and jacked up and down, in much the same manner as the old-fashioned household tool, to peel off the car's lid and expose the passengers. A reverse pincers, with jaws that spread when pressure is exerted on its handles, is designed to widen openings in car wreckage. A number of powered saws are rigged with changeable blades and teeth to rip through various kinds of metal. The survival of entrapped victims, the policemen are taught, hinges on decisions that are right the first time, with no margin for error. "You just don't go in there swinging," one instructor tells his men. "You've got to take the time to evaluate the situation and to determine what approach will involve the least danger to the victim and at the same time provide the swiftest removal route. Sometimes by removing one piece of wreckage you can pin the victim under even greater stress from other directions. Success in all entrapment rescues depends on correctly sizing up the various stresses and strains involved."

As in all accidents where victims face possible loss of life or limb, strict attention is paid in vehicular mishaps to medical considerations and the rescuers work in close cooperation with a physician. The physician on the scene is the man in charge of the operation and his advice is heeded to the letter. When necessary, after victims have been extricated, ESD mechanics saw and wrench their way into auto wrecks to locate severed arms and legs, which are rushed to hospitals for graft surgery. As they do with most modern household appliances and machinery, they constantly keep abreast of changes in car body designs and how they react under impact so that rescue techniques are always up to date.

Sometimes a knowledge of obsolete vehicles comes in handy too. One unusual case called for rescuing four women, three men and three children who were injured when the left rear wheel on a horse-drawn stagecoach collapsed in a Bronx amusement park on June 24, 1960. The ESD's frontiersmen proved equal to the task.

While the ESD has well-rehearsed contingency plans for freeing victims from various kinds of entrapment, it is mainly in innovating solutions to unusual situations that the policemen display true genius. A basic principle of physics was applied to release one worker from a bakery oven after he squeezed in to make repairs and discovered on completing the job that he could not crawl out because residual heat had swollen his body. A hose stream of cold water was played on his body until it shrunk down to near normal size. After he was slicked with lubricating oil, he was able to squirm out with the help of the policemen.

A similarly deft maneuver saved a worker who lost his footing and plunged through a chute while breaking up huge chunks of coal in the upper portion of a steel hopper in Brooklyn. Coal showered after the worker and buried him up to his neck against the hopper wall. Afraid that the victim would smother before tons of shifting coal could be dug out from around him, the ESD tried at first to reach him by burning through the hopper's steel wall with an acetylene torch, but the torch had to be turned off when the victim cried out that the heated metal was scorching him. One of the rescuers then suggested an effortless answer. Why not just open the hopper and let the man slide out with the coal? After some rusted bolts were burned away, the entire frame around the hopper's mouth was removed to provide clearance through which the trapped man was lowered down a ladder, somewhat bruised and shaken but not otherwise seriously injured.

The ESD's undiscriminating talents are available to all—even lawbreakers. When a thief, trying to burglarize a restaurant one night, snaked into a kitchen flue and became firmly stuck, a crew spent hours chipping through brick and masonry and tearing the seams of the pipe to remove him. Even as he was arrested, the burglar confessed that he never was so glad to see policemen in his life.

A number of entrapment and injury cases fall into a kind of unmentionable category that can only be classified as awkward for both the squads sent to deal with them and the clerks who are later assigned to describe them in detail. In one episode, a housewife returned from a trip to a bakery to buy some rolls and found her East Side apartment swarming with policemen, who were busy with the delicate task of separating her husband's most private parts from a vacuum cleaner hose. The project succeeded, leaving everything intact, but the official report failed to note whether the marriage fared as well. Similar assignments have involved the removal of milk bottles and, in one instance, a ball-bearing ring from an automobile wheel. "We just do the job," one ESD policeman says of such cases. "These people are in dire straits. There's not much you can say to them, and there's even less that they care to say to you."

One particularly horrible incident involved a husband who castrated himself in a fit of psychotic depression after his wife left him. He walked to a nearby station house, where he handed a box to the desk sergeant and announced, "I won't be needing this anymore." An ESD squad rushed to the station house and transported the victim to a hospital.

Of all entrapment victims, the most cunning, baffling and insidious are children, and ESD policemen are convinced that most of the fun will go out of their job if a serum is ever invented to take the adventurous spirit out of the city's Huckleberry Finns.

The ESD's records are crammed with tales of children who cannot pass fences without climbing through, refuse to let escalator threads disappear without touching them, seldom walk through revolving doors without testing the rubber gasket with their arms, and are irresistibly tempted to slam doors and jail themselves in bathrooms.

A two-year-old girl, bored almost to tears one December afternoon by her mother's conversation with an aunt about dresses, fur coats and other trivialities, escorted her twenty-two-month-old cousin on an exploratory trip into the bathroom of the aunt's Brooklyn apartment. A half hour later, the women realized the girls were missing. Squeals of delight and the splashing of water led them to the bathroom, but the door was locked. One mother, almost certain the girls would drown, ran into the hall screaming. In no time at all, all fifty housewives in the five-story tenement were crowded into the apartment, wringing their hands and chattering about what could be done to coax the girls into unlocking the door. The owner of a ground-floor delicatessen rushed upstairs and hunched his shoulder to the door, but it would not budge. A neighborhood butcher and the building superintendent barged in with axes and a cleaver and were about to break the door down when the ESD arrived and halted the mayhem, fearing that the girls might be injured when the door panels splintered. Officer Walter Whalen mounted to the bathroom window on a ladder raised outside the building and his startled gaze met two very wet little girls, both standing fully clothed in the tub and splashing each other, their blond curls plastered down with water and generous amounts of lather. All around them floated teddy bears, dolls, toothbrushes, toy wagons, one or two shampoo bottles and other bathing accessories. The older girl pointed at Whalen and giggled. A few minutes later, both dripping girls were in their thankful mothers' arms.

The bathroom lock-in caper is a heavy favorite among children, and experience shows that it can be embellished by many imaginative variations. One three-year-old not only locked himself in, but jammed his foot, for good measure, down the toilet bowl. It took a crew twenty minutes to demolish the bowl with hacksaws and chisels.

Summer is the busiest season for child-entrapment cases, since school is out and time for exploring new ways to get into trouble is practically unlimited. A common misfortune befalls children who remove gratings and get their feet stuck in backyard drains. The ESD uses an opened wire coat hanger as a makeshift extractor, working the wire down around the heel so that it acts as a skid to ease the foot out.

Excessive summer heat drove one six-year-old boy and his pet dog to the roof of a Harlem tenement, where he hauled his forty pounds atop a two-foot-high chimney after discovering a cool draft wafting up the flue. While watching his pet play with another dog on the roof, the boy toppled into the chimney, bumping down fifteen feet before his plunge was halted at the fourth-floor level by compacted debris. Terrified, the boy shouted for help for hours until he fell asleep from exhaustion. He was awakened the next morning by rain dripping down on his head, and sent up a new chorus of yells that were heard by a seven-year-old girl neighbor, who ran for help. The ESD responded along with detectives who had been searching the neighborhood since the boy had been reported missing by his mother nearly twenty-four hours before. A rope was lowered and the boy was instructed to secure it under his arms, but tugging by several policemen failed to dislodge him from the sixteen-by-sixteen-inch flue. A second line was dropped with a coffeepot of water for the boy to drink while Officer Joseph Niebuhr sweated in the kitchen of the apartment abutting the chimney to chop a two-by-three-foot hole through the brickwork. When an egress was completed four feet below the boy, the rubbish under him was torn away and he was let down until he fell into Niebuhr's arms. The boy was uninjured, his only complaint being that he was very hungry.

Rescues of children are greatly complicated by a vast pool of collective wisdom among the young that enables one who does not know how to get into trouble to learn from others. A six-year-old Brooklyn boy fell for the lure one hot July day after a rubber ball thrown wildly by one of his companions bounced into a narrow corridor between a concrete-block garage and an apartment house. The boys watched sadly as their treasure rolled about ten feet into the space, which was twenty feet deep and littered with broken glass, sharp stones and garbage. The six-year-old, handily on the slim side, either volunteered or was chosen—police favored the latter theory—to fetch the ball. While his buddies cheered his heroics lustily, the boy grunted and groaned his way in for about six feet and then came to an agonizing standstill between the walls, unable to advance, retreat, stoop or bend. His chums proffered sage advice, all of it ineffectual, and it soon became evident that wiser heads were needed. At the cost of one pound of lard and several square inches of the boy's skin, the ESD emancipated the dethroned hero by using poles with tools to chisel away all the protuberances and rough spots on the walls, grease his body from head to foot and slide and scrape him out.

The complexities of that rescue were child's play compared to those the ESD faced in disentangling a young boy whose hand was caught after he stuffed it into the outlet of a fire hydrant that had been turned on to give neighborhood children a cooling summer shower. The main valve supplying water had to be shut off and the fireplug dug out of the sidewalk. Both boy and hydrant were loaded into an ESD truck and taken to a hospital, where doctors coordinated efforts with the policemen to maintain circulation in the child's hand while heavy-duty saws chewed away the thick metal around it.

Other children exhibit an irrepressible compulsion for thrusting hands into exterior building fixtures such as mail chutes and drop boxes, many of which are protected by so-called flapper valves that lock tightly around intrusive fingers. When the buildings are closed, the unlucky victims have to wait until keys are located by police to get inside and lift the valves.

Boundless curiosity about toys, locks and other gadgetry constantly lands children in strange predicaments. A seven-year-old boy, who surreptitiously borrowed a pair of handcuffs that his customs agent father had left at home, drew the envy of other children in his Brooklyn neighborhood until he snapped them onto the wrists of a playmate. After flourishing the bracelets proudly before the eyes of his spellbound audience, the playmate was eager to have them taken off, but his friend had somehow lost the keys and neither he nor any of the others seemed to know what to do. The manacled boy wailed, and his friends ran off in all directions before parents converged on the scene. The ESD liberated the prisoner with a hacksaw.

A five-year-old girl, who was promised a ride on a mechanical horse outside a lower East Side five-and-ten on the condition that she stay by her mother's side while shopping, became restless and wandered outside to gallop all by herself. When the horse refused to giddy-up after she mounted, the girl poked her right index finger into the coin slot, where it was held fast. After her mother and the store manager tried to dismount the errant equestrienne, ESD Officer John Chakwin arrived to disengage the finger with a hacksaw, pliers and screwdriver. The girl was rewarded for bravery with an ice cream cone, and she told her mother she was no longer interested in riding horses.

A paper-cup-dispensing machine was the undoing of a thirsty ten-year-old girl, who tangled with the contraption in the lobby of a Coney Island theater where she was attending a movie. When no cup emerged after she put in a penny and yanked the lever, the girl socked her hand into the dispenser up to the wrist, then found she could not get it out. After attempting to extract the hand with screwdrivers and small jimmies, an ESD crew pried the dispenser from the wall. As the tearful child kneeled on the floor, the police shattered the device with hammer and chisels and delivered her hand intact.

Fright and hysteria are prevalent in child entrapments, and the ESD men—many with large numbers of children of their own—are trained to recognize the signs and cope with them. A four-year-old boy, watching his father at play in a Bronx bowling alley, panicked after he worked his hand into an automatic machine for returning the balls, and claimed he could not pull it out. ESD Sergeant Albert L. Schroff ordered three of his men to pick up both the machine and the boy and turn them sideways for a closer view of the mechanism. The youngster's fist was doubled over one of the bowling balls, gripping it tightly. Schroff calmed the child and explained that the way out of his difficulty was to un-clench his fist. He obeyed, and the hand came out easily.

The horror of some accidents severely tests the emotional tenacity of the rescuers themselves, who must remain calm and efficient under harrowing circumstances. One such case involved an eight-year-old boy whose lower jaw was pierced by an eight-inch picket when he tripped while tightrope-walking atop a fence on his way home from school in Queens. The spike stabbed upward to the roof of the boy's mouth as the weight of his eighty-five pounds dragged him downward and left him dangling with his feet off the ground. After positioning a box under the boy's feet for support, ESD policemen spent thirty tormenting minutes sawing through the base of the picket under a doctor's watchful supervision so that the boy could be removed to a hospital for surgery.

Cool-headedness in the midst of frenzy was crucial when an eighteen-month-old boy, sleeping in his family's cramped basement living quarters in a Harlem tenement on August 10, 1949, was buried alive beneath an avalanche of thirty-five tons of coal that burst from a bin through a plasterboard partition beside his crib. When the ESD arrived, the apartment was filled with delirious women neighbors clawing with bare hands at the huge black mound that filled the room to waist-high level. The entombed infant's faint cries could still be heard. Officer George T. Hughes dropped to his hands and knees and discovered a narrow opening beneath the shattered partition that had collapsed under the coal. He squeezed into the aperture, worming his way slowly under the tons of shifting coal until he had reached a point ten feet from the doorway, where the infant lay under jagged pieces of the partition that had formed a sheltering tent over his body. Hughes gathered the baby in his arms and inched back to safety, bracing his shoulder up against the plasterboard to protect the child from the crushing weight. A few minutes later, he emerged grimy and sweating with the crying infant. He later was awarded a special citation for heroism.

The fascination of young boys for underground exploration and the building of pirate caves and tunnels has engaged the ESD in scores of cave-in rescues over the years, most of them with tragic endings.

Children favor building-supply yards and construction sites, where the earth is heavily mixed with sand and easy to excavate. From the point of view of rescue, unfortunately, sandy ground is worst because it packs closely around its victims, leaving no pockets for air.

An eleven-year-old Brooklyn boy narrowly escaped suffocation on the night of August 26, 1968, when he sank up to his neck in tons of sand after falling down a hopper he had been playing on top of in a masonry supply yard near his home. The ESD dispatched rescuers, who were joined by firemen, and a ladder was stretched across the mouth of the hopper so that diggers could descend by ropes attached to the rungs in order to scoop away the sand with shovels and their bare hands under the glare of portable floodlights. A rope was lashed around the boy, who was pulled out unharmed after a half hour of hectic work to keep the sand from choking him.

Caves, cliffs and deep gullies, which honeycomb vast parks and recreational areas of the city and weaken under the strain of traffic vibrations or washouts from heavy rains, are other potential death traps for the young. A fourteen-year-old boy and two girls, sisters aged sixteen and thirteen, languished for more than two days in a cave, with its roof slowly disintegrating above them, one weekend in the spring of 1955, after a landslide all but sealed them in. The three were among a group of nine teen-agers who scaled the rocky cliffs of Manhattan's Fort Tryon Park one Saturday night to explore one of the many caves in the area. Leading the way with a flashlight, the boy invited the two sisters to accompany him into the cave while others kept a cautious distance. Dirt and rock poured down over the cave's mouth, leaving an opening only twelve by eighteen inches. When the shock wore off, the youngsters learned from their companions outside that the hole could not be widened without the danger of another dirt slide that might cut them off completely. The trio rounded up several empty orange crates and four kerosene lanterns that had been left in the cave and sat down to ponder their fate. One answer that was ruled out was calling for help from their parents, who would certainly not understand. The boy maintained a surface calm, but when dirt and rocks began dropping from the cave's roof, the girls became hysterical and he wound up leading them in prayer. Hours dragged by, and the youngsters outside drifted away to their homes—all agreeing on a strict pact of silence. They returned the next day to push coffee, hot dogs and doughnuts through the cave opening.

The mother of the girls thought they had gone to stay for the night at a friend's home, but when they failed to show up the next day she called the police. The neighborhood was searched with no results until a day later, when a fifteen-year-old boy told them he had last seen the girls near the cave. By the time policemen reached the cave, all three youngsters were hoarse from shouting. Fearing the trio would be buried alive if taken through the opening, the ESD used picks, shovels and pneumatic drills to batter down the entrance to an adjoining cave, where the rock and dirt formations were found to be firmer. The project took several hours because two concrete shafts supporting an elevated highway through the park were anchored in the wall that separated the two caves, and the rescuers had to burrow carefully around them. Eyes red from weeping, the boy and the two girls were led into the predawn darkness, where they fell on their knees in relief.

The predilection for running away and hiding is another youthful pastime that has embroiled the ESD in wild assignments. A six-year-old Bronx boy playing a game of hide-and-seek decided an empty garbage can was a perfect place of concealment to squeeze into until it came time for him to jump out and have the last laugh on his playmates. The youth spent an hour whimpering while policemen cut up the can to turn him loose.

A Brooklyn boy, playing with schoolmates late one afternoon, found a more serious reason to hide when he realized that it was long past his dinnertime and he faced a scolding if he returned home. He went to the roof of a nearby apartment building, where he saw an open skylight with a ladder inside. After stepping down only two rungs, he noticed an opening into the roof crawl space that seemed an ideal refuge from parental retribution. Wriggling his slim body through the hole, he stretched himself across the rafters and went to sleep. The youth had not counted on the night being so chilly and by the time he awoke he was shivering in his thin jersey and dungarees. When he began sneezing, a woman tenant in the apartment below heard him and telephoned the police. Two ESD officers mounted the skylight ladder and spotted the hole, which they enlarged by ripping away the surrounding plaster and lath. A flashlight beam picked out the youngster, who cowered as far away as he could when the men asked him to come out. Officer Edward Hoffman managed somehow to squeeze his bulk into the opening and twist toward the boy, supporting himself on the rafters, which groaned under his weight and threatened to crack through the ceiling. Hoffman talked soothingly, promising the boy that no reprisals were in prospect. Persuaded that the police had come as friends and not as enemies, the youth followed Hoffman out.

The so-called Christmas tree turnstiles in the city's subways and elevated-train stations are a perpetual—and sometimes deadly—attraction for children who view the closely spaced horizontal bars of the ten-foot-high exit gates as excellent ready-made Junglegyms. So many youngsters entangle heads, arms and legs that the ESD has routine methods for releasing them. The spokes are detached, or bolts are removed from the top to lift or reverse the turnstile when the victim is trapped underneath or inside one of the four compartments.

Turnstile entrapments are a minor aspect of a wide-ranging variety of emergencies in the subways, particularly when trains catch fire, collide or derail. In one of the most grueling rescues in its history, the ESD worked for eight hours with firemen, medical teams and disaster crews to extricate a sixty-three-year-old motorman, almost hopelessly imprisoned when his train slammed against the bumper of a lay-up track in Brooklyn on June 3, 1965. The motorman was guiding the empty ten-car train into a narrow tunnel to park it for the night when it ran out of control and rammed the bumper—a steel structure five feet high and three feet wide that is rooted in concrete at track terminals to prevent trains from rushing off the rails. The front end of the car shot into the air at a twenty-five-degree angle against the walled end of the tunnel. As it bounded back, its steel-plated roof pushed forward, folding down over the motorman. The floor of the cab peeled backward, pinning him by his legs. After doctors administered oxygen to ease the victim's breathing and blood plasma and morphine to ward off shock and pain, ESD crews labored with electric saws, sledge hammers, wrecking wrenches and acetylene torches to dislodge the four-foot chunk of ragged steel pressing in on him. Hours passed as the motorman steadily weakened—at one point he was given last rites by a priest—but the rescuers gradually succeeded in loosening the huge mass. A team of two hundred men tugging on a cable wrested the wreckage away, and the motorman was rushed to a hospital, where surgeons were able to save his limbs.

While wrecks are infrequent, the ESD is called almost three times a month to rescue subway passengers who are shoved from platforms by crowds, who jump to the tracks to commit suicide, to retrieve items such as money, dropped cigarettes and portable radios, or who engage in horseplay or meet dares from friends. Other victims fall during dizzy spells, or while intoxicated, and, panicked, fail to roll into the safety zone under the lip of the platform, trying instead to climb back up as trains roar into the stations.

The most tragic of these incidents occurred just before dawn on May 24, 1965, when three girls entered a subway station on Manhattan's upper West Side after leaving a neighborhood party. One girl toppled to the tracks as her two companions looked on in horror. A young man nearby leaped down to help the girl to her feet but was unable to lift her to the platform. He scrambled back up and tried to hoist her to safety. He had nearly succeeded when a train barreled around the bend north of the station, and the motorman, seeing the struggling girl, applied his brakes, but too late to stop the first car from screeching past the victim and mashing her against the platform edge. The ESD freed her quickly but she died on the way to the hospital.

Some victims survive similar accidents, even after being compressed into spaces four to six inches wide, since the ESD employs a rapid-removal technique developed over many years. A portion of the wooden trim along the platform edge is sawed away to reduce pressure on the trapped person's midsection, and a policeman jumps to the track and crawls under the train to support the lower section of the victim's body. Sure-footedness is essential because power is shut down on only a small section of the affected track, and nearby tracks and third rails remain alive with 660 volts of electricity to maintain train service. Huge bottle-shaped jacks capable of thrusts of 50,000 pounds each are used to tilt the car sideways, clearing a space through which the victim, held by the arms, can be moved to whichever end of the car is nearest. The operation, which consumed up to three hours a quarter of a century ago, now seldom takes more than a half hour since the ESD's invention of accessories called Z bars, which are hooked over the edge of the platform and provide close and sturdy footings for the jacks. When victims are trapped underneath trains, the jacks are strategically placed to lift only that portion of the car required to effect a rescue.

Survival is rare in cases where persons deliberately plunge from platforms to commit suicide, generally as trains are pulling into stations and there is no time for the motorman to brake to a halt or for bystanders to take preventive action. While the general public tends to adjudge subway suicides as exhibitionists because of the bedlam and inconvenience that their acts cause by snarling train schedules for thousands, the ESD sees the victims as much more seriously motivated to kill themselves than to get attention. Individual motives for subway suicides vary, but the availability of the means is an important factor and statistics show it is a relatively sure way to die. Building and bridge jumpers' acts are linked by some psychologists to a subconscious desire for a state of suspension akin to prenatal life in the womb; some subway suicides have extremely conscious and concrete fantasies along these lines. One twenty-six-year-old woman who survived a subway leap, although one of her legs had to be amputated at the hip, later claimed she saw the whole process of the train coming out of the tunnel as "the same way a child comes out of the darkness when it is born."

Subway suicides have waned in recent years, partly because death-bent persons are scared away by increased patrols of policemen assigned to combat underground crime. The drop-off itself has helped check the rate, since police believe suicides are likely to be encouraged to choose whatever style of self-destruction is in vogue at the time. The subway suicide does not fit any precise profile that the ESD can rely on. Of fifteen persons who died under trains in a typical recent year, two were women and thirteen were men, two left suicide notes, one was black and fourteen were white, four were single, three married and three widowed, and the marital status of the remaining five was never officially determined. Seven were thirty years old or younger, three were between thirty and fifty, three between fifty and sixty-five, and only two were in the over-sixty-five age group, which has the highest suicide rate when all categories of self-destruction are taken into account. One nineteen-year-old man who crouched behind a platform pillar in a Queens subway station before plunging in front of a train was a former psychiatric patient, who had been diagnosed as schizophrenic but whose family described him simply as "moody." A sister, who visited him in a mental hospital a week before his death, claimed he was not depressed, but it was later revealed that his suicidal act had come only a short time after he escaped from the hospital, telephoned his mother and found to his disappointment that she was not at home.

The ESD's most dramatic subway-accident victim by far was a forty-year-old blind, deaf and mute man who either tripped from the platform or fell from between the cars of a train to the tracks of an upper West Side subway station four days before Christmas in 1966. After the train roared off, the victim groped along the tracks with his white cane for five terrifying minutes, unseen by the few passengers waiting in the nearly deserted local station. He was almost struck by one passing train, and barely missed contact with two third rails. Two men in the station saw him crumpled in the trough of an express track and dashed to the end of the platform, where they flagged down an arriving local train. The motorman, realizing that an express was due at any moment along the rails where the victim was lying, crossed to the track and waved down the oncoming train fifteen feet from the man's prostrate form. The ESD helped remove the man and rush him to a hospital. The victim had sustained serious injuries, and attempts to determine his identity were unavailing until ESD Officer John Kelleher offered his services. Kelleher was expert in the special manual alphabet of the deaf and blind, which he had learned as a child in communicating with a neighbor who was near-blind and a deaf-mute. By tapping his fingers on the victim's hand, Kelleher spelled out questions to which he received answers that enabled police to notify the man's wife, who hurried to his bedside.

The ESD's extensive operations in the city's underground are not nearly as massive as its rescue tasks in buildings overhead, where roughly sixty thousand passenger and freight elevators are potential traps in which upward of 1,400 persons are killed, injured or stranded yearly. Many are modern high-speed lifts in skyscrapers and high-rise apartment buildings, but others are rickety, antiquated and powered by obsolete machinery in turn-of-the-century loft buildings used as factories and warehouses. Even well-maintained and inspected elevators were crippled by the unprecedented power failure that darkened the city and most of the northeastern section of the nation on November 9, 1965, turning hundreds of lifts into terrifying prisons for office workers and apartment dwellers and burdening the ESD with a monumental rescue job. Hours were spent lifting passengers through the roof hatches of halted elevators or punching escape exits through shaft walls, but when the blackout was over, only one death was recorded— that of a man who fell into the elevator pit of a midtown building. The incredibly low toll was largely attributed to a common spirit of unity among citizens confronting a major crisis for survival, a mood which oddly enough is not always characteristic of isolated elevator incidents, during which mass hysteria sometimes develops as a side effect. When a minor power lapse in one Madison Avenue skyscraper knocked out a dozen elevators and isolated scores of people, the real victims turned out to be those who were not trapped. Creatures of habit, the workers persisted in trudging twenty or thirty stories up stairwells, where the ESD found many overcome by exhaustion and had to resuscitate them. Restarting the elevators was comparatively simple since the breakdown was due to a blown fuse, which was replaced with little trouble.

Before improvements in escape hatches made evacuation of cars easier, the ESD's most difficult, dangerous and dirtiest task was repair of disabled car mechanisms. Doors were opened on the floor beneath the car and planks bridged across the shaft for the policemen to balance on while working with heavy tools on the car's greasy underside and teetering precariously above the gaping emptiness below. The procedure is now officially frowned on and undertaken only when impenetrable or inaccessible emergency exits make removal of passengers by ropes or ladders impossible.

To assure absolute safety in all elevator rescue work, standard ESD procedure calls for the precautionary removal of fuses from the electrical source supplying power so that the car cannot be started up accidentally by someone unknowingly pressing a button on another floor. The policeman who removes the fuses is designated as the only one authorized to replace them.

Ropes and ladders were utilized in the rescue of twelve luncheon-bound workers who were piled atop one another when an elevator plummeted three floors after its cable snapped in a Manhattan office building in April, 1953. A centrifugal speed governor automatically brought the car to a jolting stop by jamming brakes against the walls of the shaft. The ESD guided an adjoining elevator abreast of the damaged car and ran a plank between the side emergency exits of both. A nurse inched across the slender board to give quick first aid to the injured while police opened the door on the floor above and lowered a ladder through a trap door in the car's roof. Ten of the passengers, who had suffered only minor injuries, were helped up the ladder to avoid the hazard of evacuating them across the plank. The other two, both heavy-set men with leg fractures, were strapped in wire-basket stretchers and hoisted by rope through the roof hatch to the floor above.

An elevator case that drew worldwide attention to the ESD and embroiled it in an acrimonious legal controversy was the entrapment of Martyn Green, a British actor internationally known for his roles in Gilbert and Sullivan operettas. Green arrived at an upper West Side commercial parking garage shortly after midnight on November 7, 1959, in a light-blue MG sports car, which he insisted on parking himself, fearing that attendants would damage it. He drove the car onto the garage's obsolescent elevator and tugged a cable to start the ride to an upper level. On the way, he heard a strange rapping sound and got out of the car to investigate. The actor, who walked somewhat stiffly because of an old war wound, either stepped too far toward the edge or lost his balance, and his leg was drawn down between the elevator floor and the shaft wall as he rode past the first-floor exit. The limb was nearly torn off before the elevator went up to the second floor and stopped. An ESD crew responded to the summons and attempted to free Green's leg by prying the elevator away from the shaft with jacks and crowbars, but the technique, usually successful on lighter and less massive passenger lifts, failed on the huge garage elevator. Cutting out a section of the elevator floor around the leg was not considered feasible because the material was too tough and thick for saws and the use of an acetylene torch would risk setting fire to accumulated oil and grease on the elevator's floor and exterior. While the actor smoked a cigarette and talked to his rescuers, a medical intern deadened his pain with an injecton of morphine.

The ESD crew worked for nearly an hour and a half before the intern, who had arrived late on the scene, stepped forward to re-examine the crushed leg. "All of the bones in your leg are shattered," he told the actor. "There is a danger of gangrene setting in. I must amputate and I need your consent." Green agreed to sign a paper consenting to the surgery. The ESD crew began a last-ditch effort, while other policemen drove to a hospital and raced back with plasma and other supplies. Then, in the glare of their own emergency lights, the policemen watched as the intern severed Green's leg below the knee. During the operation, the actor's cocker spaniel, who had been with him in the car, stayed close to his master, licking his face and snapping at the policemen. When the amputation was finished, the actor was carried to an ambulance, which, to add to the difficulties, refused to start. An ESD car was pressed into service to nudge the vehicle two miles to the hospital.

Within a few days after the incident, the intern resigned in an angry public exchange of charges with hospital officials over whether he had deliberately delayed going to the accident scene and whether they had supplied him with adequate surgical instruments. When Green recovered, his attorneys filed court suits against the garage owners and the hospital, and sought monetary damages against the police, whom Green charged with aggravating his injury by moving the elevator instead of trying other methods to free him. He won a five-thousand-dollar settlement of his claim against the police and eight thousand dollars from the hospital. The suit against the garage was thrown out.

The aftermath of the Green case was especially bitter for the ESD, which had succeeded previously in saving victims in the same kind of trouble under even more challenging circumstances. Only four years earlier, a businessman had been rescued after both his legs had been locked between a doorless freight elevator and the shaft in a downtown Manhattan loft building. The victim had stepped aboard the car while it was rising past the third floor and had tripped, his legs dropping outside the elevator cab. By the time the car halted seconds later at the floor above, his left leg had been imprisoned up to the thigh and his right foot was caught at the ankle. The ESD's hydraulic jacks broadened the crevice, and within two hours the victim's right foot was out. About thirty-five minutes later, his badly mangled left leg also was released.

Even more elaborate measures were necessary to extricate a chief elevator operator when his elevator suddenly jerked upward in a West Side hotel and sent him sprawling, with his left leg protruding from the car as it rose. The leg was folded down by the top of the first-floor doorway and pinned between the shaft and the car, which stopped just below the second floor. The ESD constructed a supporting platform of ladders and planks under the car and secured it with a cable strung from the top of the shaft before acetylene torches were used to burn out a pair of heavy steel shoes stabilizing the elevator in the running tracks along the walls of the shaft. With the shoes removed, the car was swung away from the wall by hydraulic jacks so that the victim's leg could be eased out. The entire process took nearly four hours.

Several policemen risked almost certain death during the rescue of a businessman who was left hanging upside down by both feet after an elevator accident in a lower East Side loft building. The man had fallen headfirst into the gap between the shaft wall and the floor of the remodeled cage elevator, which had no doors. When the car halted at the fifth-floor landing, the victim was suspended by his ankles and left staring head-down in terror at the bottom of the pit sixty feet below. An attempt to squeeze the car toward the rear of the shaft with jacks was abandoned when the movement wrenched the victim's ankles and he screamed out in pain. The rescuers were forced to tackle the more difficult and exhausting job of gouging out a section of the elevator floor around his feet with electric saws. As the work progressed, a rope was looped around the victim, and Officer Joseph Sarlo, a six-footer, leaned into the shaft from the fourth-floor landing below to support him and take the weight off his legs. A fellow officer held Sarlo by the belt as he swayed above the deep shaft. "Don't worry, Mac, you're almost home," Sarlo assured the businessman as the saws bit laboriously through three inches of steel and four inches of wood in the elevator floor. Sarlo mopped the man's brow, gave him sips of water through a straw and kept up a steadying stream of conversation. After an hour, the left foot had been freed, but it took another hour of careful sawing before the other foot was clear and the man dropped into Sarlo's arms.

Elevator rescue work requires intricate knowledge of all types and designs, including underground freight platforms that operate from subbasements to sidewalk level and sometimes emerge without warning to entrap or injure pedestrians. One such case involved an advertising-agency secretary who took a shortcut through a four-foot-wide alley between two midtown office buildings en route to a lunchtime dental appointment. The woman was terrified when two huge sidewalk-level doors of a rising underground elevator unfolded beneath her. Before she could escape, the steel doors swung wide, one pinning her right leg against the wall of the alley. Her screams were heard by two police officers, who raced into the alley and saw her writhing in pain. One ran to the street, hailed a passing taxicab and borrowed a jack from the driver. The jack was thrust between the steel door and the wall, and expanded. An ESD squad attempted to stretch the space further with a heavier jack, but a one-and-a-half-inch horizontal crossbar in the steel framework above the elevator platform held an upright stanchion tight against the door gripping her leg. It took a half hour to sever the crossbar with an acetylene torch so that the stanchion could be bent back and the door swung away.

Recovering dead bodies enmeshed in lifting machinery or crumpled between cars and shaft walls is a grisly ordeal, and the chief goal of these assignments is to extricate the remains in a way that will prevent further mutilation. Accidents of this type are common in public housing projects, where young people are killed and injured after climbing through emergency exits to reach elevator-car roofs, which are favorite hiding places for narcotics and other contraband. The horror of the work is deepened when the person is someone who has impatiently blundered into the fatal mistake of trying to escape from a crippled car instead of shouting or pushing alarm buttons to summon help. One fourteen-year-old schoolboy, making an after-school delivery for a dry cleaner, was killed in an upper East Side apartment building when he attempted to exit through a side emergency hatch of a stalled elevator. The youth had worked the upper part of his body into the shaft when the elevator suddenly dropped, crushing him against the wall. His body was not discovered until an hour later by his father, who had shown up at the apartment house searching for him. The father and the building superintendent rode up on an adjoining elevator and removed its side panel to peer into the stuck car, where they saw the boy's legs.

A rescue that the ESD has never been overly eager to boast about occurred on the morning of June 19, 1964, in a garment-district office building, where two porters were marooned in an elevator near the fifteenth floor. ESD policemen took a companion elevator up to the floor and transferred the porters through a side emergency door. As the rescue elevator descended and congratulations were being exchanged all around on the simplicity and speed of the feat, the car came to a standstill at a point just below the third floor. The policemen aboard grew increasingly agitated when all the button-pushing in the world would not restart the car. Brief consideration was given to the unthinkable idea of summoning the ESD to rescue its own men, but reason and honor prevailed, and the repair company under contract to service the building's elevators was called instead. The company's mechanics were painfully slow in arriving, but once they did the policemen and the porters were out in a jiffy. Shrewdly calculating that no commendations were in store for their performance, the men discreetly vanished out a back entrance, spiriting the porters with them and skirting an embarrassing encounter with newsmen who were waiting out front to interview them.

Unlike many other entrapment cases, in which death or rescue generally is swift and decisive, saving persons buried alive in fallen buildings or in cave-ins is grim and fatiguing work, often stretching over hours or even days, with the rescuers toiling under danger of new collapses that might seal the doom of the persons they are trying to extricate.

The first building-collapse rescue in the ESD's history took place during the predawn hours of June 3, 1930, after a two-story brick plant housing a fat-rendering company disintegrated in a fiery explosion on the bank of Brooklyn's Newtown Creek—a barge canal bordered by oil depots and industrial plants. A lone night worker was interred under tons of brick and contorted steel beams, and his muffled cries for help could be heard above the hiss of live steam seeping from two fifteen-thousand-pound boilers that had thundered down with the building and lay on top of the wreckage. ESD Sergeant Louis J. Michaels at first considered summoning derricks to move the boilers, so that the victim could be reached by digging to him from the top of the rubble, which would be far less dangerous than tunneling in from the side. But the worker's fading pleas convinced him that there was no time to be lost waiting for heavy equipment. Michaels and members of his squad waded into the mountain of debris with picks and shovels, and burrowed a hole two and a half feet high to the entombed man, retreating for their lives several times—once when an entire section of an outer wall that had been left standing cracked from top to bottom and tons of bricks threatened to clog the tunnel entrance. No sooner had each avalanche subsided than the men were back and working, and within five hours a breakthrough was made to the victim. When it was discovered that one of the man's legs was wedged under a heavy girder, Michaels ordered jacks into the tunnel and supervised the job of moving the girder just enough to twist the man free. Exactly one-half hour after the man was carried out and removed to a hospital, the ceiling along the entire length of the makeshift tunnel fell in with a roar. At an official police hearing into the incident, one of the witnesses to the rescue said, "I believe that if the policemen had moved the wrong pipe or beam at any time, there would have been thirty to fifty tons down on them."

With the city in an almost perpetual state of construction and demolition, building collapses have been a steady problem over the years due to structural defects, explosions and fires, although recently tightened safety codes have reduced the menace.

The stage was set for the worst building-collapse disaster in the city's modern history late in the afternoon of December 11, 1946, when a gang of neighborhood boys reportedly climbed to the top of an abandoned ice-manufacturing plant in upper Manhattan and lit candles on the roof in the gathering dusk. As the shivering youths crouched and warmed their hands over the dancing flames, the candles toppled, setting the roof ablaze. When the flames spread, the boys panicked and fled.

Neighbors, observing the thick black smoke funneling from the top of the structure, turned in an alarm, and firemen arrived to drag hose lines up ladders to the roof and extinguish the blaze. After searching for hidden pockets of flame that might still be smoldering, the firemen left, only to be recalled about six hours later when the fire flared up, possibly rekindled by sparks that had penetrated the plant's cork-insulated walls. Flames engulfed the roof, forcing the firemen to retreat to positions atop an adjacent six-story tenement, from which they played hose streams down into the inferno.

Below in the tenement, ninety-five persons, comprising twenty-seven families, were asleep or getting ready for bed, and the fortresslike, twenty-eight-inch-thick walls of the icehouse seemed sturdy enough to shield them against any danger. There was no sign that an evacuation would be necessary until a muffled explosion sent a shudder through the building, and then it was too late. A sixty-foot section of the ice-plant wall buckled in the ferocious heat, and the sound of the collapse rose to a roar as the commander of the fire company on the tenement roof ordered his men to leap to the safety of an adjoining rooftop. Tons of weight shifted against the side of the tenement, bulging its rear wall, which crashed down from the roof to the second floor. Without warning, the building's sleeping occupants were hurled from their beds into an avalanche of blood-red bricks, twisted steel beams and splintered timber and plaster. Cloud bank after cloud bank of dust swirled skyward as the river of destruction carried its human cargo to ground level and below. Many were killed outright, while others were miraculously catapulted into the street in their nightclothes, stumbling about in silence until passers-by guided them to shelter. One ten-year-old boy survived when he was swept into the open oven of a gas stove that was rammed through the tenement wall into the building next door, where he fell out unharmed.

After the dust settled, the screams of people buried alive could be heard in the darkness. The ESD raced to the disaster site and joined firemen and construction workers from the neighborhood in a massive rescue operation. Thousands of persons, many of them relatives of the entombed, stood silently by in the surrounding streets while huge cranes rumbled in to swing giant steel beams and timbers off the wreckage, which was laced incongruously with Christmas packages, balls of tinsel and other ornaments for the forthcoming holiday season. The search went on through the night and for hours thereafter, with brief letups only when shifting debris threatened to slide down and crush rescuers burrowing with pneumatic drills through huge piles of brick and plaster. Some of the injured were pried loose with shovels and crowbars, but others were given morphine injections and spent hours in drug-dazed agony as ESD policemen burned through girders and other metal debris with acetylene torches to extricate them. Forty-eight hours passed before all hope was abandoned that anyone else would be found alive. The cranes began to clear away the rest of the wreckage, which ultimately yielded thirty-seven bodies.

A vast majority of earth cave-in victims are laborers digging in the elaborate subterranean network of railroad and subway tunnels, electrical, water-supply and sewage conduits and thousands of other hidden chambers that form an underground metropolis beneath the city, but the oddest case occurred on May 17, 1953, in the backyard of a house in a quiet residential section of Brooklyn. The owner of the home was walking through his yard when one of his legs sank almost knee-deep into the soft earth. He pulled himself out and went to get his brother-in-law and six neighbors to help him fill the hole, concerned that a child might fall into it. Furious shoveling failed to close the cavity, and none of the group was aware that the dirt being scooped up formed a thin crust above an abandoned cesspool that had been covered over years before. A fifteen-foot circular patch of ground crumbled under them and the six neighbors fled to safety as the home owner and his brother-in-law fell into a crater seventeen feet deep, their heads barely visible above the dirt that settled over them. Futile efforts were made by two of the neighbors to free the trapped men, and a call was put in for police. On reaching the scene, ESD policemen tested the perimeter of the crater to make certain there were no other hollows under the ground. A fire truck was summoned and a ladder positioned horizontally across the crater. Two firemen crawled to the center of the ladder and dropped in harnesses to loop ropes under the armpits of the men and keep them from sinking deeper. Dirt was dug from around the victims and passed to the surface in buckets. Wooden shoring was driven around their bodies to shield them against new earth slides. When enough dirt had been cleared, the men were towed to the surface, both in shock but neither with more than cuts and bruises.

The ESD's most agonizing cave-in assignment began shortly after noon on May 9, 1950, in a commercial garage in Brooklyn's Borough Park section, where a contractor named Dominick Atteo was sinking a well with his two sons and a friend to provide water for car-washing. When one of his helpers climbed out and reported that a jutting boulder was stuck in the well's wall at the eighteen-foot level, Atteo descended and stood on top of the rock, hacking at it with a shovel. The rock loosened and moved outward and downward about two feet, carrying Atteo with it under a shower of sand, small stones and dirt from the sides of the well that buried the lower part of his body. Atteo struggled to free himself, but he was too solidly trapped, and one of the sons ran to telephone the police.

The first of four ESD squads that were eventually to respond reinforced the sides of the well by driving a double layer of twenty-five-foot timbers down the sides of the shaft. Two fifty-gallon oil drums with tops and bottoms knocked out were sunk, one above the other, around Atteo and a steel construction helmet was put on his head to protect him from cascading stones and dirt. ESD Officer Luke McGrath was lowered by a rope to dig out dirt between the steel cylinders and the shorings, and repeated attempts were made to haul Atteo up with a heavy manila line placed under his armpits. The efforts failed.

Firemen, utility workers and two doctors joined the operation, and Atteo's courage and stamina drew nationwide attention as the story of his plight was spread by news media. Hundreds of curiosity-seekers converged on the garage, and police were swamped with telephone calls from across the nation asking for information and suggesting alternate rescue methods. The drama had stirred memories of a similar ordeal only thirteen months before when three-year-old Kathy Fiscus fell into an abandoned well at San Marino, California, and died despite a mammoth effort to save her. The public was anxious that the Atteo case end on a happier note.

When Atteo's breathing became increasingly more labored and the air in the shaft grew foul and damp, a doctor ordered oxygen pumped down the shaft to prevent him from suffocating. With an unflinching air of strength and spunkiness, Atteo chewed gum and sipped the coffee and the warm milk sent down to him. Then at one point he begged for a cigarette.

A lighted cigarette was lowered to him in a can that he was using to remove some of the dirt around him. Who passed the cigarette was a matter of dispute, but an official investigation later established that police had been emphatic in ordering that there was to be no smoking in the vicinity of the well because of the oxygen. The inquiry, which found no evidence of culpable negligence by anyone, determined that two persons, whom it did not identify, had been allowed to remain near the mouth of the well for Atteo's moral support and that two other cigarettes had been lowered to him earlier without mishap. But the result this time was horrifying. Oxygen drifting out of the well exploded in a sharp blinding flash and Atteo screamed as a ball of fire scorched his face, shoulders and arms and burned all the clothing off his back. A bucketful of water was poured on the flames, and a doctor descended immediately to smear castor oil over Atteo's seared flesh and administer plasma to keep him from going into shock.

The oxygen, which had been turned off, was turned on again only after police were certain that no further danger existed, and the rescue operation resumed in an atmosphere of growing despair. A priest donned overalls and a body harness and edged down to give Atteo the last rites of the church. As the priest was pulled up after hearing Atteo's confession, the well-digger called after him, "Don't worry, I'll be all right. Tell my wife not to worry. I'll be up soon."

Toward midnight, a longer, more tedious rescue plan was adopted, and a crane was brought in to start a long, stair-step trench thirty feet from the well. The aim was to angle the trench down at a forty-five-degree slant to a point below Atteo and to clear the boulder that was believed to be pinning one of his feet. His other leg was doubled under him. Controversy over the project mounted as the work of gouging out the six-foot-wide ditch was hindered and delayed because the garage's low roof provided little clearance for the crane's boom and the strain and vibrations of the digging threatened to collapse the ceiling, which was supported by a single pillar that stood only a few feet from the well's mouth. Massive wooden beams were propped beneath the iron girders underpinning the roof to keep it from caving in, and the trench walls were painstakingly shored up as the work progressed.

Atteo's attractive young wife, keeping vigil near the well, began to crack as the dawn of a new day broke. She swayed on her feet, and cried, "I can't stand it. I can't stand it anymore. He's dying." Then she fainted.

A little over an hour later, a cheer went up from the crowd when the trench was only a few feet from the side of the well. No lateral breakthrough was made, in fear that a new cave-in might negate the hours of work, and the rescuers continued to tunnel to reach the boulder. By midmorning Atteo's condition had weakened considerably, and two surgeons prepared instruments to amputate his leg as a last resort in the event that it was found his foot could not be freed. But Atteo seemed scarcely aware of what was going on, and it appeared doubtful that he would be able to withstand the shock of surgery.

Twenty-seven hours after Atteo had been trapped, rescuers were able to reach through a small aperture and tap him reassuringly on the back. Hope soared as the wooden shoring around Atteo was ripped away, but the incredible spirit that had sustained him was fading fast. An ESD officer leaned over the shaft mouth to ask, "How are you, Dom?"

"I'm going to die," Atteo gasped.

"No you're not," the policeman insisted. "You're going home."

Atteo's wife, clenching her rosary beads, was weeping and near collapse. One of his sons fell on his hands and knees at the mouth of the pit. "Don't you see the boards, Pa?" he shouted as more shoring planks were removed. "Take a deep breath—move your arms. Hold on, Pa, hold on. Can't you see the light in back of you? They're coming closer and closer."

There was no reply. The son got to his feet and walked away. He sat down, tears streaming from his eyes. "It's no use," he cried. "He's dead." When Atteo's wife heard the words, she screamed and fainted again.

An eerie silence fell over the crowd as a doctor went down into the trench. He came out a few minutes later, wiping sweat from his face and slowly shaking his head. With all the rescue machinery stilled, and dazed ESD policemen standing by, a priest stepped to the side of the well and intoned the Catholic prayers for the dead, then turned to the crowd and said quietly, "He kept his courage and faith to the end. There were no complaints."

Angrily refusing to accept that the well-digger was dead, the policemen tried in vain to resuscitate him after his body was extricated and brought to the surface.

When the first shock of the tragedy wore off, relatives and friends of Atteo bitterly criticized the rescue effort. His widow was not inclined at first to join them, but later filed suit for $200,000, charging that police had been derelict in allowing the lighted cigarette to be lowered. The suit never came to trial, and the city eventually agreed to settle the matter for $7,500, part of the money going toward the education of Atteo's two youngest children.

ESD Officer Michael Collins, one of the policemen who risked his life to tunnel to Atteo, was heartsick. "All we needed was another fifteen minutes," Collins said. "If he had lasted that much longer, we would have had him out alive."

5. The Living and the Dead..................

Death and scenes of physical, emotional and spiritual illness are everyday grim realities for the Emergency Service's policemen, who minister to an average of sixteen thousand so-called aided cases each year. The vast majority are victims of heart attacks in streets, offices and homes; the others are abandoned and forgotten souls found dead or dying in run-down tenements and furnished rooms and under other pathetic circumstances. Nowhere is the pathos deeper than in cases of recluses who end their bizarre existences in penurious solitude, some while hoarding great wealth. The ESD has known hermits of every shade and variety.

On a sweltering summer day in 1951, an ESD squad was summoned to a dark, musty flat in an apartment house basement on Manhattan's East Side after neighbors had not seen or heard its occupant for almost three days. A strange graying wisp of a woman who had long been an object of gossip in the neighborhood, she was rumored to have been a beautiful and vivacious girl whose life of seclusion had begun at age twenty-two after she saw her mother die of a heart attack and her father commit suicide, both on the same day.

A bag of groceries leaned against the apartment door, left there

124

by a delivery boy after repeated ringing of the bell had failed to arouse the woman, who normally answered by opening the door just enough to admit the supplies. A scrawled sign on the door read "Research, Editorial and Clerical Information Bureau," but the woman had been careful never to allow anyone so much as a peek into her private world.

The faint, nauseating odor of decaying flesh permeated the air outside the apartment. Two policemen from the local precinct station house had called for the ESD after responding to telephone complaints from neighbors and ringing the doorbell. Getting no answer, one policeman had attempted to force the door open, but had found it solidly locked.

Within a half hour the ESD squad wrenched the heavy wooden portal from its hinges with hammers, chisels and crowbars. As policemen lifted the door, an avalanche of cardboard cartons cascaded into the hallway, spilling out an odd array of clothing and household goods.

Flashlight beams poking into the darkness showed that the four-room flat was a welter of trunks, packing cases, cardboard boxes, magazines and books that rose in a solid wall from floor to ceiling. Eight policemen spent the next hour clearing the cluttered foyer and uncovering a network of narrow floor-level passageways that burrowed beneath a mountain of debris. The toppling cartons were filled with expensive artifacts and household items that had been bought and never used, including stacks of rich Irish linen still in the paper in which they had been wrapped at the store. Underneath the cartons lay a vast collection of antique furniture coated with years of dust, and many of the books and magazines scattered throughout the apartment were moldy souvenirs of a bygone era.

Worming his way through one of the tunnels, a policeman swung his portable lantern into an open area, where the rays focused on a ghastly tableau. The corpse of a frail woman, clad in men's underwear, was spread-eagled on an army cot surrounded by the carcasses of five dead cats and a dog. Guarding the makeshift bier were a gaunt police dog and a well-fed white cat.

After a medical examiner was called to certify the death as natural and to order the body removed, the policemen made an even more startling discovery. Tucked in a cardboard box were yellowing legal documents for valuable property the woman owned in New Jersey and bankbooks with recorded deposits totaling more than fourteen thousand dollars.

In another case, bankbooks listing a fortune of $62,500 were uncovered in a thirty-five-dollar-a-month fifth-floor walkup apartment on the upper East Side, where two elderly sisters had hanged themselves a month before rather than face eviction from the haven where both had lived for twenty-five years in virtual self-imprisonment. Five locks secured their front door and elaborate barricades crisscrossed all the windows. ESD policemen, using rubber gloves because the corpses were in an advanced state of decomposition, helped cut down the bodies, which were clad in long black dresses in the style of the 1890s, even to high-button black shoes. One sister had hanged herself with clothesline she had tied to a curtain rod in the living room; the other was found hanging from a skylight in the bathroom. The sisters left a note, written in Hungarian, saying that they would rather die than be evicted from their home—a dilapidated tenement that was slated to be torn down within a few months to make way for a luxury apartment building.

Other recluses have included two women known to their neighbors as impoverished rag-pickers until their deaths, when searches by police revealed them to be fabulously wealthy.

The ESD's most celebrated recluse case was that of the Collyer brothers, who had led a zealously guarded life behind the boarded-up windows of an East Harlem mansion for nearly four decades before the full extent of their misery was unveiled to the world.

The reason for the brothers' strange life style was an impenetrable mystery, but the speculation was that it dated back to adolescent trauma over the troubled marriage of their mother and father, the latter a once socially prominent gynecologist.

The younger brother, Langley, an affable and soft-spoken graduate engineer, offered no clues on the few occasions when he ventured out in turn-of-the-century clothing to shop or to consult lawyers about the brothers' long-standing feud with government officials over uncollected property taxes. The older brother, Homer Lusk Collyer, a former admiralty lawyer who was blind and invalided, remained hidden in the ghostly, tree-shaded brownstone, doted on by Langley, nine years his junior, who somehow was convinced that Homer's failed eyesight and crippled limbs could be restored by a steady diet of rolls and fresh oranges.

For nearly two decades, the brothers existed without electricity, gas, running water or heat, favoring the deprivations to paying bills. Their only sources of light and warmth were several kerosene lamps and an antiquated stove.

On the morning of March 21, 1947, the ESD was sent to the Collyer mansion after a man telephoned police with a mysterious report that one of the brothers had died. A ladder was lowered to the roof of the three-story brownstone from the top of a building next door, and policemen, smashing through two skylights and a trap door to gain entrance, were enveloped in a suffocating stench from the cluttered darkness.

Several minutes passed before an ESD officer could drop into the vast sea of junk and grope to the front of the top floor, where he sought ventilation by knocking out wooden slats covering the windows. A heavy iron grating was ripped from a rear basement door by other policemen, who penetrated from below into what one later described as a "junk dealer's nightmare."

The searchers struggled through the cobwebbed maze, blocked at every turn by ragged bundles of newspapers, cartons brimming with bottles, cans and other refuse and broken furniture stacked to the ceiling. Paths weaving through the mansion were mined by elaborately contrived booby traps, fashioned of tons of debris wired together so that its crushing weight would crash down on intruders. Tin cans were strung on the wires to rattle as burglar alarms.

Several hours of work failed to put a significant dent in the choking mass, and a ladder was raised to a second-story window so that ESD Officer William Barker could climb up and rip off the barrier of rotting boards.

Once inside, Barker discovered the body of seventy-year-old Homer, dressed in a dirty threadbare gray bathrobe and lying on the floor about six feet from the window with his legs drawn up to his chin. Homer's white hair and beard reached almost to his waist. He had been dead about a week.

There was no sign of Langley, and although there was some belief that he might have wandered off in stunned grief over his brother's death, overalled policemen spent the next three weeks extracting more than 120 tons of rubbish from the mansion in an effort to locate him. The only evidence of life found were eight ailing cats wandering in the building's basement.

A building inspector was summoned to supervise the project when the brownstone was threatened with collapse by the dislodging of debris that had become an integral part of the structure and was holding up weakened walls and floors. The sagging areas were shored up as the work progressed. Legal entanglements arose after a host of distant cousins in the Collyer family descended on police to challenge them on what articles were heirlooms and what was worthless and could be carted away.

Samples in the Collyer collection included the well-preserved jawbone of an ass, a bumper, hood and crankcase from a model T Ford, a doll carriage, fourteen grand pianos, a raft of dressmaker's dummies, two ancient potato-peeling machines, a 1908 telephone directory, a box of model airplanes and toy tops, pictures of pinup girls, several World War I–vintage gas masks, the battered roof of a horse-and-buggy carriage, a set of twenty-five-cent tickets to the annual boat excursion of the Trinity Episcopal Church School of July 8, 1905, more than 2,500 books, and newspapers carrying advertisements for men's shirts at seventy-nine cents each and whiskey at $1.75 to $2.50 a gallon. Numerous legal papers documented a personal fortune of over $100,000.

On the nineteenth day of the search, Langley's body was extricated from beside an old-fashioned wooden trunk, where he had smothered under tons of refuse that had thundered down on him from one of his own booby traps. He was attired in an old sweater and rumpled pants. His legs and feet had been gnawed by rats. A bag of oranges beneath the corpse led police to surmise that he met death while bringing a meal to Homer, who apparently starved to death when no one was left to feed him. For his role in helping recover the bodies, Barker was cited for excellent police duty, along with seven other ESD policemen—Lieutenants Edward M. Reedy and John R. Hudson, Sergeant Valentine Braun and Officers William F. McAdam, Thomas J. Tighe, Joseph Niebuhr and Richard W. Finnin.

However Gothic the aspects of the Collyer case, they did not overshadow an earlier discovery, on March 15, 1942, when the superintendent of a lower East Side tenement called police on the suspicion that the bizarre tenant of one of the apartments in his building might be dead. His fears stemmed from several days' absence of an unearthly clang that had sounded from the flat every night at bedtime.

The tenant, a raw-boned six-footer in his fifties, had lived in the flat for thirty-five years, the last five without a single visitor except one insurance adjuster. Once a month, he would open his door just a crack and push out fifteen dollars in cash with the sole sepulchral word "Rent." The neighborhood knew him by the nickname "Dracula" because of his long, taciturn strolls along its streets in a black top hat, black suit and flowing black cape. Legend had it that the marked aversion he displayed for women was traceable to a tragic romance in his youth. Every two weeks with regularity he visited the corner grocery, closing his eyes before confronting the woman clerk and whispering an order that included one crate of eggs, two boxes of apples, twelve dozen oranges, 216 candles, fifteen pounds of baking soda and a case of ketchup. He paid for the merchandise in twenty-dollar bills, but no one ever knew where he got the money or what happened to the supplies. Rumored to have been employed at one time by a railroad, he was said to have run into job difficulties when he refused to do his night cleaning work in brightly lighted cars, insisting instead on using a flashlight.

An ESD crew entered the two-room flat by crashing in the door with sledge hammers. It was sparsely furnished with two broken and dirt-encrusted tables and chairs, and all the windows were nailed shut and opaque with decades of grime. A bowl of stale cereal rested on one of the tables, but there were no other signs of food. Neither the electricity nor the gas in the apartment was turned on.

In the center of one of the squalid rooms stood a coffinlike metal box, four and a half feet high and four feet wide, with holes punched in its two-inch walls at various points for ventilation. Fashioned of riveted sheet iron, the container resembled a medieval torture device. One end was equipped with a hinged door that would not budge until the policemen pried it from a padlock that clamped it shut from the inside. The door of the chamber swung back to reveal a corpse in trousers, undershirt, galoshes and earmuffs, curled up in fetal position so that the knees rested under the chin. A medical examiner later ruled that the man had died naturally while following an apparently nightly routine of imprisoning himself in the box in an eerie ritual of self-punishment.

While the majority of recluses found by the ESD are victims of self-imposed squalor, one thirty-two-year-old hermit was encouraged in his lonely exile by his anxiety-ridden mother, who evidently feared he would be drafted for Army service during World War II unless she helped him hide. The drama of warped minds and bitter emotions came to light late in April of 1949 in the family's ramshackle brownstone in Brooklyn's Greenpoint section after the mother, facing a hospital stay for treatment of cancer, asked a woman neighbor to care for her son while she was gone. The neighbor listened in stunned silence as the mother led her to the son's hideout in a cramped cubicle inside one of the building's walls and painstakingly explained how food was to be lowered to him by rope. The neighbor kept the secret until after the mother left for the hospital and then notified police.

When ESD policemen tore away plasterboard from the five-by-three-foot hollow behind a living room wall, a bundle of rags arose from the darkness inside and lumbered out, slowly assuming a human form greatly resembling traditional pictures of Robinson Crusoe. The son's leathery face was half hidden by a reddish beard that was long and wild, and his dark eyes blinked at the light from behind spectacles that were held together with pieces of wire. Despite his long internment with no sanitary facilities and only a soft mat and thin blankets for sleeping, the husky man betrayed no signs of physical illness or malnutrition—a tribute to his mother's faithful trips on hands and knees each day through a three-foot-high crawl space above the apartment's hanging ceiling to drop jars of food to him through a hole in the side of an eight-by-six-inch chimney that formed one of the sides of his cell. On the floor of his cubicle was a book entitled *Man the Unknown* and several shorthand training manuals, plus a flashlight for reading.

A thin, watery-eyed proprietor of a tailor shop on the building's ground floor turned out to be the recluse's father, but he was completely unaware of his son's presence in the house. The father said that he had last seen his son ten years before when the lad—then twenty-two—helped him install a new electric socket in his store one day and then left, never to appear again. Told by his wife that the boy had gone to Canada, the father said violent arguments developed over the matter and he had moved down to live in the rear of his store. He had not been back upstairs for seven years, he said, but had contributed to his wife's support, turning money over to her regularly for taxes, gas, electric and food bills.

The police were really astounded when the recluse, after a glimpse of the outside world, announced that he wanted to go back into his hole, explaining that he was not satisfied with "the way things are going." Psychiatrists reportedly diagnosed his case as dementia praecox of the paranoid type and his past disclosed adolescent trouble with obesity, fear of girls, poor grades that put him last in his class in school and overprotectiveness by his mother, who became obsessed by fear of losing him after another son had died of blood poisoning. After her cancerous condition was arrested, the mother was confined to a mental institution, convinced "My son is dead." The son underwent psychiatric counseling, and after seven months resumed life in the outside world as a helper in his father's shop, a clean-shaven, neat but forlorn figure who still preferred a quiet life of privacy. Although expertly adept at shorthand due to his long solitary studies, he complained that he could not secure a job with the skill because prospective employers "all wondered why I had been out of work for ten years."

The incredible circumstances of filth and deprivation under which the city's bereft, aged and indigent are found sometimes invite brusque black humor among ESD policemen, who know that not to laugh would be to cry. One case involving the removal of an aged woman from a filth-infested home in Queens inspired this parody that was submitted by an emergency squad on June 19, 1969:

Upon arrival at above location was informed by some nasty sergeant that there was a little old lady that lived in this dirty old run-down house with a lot of rats, mice and cockroaches. Above-mentioned nasty sergeant ordered crew to gain access to residence and see if said little old lady needed medical attention. Also at above location a nosy little old nun from some nearby church wanted to know from the nasty sergeant if the dirty little old lady was okay.

At this point the above-mentioned emergency crew ordered three bright-red ambulances from Jamaica Hospital to remove the dirty little old lady, the nasty sergeant and the nosy nun. The above-mentioned nasty sergeant canceled two of the above-mentioned ambulances and had just the one shiny bright-red ambulance respond for the little dirty old lady.

One patrolman gained access to above rat, mice and cockroach-infested residence by being thrown through window of porch by another patrolman of this squad. At this time above little dirty old lady was placed in body bag and walked to shiny bright-red ambulance by the above-mentioned resident cockroaches of said apartment.

Door of above-mentioned residence was secured under supervision of said nasty sergeant by the rat and mice residents of said apartment by leaning against same and slamming shut. No further services by members of this squad.

Other aided cases ministered to by the ESD encompass a variety ranging from persons suffering from pneumonia or malnutrition to others whose life breath is cut off by injury, electrocution, drowning, poison or toxic gases.

Resuscitation is an essential element in most aided cases, and the ESD boasts one of the most elaborate oxygen services in the world, yearly dispensing more than five thousand cylinders containing more than eighty thousand cubic feet of the life-saving gas.

The service is the product of years of research and testing that began with the ESD's birth in 1930 in the midst of a controversy raging over the old Pulmotor, which had been invented in 1912 and until the early 1930s was widely used on victims of drowning and persons overcome by smoke and fumes. Critics had branded the Pulmotor a "death-dealing" machine because of its pump action, which forced air into the lungs at heavy pressures and withdrew it under suction in a pulsing cycle that fatigued the victim, reduced the prospects of restoring normal breathing and threatened internal hemorrhaging. The dispute over the device grew so intense at one point that lifeguards at several city beaches fought off attempts to use it on people rescued from drowning, insisting instead on employing only manual artificial respiration, which was considered much safer.

The ESD from the outset adopted a newly developed invention called the inhalator, which exerted no pressure, and merely supplied a mixture of 5 percent carbon dioxide and 95 percent oxygen that was drawn into the lungs by manual artificial respiration to coax heavy breathing. The body's natural reactions were triggered by the carbon dioxide, which stimulated the lungs into inhaling more than their normal 20 percent quota of oxygen and exhaling toxic substances.

While the inhalator was less risky than the Pulmotor and its two gas cylinders afforded far greater capacity, one disadvantage was the need for a three-man crew to operate it. A second drawback was its bulkiness and weight (seventy-eight pounds), problems that later were solved by ESD Sergeant Felix Hanratty, whose research resulted in lightening and reducing the size of the device. Hanratty also developed a manifold apparatus to speed the recharging of depleted oxygen tanks, a process that had been long and tedious. A third drawback was not detected until years later, after new research determined that the lung-stimulating effect of the carbon dioxide was sometimes offset by a tendency to depress the victim's brain-control center and undercut the resuscitation process if his system already was overloaded with the gas. The discovery led to the ESD's acquisition of the more modern resuscitator, a compact machine that can be operated by a single policeman. The resuscitator supplies pure oxygen in cycles of input and withdrawal under pressure carefully controlled by a sophisticated mechanism that regulates to the victim's needs and forestalls any damaging surges. When pressure is deemed inadvisable, a simple flick of a switch converts the machine to inhalator action.

The ESD has a strong tradition of never giving up on resuscitation as long as there is a chance in a million of saving a life. Even though there may be no trace of heartbeat or flutter of breath, the crews prolong the process until all hope of life has fled. Legend has it that rigor mortis is the only positive proof of death that some crews accept, and, more than once, seeming miracles have resulted, with victims restored to consciousness when life, according to any standard medical tests, has faded.

Each squad averages about four cardiac calls during an eight-hour tour. Assignments often entail lugging equipment up four or five flights of stairs, reviving the stricken and carrying them down to waiting ambulances while administering oxygen and first aid. The heaviest victims seem invariably to live on the topmost floors, and when patients are not built for ordinary stretchers, novel methods are employed to remove them for hospitalization. One three-hundred-pound woman posed a special problem after an ambulance doctor cautioned that she might die of visceral congestion if left in a reclining position for any length of time. She was bound with sheets to a parlor chair, which was balanced on two stretchers so that she could be carried upright.

The resuscitation crews are trained to search for objects that might be blocking the victim's throat since the symptoms of choking can often be confused with those of heart attacks. Choking cases are especially prevalent among persons with dentures, who swallow food they have neglected to chew properly, particularly after the relaxing effect of a few drinks before dinner.

Over the years, the ESD has achieved a high rate of success in all kinds of resuscitation cases, with the exception of electrocutions that usually result from industrial accidents, from young boys' stumbling into high-voltage lines and third rails while exploring railroad yards and subway tunnels, or from adults' being shocked by radios, hair dryers and other electrical appliances that they touch or that topple in on them while they are bathing.

One crew worked for hours in a vain attempt to revive an eighteen-month-old girl who was electrocuted on April 7, 1955, in the kitchen sink of a Queens home where she was being given a bath by her grandmother. The baby, who was visiting the grandmother's home for the Easter holiday with her parents from Virginia, grasped the cord of an electric toaster that was still plugged in after breakfast and pulled the appliance into the bath water when the grandmother went to answer a ringing telephone just a few feet away.

Lightning strikes have accounted for a significant number of electrocutions. Massive resuscitation by the ESD saved thirty bathers struck by lightning bolts in two separate incidents on the beach at Brooklyn's Jacob Riis Park within the space of one year—a phenomenon that shattered the popular notion that the fiery flashes never hit twice in the same place. The first bolt stabbed into the sands shortly after 1 P.M. on Sunday, August 8, 1937, killing three bathers and shocking fourteen others into unconsciousness. The tragedy prompted the ESD to station one of its trucks on temporary duty at the beach during the following summer, and the vehicle was on hand on Sunday, August 7, 1938, when a three-forked tongue of lightning streaked down at almost the same spot and time as the fatal bolt of exactly one year before. Fifteen bathers were revived, and three others were given inhalator treatment for more than six hours before the ESD accepted a doctor's pronouncement that all were beyond hope.

Most lightning strikes nowadays are in parks and outlying areas, and the ESD's tasks in the interior city are confined to examining struck buildings for damage, shoring up loose cornices and correcting other dangerous conditions when necessary. Nearly all deaths and injuries from lightning in recent years were bunched mysteriously into a three-month period during the summer of 1959. In June, two children were killed and four persons injured while picnicking in Central Park. Six weeks later, four persons were killed at Orchard Beach in the Bronx and another four injured outside the Bronx Zoo by bolts that struck six miles apart and within fifteen minutes of each other. All the victims had scurried for shelter under trees—the worst possible refuge in an electrical storm. An emergency police squad was already on the way to the beach when the bolts struck. Exactly six weeks later, twin bolts struck again at the same sites, killing a bather at Orchard Beach and injuring a refreshment-stand vendor at the Bronx Zoo. The bather was hit as he hurried across the sands with a beach umbrella under one arm and his three-year-old daughter under the other. The girl slipped from his grasp when the bolt struck and survived with only a slight cut on her forehead. The accident occurred exactly nine years to the day and hour after a man and his wife were killed by lightning in the same area.

During the 1930s, when hospital oxygen equipment was not as plentiful or as highly developed as it is today, the ESD's pioneer resuscitation techniques frequently spelled the difference between life and death for newborn and premature infants with respiratory difficulties and others suffocating from a variety of causes ranging from swallowing their tongues or foreign objects to lung congestion.

"Kiss of life" mouth-to-mouth breathing was used with success in many cases, and on January 20–21, 1933, an ESD team spent seventeen hours in a lower East Side tenement administering oxygen to save a baby after it was born, apparently dead, to a thirty-year-old housewife who had lost four other infants at birth. The six-and-a-half-pound boy's face was black and there was no evidence of breath, heartbeat or pulse. A doctor started mouth-to-mouth respiration after administering a shot of adrenaline to the infant. An inhalator was rigged and oxygen was flowing into the child within forty minutes after its birth. ESD Officers Harold Pritchard, William Englehart, Raymond Taylor and Joseph Barron maintained the oxygen in relays through the night and into the next morning until the baby had strengthened its grasp on life enough to be transported to a hospital nursery.

A police officer's almost fatal choking from pneumonia in 1935 was responsible for the ESD's establishment of an oxygen-tent service that was operated by the men in their spare time with money donated by a police relief fund. The officer was kept alive by an inhalating crew while ESD Lieutenant William Schnabel contacted an oxygen-tent manufacturer and borrowed the equipment, which was then in short supply at hospitals and rented for thirty to fifty dollars a day. The manufacturer donated the tent to the police, and the officer recovered. As a result, several ESD policemen volunteered to learn the operation of the tent and in the first year cared for twenty-three similar cases. By 1937, other policemen had learned of the work being done with one tent and donated $1,350 for five others. They were used to save scores of victims suffering from pneumonia, cardiac ailments and asthma.

The ESD has assisted at the births of hundreds of babies in everything from theater balconies to taxicabs, and rescued scores of unwanted infants close to death from pneumonia and other complications after being abandoned on church doorsteps or left to die in trash cans and incinerators. In the early days, the policemen were trained in midwifery up to and including cutting and tying umbilical cords, but current procedures call for taking no measures beyond delivery that might infringe on medical responsibilities. The umbilical cord now is left intact and the baby placed on the mother's abdomen to await an ambulance or an incubator. When incubators are scarce or delayed, the policemen are trained to simulate the machines. After finding one mother already had given birth to a baby that was gasping for life, ESD Officer Frank Novak improvised an incubator by resting the infant in a dresser drawer under a plastic raincoat and running an oxygen hose into the shelter. To warm the oxygen so that it would not damage the child's eyesight in its cool, raw form, Novak filled a hot-water bottle and wrapped it around the hose, closely approximating incubator conditions.

For infants and children overcome after consuming toxic substances, the ESD relies heavily on the city health department's Poison Control Center, a round-the-clock agency that was set up in 1955 to provide information on antidotes after a rash of poisoning cases from misuse of aspirin and other pills as well as careless storage in the home of commercial products, including cleaning fluids, insecticides, furniture polishes, paints and cosmetics. Children, who under a certain age have no real taste at all and will ingest any fluid or substance without repugnance, were the chief benefactors.

The ESD also draws copiously on the center's ready file of hundreds of toxic formulas and their remedies to aid persons who attempt suicide by overdoses of patent and prescription medicines or illicit drugs. Between 800 and 1,200 persons kill themselves in the city each year and about ten times as many try. Pills have fast outpaced all other means of self-destruction, with the burgeoning use of barbiturates and tranquilizers, and are favored by women over messier and more gruesome methods.

"Sometimes the victims are very prominent people," says Officer Eugene Corcoran, who works out of a squad covering one of the affluent areas of Manhattan. "It really wouldn't be fair to say who they are. A lot actually are accidental overdoses, you know, people who are upset because they can't sleep and then take these pills. They simply forget and lose track of how many they've taken."

The most tragic cases in recent years, according to Corcoran, involve young boys and girls caught up in the drug culture. Corcoran and his fellow officers frequently have been cast in the unenviable role of breaking the news to shocked parents that their children are on drugs.

"A lot of parents don't recognize the signs for what they are," Corcoran says. "They think the kid is just being moody or something like that. By the time we get there, the kids have reached the stage where they're in convulsions and in very bad shape. That's when the truth dawns on the parents."

Classic among the overdose victims are aspiring models and actresses from hometowns too small to contain their ambitions, who ignore the pleas and arguments of parents and travel to the city certain they can take it by storm. Few wind up on Broadway and many more drift into dreary nine-to-five jobs because they have to eat. The fortunate ones go on to other occupations and forget about fame and riches, but there are those who gravitate to dimly lit flats, where the ESD sometimes finds them after they have gulped stupefying doses of pills and written regretful notes over failures in careers and romances.

"They're impatient to set the world on fire," one father said. "They're driven by some kind of ambition. They're trying to prove something. And there are so many. I've never been able to figure out what they're trying to prove."

Besides the usual suicides by overdose, wrist-slashing, gunshot and hanging, the ESD was confronted during the late 1950s with a new wave of asphyxia cases—both suicidal and accidental—when polyethylene bags gained widespread use for dry cleaning and food packaging. The bags, especially those with drawstrings, had a fatal fascination for the suicidal as a handy and quick bonnet of death that could be fitted over the head with the cord pulled tight to capture poisonous carbon monoxide expelled from the lungs. Others hastened the oblivion by inserting into the bags hoses from gas jets or automobile exhausts.

Infants rolling over in cribs or on pillows covered with plastic met accidental death when the material was masked to their faces by static electricity. Several adolescents were suffocated during weird experiments, one while staging a Houdini-like trick to determine how long it would take him to free both hands tied behind his back and rip the bag from his head. In almost all cases, death was swift and the ESD resuscitation crews were powerless to help.

The crews were equally unsuccessful in aiding victims of immolations, another spectacular form of public suicide that cropped up during the tumultuous 1960s among Vietnam war protestors and the mentally unbalanced who followed their example after reading about the blazing deaths in the newspapers. At the height of the incidents, a specially trained team of ESD policemen kept vigil outside the United Nations compound, ready to move in at a moment's notice with dampened blankets to smother flames enveloping the victims and take first-aid measures.

Until the city's utilities converted to natural gas in the 1950s, thousands of persons were overcome accidentally or attempted suicide by manufactured illuminating gas—a mixture of highly explosive hydrogen and poisonous carbon monoxide. ESD policemen faced the hazards of plunging through the toxic vapors to drag victims to safety before a blast could be set off by a neighbor flipping a light switch or casually lighting a cigarette.

Scores died in explosions, but one ailing sixty-year-old wife of a retired stockbroker survived by an unwitting act of self-preservation. After opening five jets on the kitchen range, she lay on the floor, where the full force of the shock swept over her body when the gas blew up, wrecking her apartment and several empty neighboring suites in her Park Avenue building. Hauled unconscious from the rubble, with only a cut lip and bruises, she was resuscitated by an ESD crew.

Fear of killing or injuring others persuaded a death-bent twenty-one-year-old housewife to tape a cautionary note to the door of her Manhattan apartment before turning on the jets after a quarrel with her husband. Policemen fanning through the building to trace the gas spied the neatly printed message, which read: "Do not light the lights and do not come in with a lighted cigarette—for your own safety!"

A beauteous nightclub singer, who was revived by an ESD crew after she was found overcome in her gas-filled East Side apartment, told the rescuers that she had turned on several gas jets in the kitchen, but turned them off again because she was fearful that the fumes might touch off an explosion in the structure and endanger the lives of other residents. The woman had been depressed after a quarrel with her boyfriend, who had broken off their engagement and had started going with another show girl.

The will to die is exceptionally strong in some cases. A young mother, unstrung by separation from her husband, pleaded hysterically with an ESD crew to let her die after she was revived in her gas-filled East Side apartment on a summer evening in 1958. The policemen, summoned by a neighbor with whom the distraught woman had left her four small children, ignored the victim's appeals.

One of the strangest illuminating-gas accidents claimed the life of a Navy veteran on March 21, 1949, in his off-campus apartment near New York University, where he was enrolled as a student. The victim had put a sealed can of beans in a saucepan of boiling water on the kitchen stove and relaxed on a sofa while he waited for the food to heat. The water boiled away and the can blew up, cracking the gas burner beneath it. The student leaped up to investigate and was overcome by the fumes. An ESD crew worked more than two hours in an unsuccessful effort to revive him.

In one of the last illuminating-gas cases, an ESD crew revived a Bronx housewife and her two daughters, who were overcome by the fumes in their four-room bungalow, even though a pet canary was still chirping away robustly in its living room cage. The fumes had seeped through the house from the basement, where equipment was undergoing adjustment for conversion to natural gas. The canary apparently had not been advised that it was his traditional duty to keel over at the first sign of dangerous gas fumes.

Natural gas sharply reduced the toxicity of kitchen-range fumes, but did not discourage the suicidal, who merely found the task of self-destruction longer and more difficult. Unlike the carbon monoxide in manufactured gas, the methane content of natural gas tended in small doses to stimulate victims rather than make them drowsy. Many turned on jets and lay down to die, only to remain awake and alive after hours of waiting. A psychology teacher who was still conscious more than three hours after opening four jets in his Greenwich Village apartment took out a cigarette to calm his nerves while he puzzled out what had gone wrong. The match flame ignited an explosion that blew out a wall and the front door of his one-and-a-half-room flat, and he was pulled alive from the charred ruins with burns over 45 percent of his body.

While no ESD policemen have died as a result of gas suicide cases, several have been killed or injured in accidents caused by the fumes.

ESD Sergeant George D. Nadler, married and the father of four children, was crushed to death in an explosion at dawn on February 1, 1935, after helping remove the body of a night watchman and two unconscious men from the basement of a downtown Brooklyn furniture store that was seething with gas from a broken street main. A huge steel marquee over the store's entrance crashed down on Nadler after it was torn from its moorings by a blast set off by a spark of unknown origin. ESD Officer George Hubner and nine other persons, including three newspaper reporters, escaped alive from under the canopy, some suffering from fractured skulls and other injuries, and some in shock.

Two other ESD officers were killed on the evening of November 25, 1946, while attempting to check gas leaking from a pipe valve in the basement of a private home in Queens. Sergeant Paul F. Roschke and Officer Peter J. Knudsen arrived at the home after two utility workers had grown dizzy and another had been overcome. The workers had attempted to plug the leak with a screwdriver and had also searched unsuccessfully for hours along the snow-covered ground outside the house to locate a main valve and shut off the fumes, which were billowing into neighboring homes and endangering the entire neighborhood. Joined by Officer Francis M. O'Hara, who was assigned from the local precinct station house, the gas-masked policemen entered the basement and tried in vain to stuff the leak with a wooden plug. After retreating outside for fresh air, the men headed back into the basement with soaking-wet towels to swathe the leaking pipe with the dampened material. By some freak, the gas had failed to reach the glowing coals of a hot-air furnace in the rear of the basement until that moment. A terrific explosion demolished the two-and-a-half-story brick structure. Knudsen and O'Hara were entombed under an avalanche of falling bricks, timber and plaster. Roschke, critically scorched over his entire body, was dragged from the wreckage into the street, where flying debris had just injured two teenage boys and two men walking past the house. ESD Lieutenant Charles R. Mitchie, arriving in a car from Manhattan to supervise the operation, saw the holocaust and leaped out to race into the rubble and claw a path to the victims. As he tore away at the wreckage, he was felled by a fatal heart attack. Mitchie, Knudsen and O'Hara were posthumously awarded the Medal of Honor—the department's highest decoration—and Roschke received a citation for bravery.

The ESD's first experiences with natural gas came long before the fuel was commercialized for home and industrial consumption. Known colloquially as marsh or fire gas, the colorless, odorless fumes are an ever-present threat in construction work underground, where methane, generated by the decomposition of buried organic matter, collects in hidden pockets. Relatively harmless in low dosages from kitchen ranges, methane can be deadly when released in dense masses, and the danger was especially acute during the 1930s, when sandhogs were felled by the gas while laboring in compressed-air caissons on tunnels and on foundations for bridge towers and highway pillars in land-fill areas created by the dumping of garbage.

A caisson operation to construct footings for an extension of Manhattan's West Side highway ended in death for one construction worker on August 27, 1937, but ESD policemen saved six others overcome by methane. In another incident, ESD Officers John Liston and Philip Cooper donned masks to recover the bodies of three Department of Sanitation workers who were suffocated by the gas in a Washington Heights incinerator plant on July 23, 1944, after descending a ladder into a forty-foot garbage pit to retrieve a dropped tool. Two other workmen, who detected the gas after scrambling into the pit to rescue their comrades, staggered out alive and were resuscitated by ESD crews.

Natural gas still sends the ESD on upward of three hundred calls yearly, to stem leaks in street mains or in old or defective cooking and heating equipment in homes, restaurants, factories and other buildings. The fuel also is responsible for asphyxia accidents when incomplete combustion produces the same carbon monoxide contained in manufactured gas and gradually consumes all the available oxygen in poorly ventilated rooms and apartments. The danger is particularly prevalent during winter in the cold-water flats of the ghettos, where tenants, failing to receive adequate heat from landlords, misuse clogged or rusted appliances and weather-strip windows to keep cold air out and heat—and carbon monoxide—in. Do-it-yourself repairs or adjustments on gas equipment by home owners in other areas also lead to mishaps when the gemlike blue flame that is a sign of safe combustion is flecked with orange tints that forebode trouble.

The ESD also encounters carbon monoxide poisoning in cases of persons overcome by smoke at fires or by fumes that escape into homes and apartments from defective oil-burner or coal-furnace flues. The invisible and odorless gas causes death within thirty minutes by a kind of internal suffocation, infiltrating the bloodstream and interrupting the flow of oxygen to the body's tissues. The lethal effect is termed the "cherry red death" because the lips of those overcome turn bright scarlet and their corpses glow with a pink hue.

Research by the ESD into other gases and chemicals has played a vital role in developing techniques to combat their effects and in shaping laws to ban or control them. As a direct result of ESD experiments and expert testimony, the city's ordinances governing professional exterminating have been amended several times to impose stringent curbs on highly dangerous fumigants.

The most widely used commercial exterminant in the ESD's early days was HCN, a blend of hydrochloric acid and cyanide, of the type common in gas-chamber executions. It was potent enough in concentrated form to seep through twelve inches of solid brick in four hours, penetrate the heaviest rubber boots and coats and deliver a toxic dose through the skin of a human being within fifteen minutes.

When HCN vapors drifted from a furniture warehouse under fumigation on Manhattan's upper East Side on November 16, 1930, the ESD was called to resuscitate five persons overcome in an adjoining cafeteria. Ten employees were reeling in the cafeteria's basement kitchen, all complaining of throbbing headaches but unaware of the cause. Inhalator crews worked on the unconscious victims while an ESD sergeant and five other men donned masks and dashed into the three-story warehouse. Two fifty-gallon vats of HCN were hauled out before the fumes pierced the masks. The policemen stumbled out, gasping for breath. One collapsed on the sidewalk, but the others adjusted fresh masks and went back in. Within an hour's time, all had changed masks three times to drag out fifteen tubs of the poison and several smaller casks. No one died in the ordeal, but five of the cafeteria's patrons were hospitalized and for three days afterward the policemen experienced severe chest pains and cracked and dry skin. Hardier souls in a poolroom above the cafeteria had managed to flee without paying their scores.

The incident taught the ESD some important facts about HCN, but Deputy Inspector Louis F. Dittman, who was second in command of the unit at the time, was not satisfied that enough had been learned about the progressive effects. Dittman, a slender 150-pounder whose diminutive build had almost led to his rejection for police work, offered himself as a guinea pig.

Without any protection at all, he went into a specially built chamber filled with HCN. Dragged out when he was nearly unconscious, Dittman later appeared as an expert witness at official hearings which ended in enactment of regulations to curb use of the gas. Current laws require that the ESD receive detailed forty-eight-hour advance notice of all major extermination projects in the city. Minor incidents still persist in slum areas, where tenants are overcome while burning pungent sulfur candles in poorly ventilated apartments to chase roaches and other pests. Oddly enough, the candles are legal to sell even though illegal to use.

Dittman's experiments with other noxious chemicals led to similar controls. At one point, he temporarily lost his voice while testing various types of tear gas for police use. He spearheaded efforts to ban sale of the gas to the general public and to agencies other than the police. Although it is now illegal to sell or use, tear gas could be purchased easily by anyone during the early 1930s and was used by banks and other businesses in security systems to protect vaults and safes.

One spectacular incident that helped speed controls on its general availability occurred at noon on August 4, 1933, when a band of young political radicals, led by a Harvard graduate lawyer, teargassed the New York Stock Exchange. Two thousand persons were driven coughing and choking to the street by fumes drifting through the building from two gas bombs that had been triggered near a cooling-system intake vent on the fifth floor. An ESD crew wearing gas masks located and removed the bombs, but trading was suspended for the day. It was later determined that the bombs had been purchased for twelve dollars each at a sporting goods store.

Dittman paid dearly for his daring. Three years after he took full command of the ESD in 1932, he came close to death after undergoing an appendectomy because his natural defenses against infection had been sapped by the effect of the gas tests on his internal organs. He recovered, but two years later, in 1937, he died suddenly of a heart attack in his Brooklyn home at age fifty-five.

Despite gas masks and other protective gear, ESD policemen were exposed to serious hazards during the 1930s, particularly at homes and at ice plants, breweries and other commercial establishments where leaks in refrigeration and air-conditioning equipment exuded sulfur dioxide and ammonia.

ESD Officers William J. Sullivan and John C. Stewart were hospitalized for days after racing through vapors of ammonia on March 4, 1938, to rescue workers injured when coal dust exploded in a Harlem brewery complex and shattered refrigeration pipes. Ammonia fumes spewed over a wide area. The two officers were nearly overcome as they groped through the rubble to help shut off valves leading to the broken pipes and to remove some of the seventeen workers injured by the blast, which killed three men outright.

Carbon dioxide, a third refrigerant in vogue in those days, was relatively harmless when put to such uses as carbonating beverages, but it acquired deadly tendencies when frozen into dry ice, which evaporated into heavy, suffocating fumes that were perilous in poorly ventilated areas. Melting dry ice turned the forward hold of the Buffalo-based inland-waterway freighter *Empire State* into a death trap on November 24, 1936, after the ship berthed at a Brooklyn pier with a cargo of cherries packed between layers of the processed refrigerant. The ESD was summoned after two longshoremen collapsed on entering the cargo area and five other stevedores and two crew members were overcome trying to drag them to safety. ESD Sergeant Charles J. Graf and six officers donned masks and descended to the victims, four of whom still showed signs of life. A dockside crane was swung over the bow of the ship to hoist the men up, but ESD resuscitation crews succeeded in reviving only three. Citations for the work were awarded to Graf and Officers Joseph E. Flanagan, Ernest Peters, Bernard E. Esker, Matthew F. Kelley, Francis E. Underhill and James F. P. Duggan.

By July, 1947, the ESD had acquired a Navy-developed breathing device that generated its own oxygen by chemical reaction in a rubber pouch containing potassium textroxide. Two hoses connected to his mask recycled the wearer's breath through the pouch strapped to his chest in a freshening process that lasted up to an hour. The gear, still part of the current equipment inventory, was used by ESD officers to reach two workers overcome by carbon dioxide that collected as a by-product of fermentation in crushed grape skins at the bottom of a four-thousand-gallon oak-stave vat in a lower East Side kosher winery in October, 1961. The men were rigging a platform for a grape-grinding machine above the fourteen-foot-high vat to begin the traditional fall process of wine-making when a plank fell and one of them descended a ladder to retrieve it. When the worker crumpled to the floor of the vat, his companion—in a familiar pattern that multiplies casualties in nearly all gas cases—rushed down after him and met a similar fate. The victims were lifted out by Officers John Prendergast and Frederick Mahler, but forty-five minutes of resuscitation failed.

Eight years to the month later, ESD Officer Salvatore Spinola, a father of four, died on October 2, 1969, while attempting to rescue an unconscious man in similar fashion from a gas-filled Brooklyn manhole. The victim, a city inspector, had descended into the ten-foot-deep underground chamber to make a routine check, and collapsed after inhaling noxious gas fumes. Spinola, a policeman for fourteen years who held three citations for bravery, donned a mask and went down after the stricken man. He also was quickly overcome. His partner, Officer David Hayes, was driven back by the fumes when he attempted to reach both men. A combined effort by policemen and firemen finally succeeded in bringing both men to the surface, where they were pronounced dead.

Another piece of equipment quickly adopted by the ESD was the Scott Air-Pack, a totally self-contained demand-type breathing apparatus that supplies the wearer with oxygen from a cylinder strapped to his back. An outlet valve with a gauge to monitor the gas flow in the mask is attached to the front of the harness. Standard equipment for fire rescues and for entering buildings filled with toxic fumes, the masks provide almost foolproof protection against all kinds of gases.

Except for leaks in gas refrigerators, mishaps involving cooling equipment fell off measurably after World War II with the introduction of Freon, a safer and cheaper freezing element that had previously been restricted to military use in mobile refrigeration units and as a compressed gas to charge insecticide sprayers.

But new danger emerged with mounting traffic through the city of tanker trucks transporting highly volatile and poisonous gases. The ESD, in cooperation with fire officials, supported stringent ordinances requiring that the vehicles be rigged with elaborate safety devices and that advance reports be filed on the type of cargo and the route to be followed. In some cases, special standby escorts were provided by the ESD, which also prescribed itineraries through least populated areas for trucks carrying particularly hazardous chemicals. While the policies are still in effect to this day, on two occasions flagrant violations nearly ended in disaster.

A truck carting chlorine through Brooklyn on June 2, 1944, sent clouds of yellowish-green vapor drifting over a ten-block area when the chemical escaped through a one-eighth-inch hole eroded by rust in one of twenty tanks of the gas aboard the vehicle. A motorist behind the truck saw the fumes streaming from the tank and pulled alongside to inform the driver, who was transporting the water-purifying substance from Bayonne, New Jersey, to a pier for shipment to Cartagena, Colombia.

After telephoning his employer and the police, the driver, joined by a foot patrolman in the area, lifted the slender four-and-a-half-foot-long tank from the truck and rested it in a sidewalk trash basket above a subway grating. The heavy fumes seeped downward, and hundreds of passengers aboard an arriving subway train, mostly women with their children, were sent staggering, coughing and choking onto the station platform.

The chlorine mushroomed rapidly throughout the neighborhood and by the time ESD and other rescuers arrived, more than a thousand persons had been affected. Resuscitation crews worked frantically, concentrating on the more seriously overcome, while other ESD teams stifled the leak in the tank and shoveled sand over residual patches of the thick gas on the street to prevent further spreading. More than four hundred of the victims were rushed to hospitals for further treatment but only 195 remained and none died from the effects of the gas.

The absence of fatalities was due largely to the Army's contribution of the so-called wonder drugs penicillin and sulfadiazine, which were not yet available for civilian use, to treat victims in danger of pneumonia infections from the deteriorating effect of the gas on their lung tissues. The ESD and other agencies gave the Army vital data gathered during the rescue effort that aided in military research into techniques for resuscitating possible gas casualties during World War II and for improving the effectiveness of military gas masks.

A subsequent investigation disclosed that the truck had been operating with an expired permit and had fulfilled none of the legal requirements, which called for covering the tanks with a heavy tarpaulin and carrying masks for the driver and fifty-foot hoses that could be connected to fire hydrants in case of emergency. The vehicle also lacked signs warning of the nature of its cargo.

The south tube of the Holland Tunnel between Manhattan and New Jersey was turned into a giant gas chamber on May 13, 1949, when a city-bound truck carrying an illegal load of carbon disulfide caught fire and exploded with a force that ripped out the tile walls down to the structural steel for a distance of more than 230 yards. ESD and other rescuers turned out en masse to aid motorists, who stumbled to the exits with handkerchiefs clutched to their faces to ward off the poisonous yellow vapors and other acrid fumes released by exploding bottles of bleach on another truck in the tunnel. Fortunately, the tunnel's powerful air-ventilating system sucked the fumes away before a deadly concentration could build up in the two-mile tube, which burrows ninety-three feet below the surface of the Hudson River. Harbor Unit launches raced to the site to scout the surface for telltale bubbles from a possible puncture in the tube, but no leak developed. The damage was confined to twenty-three trucks and cars and about seven hundred feet of the tube's interior, which cost $600,000 to repair. An investigation showed that 4,400 gallons of the chemical, which is used in rayon and cellophane manufacture as well as being a rubber solvent and fumigant, was aboard the truck in eighty fifty-five-gallon drums, in violation of laws limiting the maximum single load permissible in the tunnel to one hundred gallons. Sixty-six persons were injured in the incident—none seriously—nearly all of them ESD policemen, firemen and other rescue personnel.

Despite tightening of restrictions and surveillance procedures, tanker-truck accidents still occur on occasion due to unforeseen circumstances. In October, 1965, a tank trailer loaded with 8,600 gallons of explosive propane gas—enough to devastate an area a half mile square—disconnected from the tractor truck that struck a bump while towing it through the northeast Bronx. The tank dropped onto the tractor's rear wheels. The driver slammed on the brakes in time to prevent the tank from slipping off its precarious perch on the wheels and crashing to the roadway and rupturing. ESD squads and firemen rushed to the scene of the predawn accident and immediately evacuated about sixty persons from two neighboring motels and forty others working the grave-yard shift at a nearby plastics factory. As a precaution, all service on a nearby elevated-train line, 150 yards away, was stopped in fear that rumbling trains might dislodge the propane tank from its delicate position. All streets within a half-mile radius were blocked off to traffic. After deflating the tanker's tires and wedging chocks under the wheels to prevent further slippage, ESD crews used jacks to raise the tank and reconnect it to the tractor. The operation took four hours.

The bulk of propane accidents nowadays occur at construction sites, where the gas is stored for heating tars and other materials. The gas was responsible for one of the most spectacular accidents in the city's history when a propane tank tore like a blazing rocket through a midtown area on August 21, 1968. The one-hundred-pound tank, four feet long and one and a half feet in diameter, was being used to melt tar for repaving a terrace outside the penthouse offices of a Madison Avenue public-relations firm when the tar over-heated and burst into flames. Workmen called police and the ESD responded along with firemen.

The leaping flames spread to the tank, which rocketed across the terrace, shattering the penthouse windows and shaking the en-tire building before plunging northward into Madison Avenue and crashing through the window of a coffee shop a block away. Thirty customers and employees in the shop had rushed to the front win-dow on hearing the explosion and saw the flaming missile coming straight at them. All scattered toward the rear and dived to the floor, as the tank crashed through the plate-glass window, hit the front counter and exploded, spewing flames over a waitress and setting her hair and clothes afire. She ran screaming around the shop until the manager and two customers grabbed her and beat out the flames with their jackets. ESD policemen helped remove her to a hospital.

Of all the deadly vapors ESD men encounter in their work, one of the worst is live steam. Several emergency policemen have been seriously scalded plunging into factories, homes and office build-ings where broken heating and pressure pipes have released seeth-ing clouds of steam, but one of the most gripping ordeals occurred on the bitter-cold evening of December 22, 1955, at a street inter-section on Manhattan's East Side.

A pedestrian crossing the intersection side-stepped a swerving car, slipped on ice and plunged under a barricade ringing the mouth of an open pit that had been dug by workmen to repair a cluster of underground steam pipes. As the man landed at the bottom of the pit, his body smashed one of the pipes and the hole was almost instantly filled with boiling vapors. The victim's agonized screams attracted nearby Traffic Officer Joseph Citelli, who dropped into the pit but was immobilized by the intense heat.

Passers-by called police, and ESD Officers Arthur Bonte and George Heaney were ordered to the scene. Bonte leaped into the pit and swiftly located Citelli, whose right hand was so badly scalded that the bones showed through the flesh. He boosted the policeman up to Heaney, and then groped his way to the pedestrian, who lay motionless at the bottom of the pit, his legs wedged into a small crater.

"The steam was agonizing," Bonte recalled later. "I managed to drag his body over to the wall. I pushed him upright, using him as a prop, but even that close I couldn't see him, the steam was so thick."

Heaney reached down to pull the pedestrian out and then helped Bonte to the surface. "We didn't need a doctor to tell us he was dead," Bonte said later. "He'd been cooked alive."

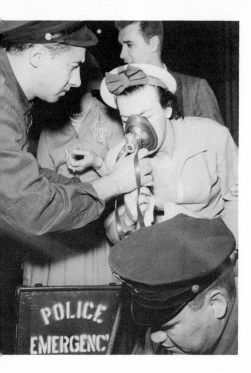

A patrolman administers oxygen to a passenger overcome by smoke during a subway fire.

New York *Post* photograph by Louis Liotta © 1960 New York Post Corporation

Moments after he'd tried to jump from a cable atop the Manhattan Bridge, a would-be suicide (second from right) is brought under control by three patrolmen.

New York *Post* photograph by Vern Shibla © 1973 New York Post Corporation

These high-speed fiberglass boats, each twenty-five feet long, are part of the police beach patrol fleet.

New York *Post* photograph by Louis Liotta © 1968 New York Post Corporation

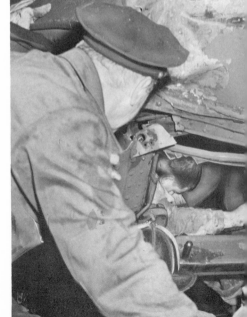

A subway yard motorman lies trapped in the wreckage of his train, April 15, 1960. Rescuers finally reached him but he died on the way to the hospital.

Wide World Photos

The Emergency Service bomb truck, used to transport bombs and other explosives that cannot be deactivated on the spot.
Courtesy of the New York City Police Department

A sixteen-year-old girl is safely caught in a police emergency net, April 14, 1964, after she had jumped from a fifth-floor ledge of the Salvation Army headquarters in Harlem.
Wide World Photos

An emergency crewman tries in vain to free a man buried in the collapse of two West Side rooming houses, June 22, 1964.

New York *Daily News* photo

A youth jumps from the seventeenth floor of the John Adams Houses into an emergency net. He survived, although his fall stretched the net to almost three times its pretested strength.

New York *Daily News* photo

6. Metropolitan Safari

The roughly 7.8 million human beings who inhabit New York and are vulnerable to suicidal urges, undersize bathtubs and other assorted misfortunes are not the only living creatures who require the expertise of the Emergency Service when they blunder into or cause trouble. By latest estimate, there are 313,000 licensed dogs, countless cats and a wild and weird array of other beasts that amply qualify the metropolis as a jungle in the literal rather than the derogatory sense.

The ESD has faced thousands of droll adventures over the years with a bewildering assortment of animals and birds that roam the city—many domesticated pets, others escapees from planes and ships, and still others that appear with a kind of ghostly magic.

One of the ESD's earliest safaris into the animal kingdom began on a balmy spring afternoon in Brooklyn when a housewife returned home from a shopping trip to find that her apartment had been burglarized by a thief whose tastes ran more to food than to cash and jewelry. As the woman was about to enter her apartment, on the second floor of a two-family house, she looked inside and noticed that her refrigerator, with door open, was tilted against the kitchen wall. Scattered on the floor were a butter dish that appeared to have been licked clean, an empty bowl, which had previously been filled with chicken legs, and a quart milk bottle, drained dry. The housewife heard scraping noises behind her and, glancing around, saw a five-hundred-pound bear, with butter smeared on its nose, lumbering up the stairway. The bear made a sort of courtly bow. The woman was unimpressed by this seeming gentility and fled screaming into the flat, banging the door shut and locking it. Her shrieks rose in intensity as she raced to a front window and shouted into the street.

A neighborhood policeman heard her screams and ran to the house. He listened in astonishment as the housewife gasped out from the window the incredible claim that a bear was chasing her. Uncertain whether her situation demanded a restraining jacket or an armed posse, the officer knew that in either case the ESD would satisfy the need.

He ran to a nearby call box to telephone for help. An ESD squad under the command of Sergeant Hugh McGuire responded.

Soon convinced that the housewife was telling the truth when they heard the bear growling wildly inside the house, the squad raised a ladder to the window and brought the woman down to the street.

McGuire then mounted to the roof with his men and lifted a skylight over the stairway where the bear was lurking. After four attempts, he succeeded in dropping a lasso around the bear, but the rope snapped and the huge animal tumbled head over heels down the steps. When the policemen rushed to the door, the bear, furious over the rough treatment he'd been receiving, refused to come out. At this point, a pet-shop owner who lived next door and was keeping the bear in a backyard pen for some circus friends arrived home and was told by police that the animal had escaped. The man went to the door behind which the bear was barricaded, kicked it open and offered the animal some cookies as an enticement to surrender. Eager for the treat, the bear came out only long enough to grab the cookies, then dashed back into the house, slamming the door and leaning against it to keep it tightly shut. The cookie lure was tried twice more and failed, but the policemen were not about to admit defeat. While the unsuspecting bear sulked inside, one of the officers crept up to the door and secured a rope around the outside knob. The pet-shop owner was

instructed to offer more cookies. When the bear emerged to retrieve them, a team of policemen yanked the rope and the door
slammed shut behind the animal. The mouse-trapped bear found
himself being wrestled toward the hole in the fence through which
he had escaped. He turned for one last sneer, growling his distaste
for all assembled, before he was thrust back through the hole,
which was quickly boarded up.

Since that early foray, the ESD has dealt with an ever-widening
variety of pets and wildlife. The incidents have grown to an annual
total of nearly four hundred, due to a steady upsurge in the city's
dog and cat population and increased travel, which allows pet fan-
ciers to return with all sorts of strange creatures that they later
discover are dangerous and turn loose on the streets. Cats and
dogs far outnumber all other pets in the city and are notorious
for poking heads and paws into drains and containers, squeezing
into narrow crevices between buildings and apartment water pipes
and scampering up into trees and other lofty perches without fig-
uring out beforehand how to get down. The entrapment cases
usually call for slicking down the animals with lubricating oil to
slide them free from whatever is imprisoning them. But some rescue efforts are much tougher and require the more exhausting work
of chiseling away brickwork, sawing through metal and disman-
tling plumbing fixtures.

A majority of the animals are released unharmed, but the ESD,
which cooperates closely with agents of the American Society for
the Prevention of Cruelty to Animals, maintains a standby list of
expert veterinarians to treat those that are injured. When the animals scoot up into trees and other high places, or run wild with
rabies and threaten the public safety, the policemen often risk
life and limb chasing them. A fairly common and dangerous assignment in the present era of high crime involves rescuing children from trained attack dogs kept by home owners as a defense
against burglars and other intruders.

Hundreds of abandoned, garbage-strewn tenements in Harlem
and in slum areas of Brooklyn and the south Bronx afford food
and shelter for an estimated hundred thousand other vicious dogs.
Some have been wild for generations. Others are mistreated animals that are thrown out by owners and wander the streets, ter-
rorizing people. The ESD had long considered acquiring the kind

of tranquilizer dart guns already used in less densely populated sections of the country to deal with animal packs when they run amok. The program was held in abeyance for years by the customary ESD concern over whether the effectiveness of weaponry is offset by the danger of injuring bystanders in crowds.

The policy on tranquilizer guns was swiftly reversed after a three-year-old girl was torn to pieces by a pair of wild dogs in Brooklyn's Bedford-Stuyvesant ghetto in the spring of 1972. A training program was begun in the use of weapons that fire a compressed carbon dioxide charge to propel a needle-tipped dart loaded with a nicotine-alkaloid-based tranquilizer. The drug inflicts no permanent injury, but merely immobilizes the animal for up to an hour so that it can be removed and turned over to the ASPCA. Marksmen are under orders to corner the animal where possible and fire at close range to reduce the chances of hitting bystanders, although the drug rarely causes ill effects in human beings, except those suffering from respiratory or heart ailments. While the guns are standard equipment for veterinarians and animal handlers at the zoos, the ESD is the only citywide unit to possess them.

"You don't find many veterinarians working at midnight on an emergency call," explains ESD Sergeant James Heller, who supervised the first experimental use of the guns. "If a lion escapes somewhere, we're it."

Runaway monkeys closely rival cats and dogs in their talent for eluding capture. The humorous antics of the primates are painfully frustrating since they tend to attract audiences, which encourages greater virtuosity of performance and makes them more difficult to catch. Entrapment depends on quickly isolating them from crowds. In one case during the late 1960s, the ESD spent a month recapturing all but one of six high-strung experimental monkeys that ran wild through an area of upper Manhattan after fleeing from a scientist's automobile. The last of the fugitives vanished completely and hasn't been heard from since.

Chimpanzees pose an even greater challenge than monkeys, since they combine dexterity with weight and strength. The ESD recalls as one of its worst animal cases the escapade of a buxom, seventy-five-pound female chimpanzee named Minnie, who was featured in an animal exhibition at the old Manhattan Hippodrome. When a keeper entered Minnie's cage one morning to give her fresh bedding, the animal capered about, chattered in high excitement and bit him. The keeper hastily backed out of the cage, failing in his panic to fasten the door securely. Minnie was quick to take advantage of the oversight. She loped down the corridor behind the keeper while charwomen working nearby brandished their mops and shouted at her to stay away. Hearing the commotion, the keeper turned around to see the chimp dart into the unoccupied office of the exhibit's proprietor.

She was restored to good temper for a time when she knocked over an inkwell on the desk and discovered that she left perfect finger and toe prints at every step, but her mood darkened considerably when other menagerie employees converged on the office. She dodged back out into the corridor and swung up on a set of large iron pipes suspended from the ceiling about eight feet above the floor. For the next two hours, she taunted her pursuers by steadfastly rejecting lures of bananas, sugar and other delicacies. The menagerie employees finally gave up and called for outside help.

The ESD arrived and attempted to lasso Minnie. The tactic backfired when she retreated indignantly into the duct of a ceiling ventilator shaft, pouting and aloof, while the policemen pondered what to do next. Several desultory and useless suggestions were made by bystanders. Various enticements were tried. Minnie was offered more goodies. Thoroughly contemptuous, she tossed the food back at her would-be captors. There was some talk of using tear gas to flush Minnie from her hideout, but the plan was discarded when a lion tamer loudly protested that he was not going to watch as all his cats were reduced to tears.

Nearly seven hours elapsed before the idea was advanced that Minnie might be scared into the open if someone sneaked up on her from the opposite end of the ventilating shaft.

The maneuver was more than Minnie had expected. When the intruder neared, she grew extremely nervous and began to back away. As the chimp gave ground, a chain attached to her collar slipped through a vent and policemen leaped to grab it. She was tugged down through the opening. With handcuffs snapped on her wrists, she was taken back to her cage, where she settled down to her normal routine with the air of a chimpanzee to whom liberty meant nothing.

The ever-changing fads in exotic animals owned by city-dwellers has kept the ESD constantly boning up on new techniques of capture. The years have brought an ebb and flow of strange pets, including raccoons, foxes, ocelots and skunks. Raccoon chases, still common on Staten Island and in the upper reaches of the Bronx, are a perilous task since the speedy little animals have strong tree-climbing instincts as well as razor-sharp teeth capable of snapping through nets and inflicting painful bites. In the ESD's fledgling days, a pet raccoon demonstrated this strikingly after escaping from a Brooklyn home one summer afternoon and climbing a nearby tree. Two agile officers shinnied up after the animal. Two others stood below with an outstretched blanket. The men in the tree shook the limb on which the raccoon had taken refuge. The pet lost its grip and fell into the blanket, but bounced out and scrambled to a loftier limb. The policemen followed. The limb broke under their weight, crashing down and knocking a bystander unconscious. Grounded and enraged by the debacle, the raccoon bit one of the policemen and bolted back up into the tree. After restoring the bystander to consciousness, the policemen doggedly resumed the coon hunt, this time with a strong leather loop at the end of a pole that proved too tough for the wily animal to gnaw through.

A similar noose was used successfully a short time later to ensnare a two-year-old silver fox when it made the first of three escapes in the space of one week from a cage in the backyard of a Brooklyn home. The fox grew foxier on its second flight. Ducking away from the noose, it led panting police to nearby Newtown Creek and dived into the water. The ESD commandeered a small boat and paddled furiously to overtake the animal. The fox was removed to an ASPCA shelter, but was quickly sprung by its owner and taken home. Within a few days, it broke loose again and disappeared into the ruins of an abandoned house. The ESD surrounded the site, but the fox somehow slipped through the cordon, never to be seen again. Foxes still turn up at times and lead the ESD on tally-ho hunts, especially in forested areas of the Bronx.

For capturing such animals, the men now employ a noose device consisting of a four-foot length of pipe through which a strong doubled-over cord is threaded until it emerges as a loop at one end. The loop is cast over the animal and drawn tight by pulling the loose cords at the other end of the pipe.

In the early 1960s, the ESD experienced increased trouble with pet skunks, which had become so popular that the health department found it necessary to issue a warning against the danger of the animals' contracting rabies and creating a public hazard. Fortunately, most domesticated skunks are deodorized, but gas masks are always handy whenever the wild and fragrant variety turn up.

Other aromatic animals the policemen view with little enthusiasm are hogs and goats, which boast another unseemly trait— obstinacy. A hog of magnificent physical proportions, but somewhat retarded mentally, snarled rush-hour traffic on the George Washington Bridge one March evening until its stubbornness was overcome by sheer weight of force. The 850-pound hog, reared on the choicest garbage, had caught the eye of a New Rochelle ice dealer when he drove to a New Jersey pig farm to pick up a porker to butcher for his family. He loaded the animal aboard his ice truck and headed for home.

Lost in dreams of roast pork, he was driving across the bridge at the height of the rush hour when the tailboard dropped from the truck and the hog crashed to the roadway. The ice dealer was unaware of the loss until he heard the screech of tires as motorists swerved and braked to avoid striking the animal. The hog squatted stolidly in the center of the traffic, grunting and refusing to move. Drivers and spectators choked the Manhattan end of the span. The hog owner saw at once that the problem was too much for him and called the police. ESD Sergeant John Casey and his men arrived and constructed a slanting runway of wooden planks leading from the pavement up into the truck. The ramp conveyed no idea whatever to the hog. The best hog-callers among the policemen tried to lure the animal back into the vehicle with no success.

The hog made no attempt to get away, but neither did it yield an inch to coaxing. Four policemen mounted the truck and ropes were hitched to the hog to haul it in. Other policemen applied themselves to the animal's rear end to encourage its progress. After much pulling and pushing, the hog was dragged back and the truck's broken tailboard was lashed down. The hog's owner started off for home, but the first jounce tore off the tailboard. There was another delay while it was repaired. As night fell, the ice dealer and his hog departed and traffic on the bridge returned to normal.

Similar chaos erupted on Manhattan's lower East Side one fall day when a goat that was to be the *pièce de résistance* at a Puerto Rican family feast balked at the menu plan. The animal, stored in the basement of a neighborhood grocery to await its fate, was terrified when the grocer's seventeen-year-old son showed up to slaughter it on the morning before the scheduled feast. After one glimpse at the huge butcher knife, the seventy-five-pound, eight-month-old goat bounded out of the basement to the street, ran east and plunged into morning rush-hour traffic on the East River Drive. The grocer's son hailed a taxicab and trailed the fugitive. ESD Officers Theodore Motz and Patrick O'Connor were cruising nearby when the radio crackled with an alert that traffic on the drive had been thrown into turmoil. Motorists were careening in all directions to avoid hitting the prancing creature. Near the Brooklyn Bridge, the officers spotted the animal gazing perplexedly at ribbons of traffic stacked bumper to bumper along the highway. O'Connor got out to approach the goat. The animal vaulted a three-foot safety barrier in the center of the highway and raced north. O'Connor hurdled the barrier to chase on foot, while Motz sped ahead in the ESD wagon to cut off the goat at the nearest crossover point. The goat reversed direction several times to elude capture. At one point, O'Connor commandeered a taxicab and instructed the driver, "Follow that goat." A startled passenger in the cab's rear seat whispered faintly, "Oh, my God, this could only happen in New York." Laughing motorists left their cars to watch as the goat scampered two miles to the north and then two miles to the south before leaping off the highway and heading for the financial district. Motz and O'Connor abandoned their vehicles and took up pursuit on foot. Exhausted and frightened by traffic noises, the goat collapsed in a heap in front of the New York Stock Exchange. The officers, both shaking with laughter by this time, advanced from either side and grasped the animal's horns. The grocer's son arrived soon after in the taxicab to claim it.

Horse rescues were a major assignment of the ESD in its early days, before the animals gradually dwindled in number with the growing use of automobiles. The most memorable occurred in 1938 after a disastrous fire swept a lower East Side stable, destroying 130 peddlers' horses. Workers searching through the ruins discovered that nine horses had miraculously survived the blaze. They were marooned in a darkened corner on the second floor of the building's blackened shell.

The flooring on which the horses were stranded had been seriously weakened when supports were burned out under and around it. The boards threatened to collapse and plunge the animals to death or injury. The ESD was directed to shoot the horses to save them from further suffering, but the policemen were repelled by the idea and set about to rescue them. A call was put in for two Sanitation Department wreck trucks with steel I-beam tops. One was backed under the shaky flooring. Jacks were positioned under its chassis and it was raised four feet off the ground until its top firmly supported the sagging boards. Brickwork around a window near the horses was broken away with sledge hammers, and the second truck was driven alongside the building's wall just under the enlarged opening. After a wooden ramp was constructed between the window opening and the top of the truck, the horses were paraded down one by one to be strapped in horse belts and lowered to the ground.

One of the ESD's numerous innovations in equipment evolved from the complex job of saving horses trapped in excavations. The animals usually were dragged out by block and tackle—a method that was slow and arduous and exposed them to further injury by jostling against the sides of the pit. To lift the horse straight up, a derrick would have been ideal, but the equipment was too heavy and cumbersome to be moved swiftly to rescue sites. One of the officers invented a giant tripod, made of telescoping steel pipes, that was compact, mobile and could be set up quickly over a pit with a pulley at its apex to hoist any heavy object to the surface. The tripod has since been removed from all of the trucks to make room for more urgently needed equipment. In its stead, ladders, which are always carried on the vehicles, are lashed together in tepee style. The tripod is held in reserve at ESD headquarters and utilized only when specifically required.

No equipment is ever considered obsolete. All rescue devices that fall into disuse are eliminated from the truck-equipment inventory, but are stored in case the situation for which they were originally intended should arise again. The unit still keeps a horse belt on hand to rescue steeds on the Police Department's own mounted force or on the city's bridle paths.

Although the ESD has had little direct experience with jungle animals in recent years, it is alerted to stand by with weapons and other equipment whenever dangerous beasts are transferred from one location to another in the various city zoos. It also provides escorts for trucks transporting wild animals through the city and lends assistance when zoo animals are injured or overcome. Not long ago, the men were called to the Bronx Zoo to resuscitate a five-hundred-pound gorilla that had fallen into a moat surrounding its isolated preserve. Ten policemen tugged the gorilla out of the water by ropes and trussed up its arms and legs. A resuscitator was applied to its face, and hours were spent in an unsuccessful attempt to save the beast. A few men later confessed to mixed emotions about whether they had been eager for the revival effort to succeed. If the animal had regained consciousness and had broken its bonds, they might have found themselves running for their lives.

The ESD fared better with nine prized chimpanzees that were overcome by carbon monoxide in the cellar of a Queens home. The policemen entered the cages where the chimps were being kept and sat astride the prostrate primates, pouring oxygen into them and administering artificial respiration. The problem was to know exactly when to stop the resuscitation efforts and get outside the cages. In the end, all of the policemen and eight of the chimpanzees were alive.

None of the animal expeditions of the present day can match, for sheer danger and excitement, pursuits of jungle beasts and other wild creatures that escaped from loosely guarded zoos, circus sites and private compounds in the service's early days. A full complement of armament—including machine guns, tear-gas bombs and shotguns—was mobilized one spring night in 1937 to track down a four-hundred-pound tiger running wild in Queens. While awaiting shipment from a circus grounds, the animal gnawed through the wooden planks of its crate and broke free by ramming its head against the weakened timber. As it roared off into predawn darkness, circus attendants shouted the alarm. A few minutes later, police received a telephone call from an excited truckdriver.

"Listen," he said. "I'm not drunk, so please believe me. I'm driving my truck just now, and I see a tiger—a big tiger. I see three men chasing a tiger."

"Wait a minute," the policeman on the other end of the line said. "You mean you saw a tiger chasing three men."

"Look, don't argue," the truckdriver shouted. "I'm in a hurry and it don't matter who's chasing who. Only it's a tiger and he's loose. Good-bye—I'm going."

The ESD was joined in the tiger chase by a circus posse of sixty men with pitchforks and other makeshift weapons. The pursuers lost the animal several times in the darkness before cornering it in a tree at the rear of a private home. Policemen and a circus trainer encircled it with nets. The tiger was dragged from the tree, hauled back to the circus site and placed in a new crate for shipment.

Lions are another jungle quarry the ESD regards with the utmost circumspection, even though up until very recent years it was technically legal for a child to walk New York's streets with a lion. A law enacted sometime before 1850 stipulated only that the lion be on a leash with an adult walking one-eighth of a mile ahead to warn passers-by that the king of the jungle was at hand. Lion-walking in the city was permissible at night, under Section 1425, Subdivision II, of the Penal Law, provided that the lion-walker was preceded by a person carrying a cautionary red light. The law, which astute legislators have since repealed, was still in force on a summer morning in 1961 when an attendant checking cars in a West Side parking lot peered into a white Cadillac and saw a lion poised regally on the back seat. Nary a child or adult was in sight. The attendant stared in disbelief at the tawny beast, then he fled out into the street shouting for help. He stuttered out his story to a police officer, who was somewhat skeptical, but agreed to accompany him back to the car. The policeman's doubts were soon dispelled. He took one look at the lion and, with gun drawn, backed away to summon reinforcements. Two ESD trucks sped to the parking lot along with ten police radio cars and an ASPCA wagon. Several of the policemen took out shotguns, while others encased the car in a suicide net secured with extra-heavy rope lashed over and under the vehicle. Not long after, a lion-tamer named Flynn, from Saint Louis, showed up to claim the beast. He was amazed by all the fuss. Flynn insisted that the lion, whom he identified as King Kado, was good-natured and deserved a friendlier welcome to the city. He intimated that police in particular, and New Yorkers in general, were a little unsophisticated and very hostile.

"We do this everywhere we go," he explained. "Generally, we have to fight the crowd around the car to get to him. People want to stick their arms through the open window to pet him."

The tamer said that he had been on his way with the "completely docile" King Kado to a county fair in Maryland. He had detoured into the city to see a former sweetheart. The girl was the light of his life, he sighed. She also had been sorely missed in his lion act by the thousands who had thrilled when she put her head in King Kado's mouth. At this point, one of the policemen spied some blood on the Cadillac's door and wondered aloud whether King Kado had momentarily forgotten his genteel manners and munched on some overtrusting admirer. Flynn angrily defended King Kado. He protested that the lion shunned violence and the blood had been spilled when his sweetheart's mother had cut her ear getting out of the car. While Flynn was voicing his indignation, his former fiancée-partner arrived with her mother from a nearby restaurant, where they had been talking over a possible patch-up of the broken romance. Both backed up Flynn's story. The ASPCA agents meanwhile were chiefly concerned about the lion's plight. They complained that the beast looked hot and uncomfortable in the back of the car and that it was cruel to leave him there.

"What do you mean, cruel?" Flynn fumed. "The normal temperature where lions live is 120 degrees. It's only ninety-one here. He's very comfortable."

All the while, King Kado sat patiently in the back seat, purring with a sound resembling a motorboat in low throttle. He did not seem in the least upset, even when police handed out summonses all around and invited Flynn and the beast to leave the city. Flynn was cited for health-code violation and cruelty to an animal. He and King Kado were given a special police escort through the Lincoln Tunnel to make sure they would not wander astray before reaching New Jersey. Not three days had passed before Flynn, apparently still ardently intent on reconciling with his ladylove, was back. King Kado was spotted ensconced in the Cadillac in a parking garage close to Times Square by someone who called police but didn't take the time to leave his name. With shotguns at the ready, ESD policemen again wrapped the car in a net. An ASPCA wagon had been summoned by the time Flynn returned, and he helped walk King Kado to the vehicle, which removed the lion to the Central Park Zoo where he was lodged in the only cage available, which was marked "Lioness." Flynn was arrested.

"We're not going to allow our citizens to be terrorized because of someone's desire for publicity," a judge later scolded Flynn in court, and sentenced him to thirty days in the workhouse. Flynn was led off to jail, with no further word on the progress of his love life. His sweetheart, who had switched from lion-taming to exotic dancing under the name Bon Bon, sniffed when asked about her former suitor. But she grew wistful at the mention of King Kado, murmuring, "I love that lion."

Fearsome as lions, tigers and other wild animals are, the ESD has experienced its stormiest adventures with escaping bulls, a common problem before the last of the city's slaughterhouses closed and shifted operations to New Jersey and elsewhere in the mid-1950s. The Hudson River waterfront area west of Times Square was one of the nation's busiest cattle runs. Livestock, led by "Judas" steers or goats, were herded off barges and railroad cars and guided through the streets to slaughterhouses. Escapes were fairly frequent.

The biggest, toughest and worst-tempered bull ever confronted by ESD matadors was Rhoderick Dhu, a black-and-white Pennsylvania Holstein. He was driven to the city by his owner on the morning of July 5, 1930, in a crate in the rear of a small truck. The owner, who intended to transship the animal to Puerto Rico for a show, drove across the bridge from New Jersey to Staten Island and north to the ferry then operating to Brooklyn. As the ferry put out through the morning mists, a hired man on the truck noticed that two slats of Rhoderick's crate had loosened. He set to work refastening the boards with hammer and nails. When the hammer began to pound, Rhoderick began to roar. The bull lost his temper completely when the pounding kept up. Halfway across the bay, he gave one great bellow and burst the crate apart. The hired man ran for his life. Rhoderick rampaged after him.

Passengers in cars near the truck leaped out and stampeded up the stairs for the second deck. A mate aboard the ferry, fancying himself somewhat of a seagoing cowboy, fashioned a lariat to lasso the bull. The looping rope missed. Rhoderick forgot the hired hand and took a sudden dislike to the mate. He chased him up and down the decks with head lowered and horns ready for the kill. The bull then sighted his own reflection in a deck window and charged. Crashing through the glass-and-wood frame, he plummeted like a bomb into the water. The ferry stopped and passengers reappeared from hiding places. The crew tried in vain to rope the floundering Rhoderick. An alert was radioed to police, and the ferry continued on its journey. Three Harbor Unit launches converged on Rhoderick, who thwarted rescue, swimming out of range and eventually disappearing in the mists. The bull was not seen again until six hours later. Weary and subdued, he was sighted and helped ashore by a fisherman six miles away in Coney Island. The police arrived and Rhoderick was taken to an animal shelter for submersion treatment.

The ESD faced its biggest cattle roundup on May 3, 1973, when a truck transporting forty Norwegian red heifers from Kennedy International Airport overturned in the Bronx, scattering the steers into a flood of morning rush-hour traffic. Twirling lassos, the policemen captured the heifers and tethered them to metal railings along the road until help came in the form of a couple of other cattle trucks. The escapees were loaded aboard and taken to their destination—a U.S. quarantine facility in Clifton, New Jersey—along the overland trail of the Interstate Highway System.

A few animals with popular images of ferocity have turned out to be surprisingly submissive in the hands of the ESD. A coyote that roamed from its cage in Brooklyn's Prospect Park Zoo one day seemed grateful to be rescued from two whooping boys who had chased and cornered it in the lobby of an apartment house. The police gently lifted the frightened coyote into an ashcan and carried it back to the zoo. It was discovered that the animal had run off after crawling under a wire fence to play with a group of young children. Seven companion coyotes had stayed in the com-

pound, apparently preferring the peace and quiet of their sur-
roundings to the hectic outside world.

Snakes, even when perfectly harmless, always strike terror into
the public. When startled citizens telephone to report seeing the
reptiles on streets, in apartments and in stores in the city, the ESD
has learned that it is not always a signal to rush over with restraining jackets or to advise the callers to contact Alcoholics Anonymous. While snakes, which often travel in pairs, normally stay out
of sight in the moist earth and underbrush of vacant lots or wooded
sections, the records of the unit show that they are liable to turn
up in any place at any time. When thirst forces them to search for
water close to human habitation in time of drought, snakes seek
out lawns, golf courses and other places kept damp artificially.
When deprived of these sources of water, they start to move in-
doors and telephone calls light up police switchboards. Many are
harmless garden snakes, but some are copperheads, rattlesnakes
or similarly poisonous species. Still others are wildly exotic types
that escape after being imported by zoos or surreptitiously spirited
into the country. Although there is a law against owning pet
snakes in the city, snake enthusiasts often harbor the reptiles for
scientific study or companionship.

Never satisfactorily explained, even speculatively, was a boa
constrictor's visit one summer night to an apartment near Colum-
bia University. A studying student glanced around to see the six-
and-a-half-foot reptile slither out of a bookcase and drop onto his
bed. The snake was beautiful in a way, being green, gray and blue,
but the student, recognizing instantly that it was no bookworm,
bounded out the door to call police. After five minutes of brisk
grappling, ESD Officer John Greaney snared the boa with a noose
and turned it over to an ASPCA agent for removal.

Besides the dog-noose method, the ESD uses a number of techniques to trap snakes, including a frontal assault with heavy bear-
skin gloves—an approach that is necessary in unwinding reptiles
coiled tightly around hot water pipes or securely entwined in air
conditioners.

Snake hunts sometimes last as long as thirty days. The more
wily reptiles slide back into hidden haunts inside walls and other
cramped places after being sighted, and are gone when the po-

licemen arrive. The complainant is advised to telephone when the snake reappears. It is then a matter of a very quick response to capture it before it vanishes again.

In Brooklyn's Coney Island, where practically anything goes, ESD police are used to getting calls to corral wandering serpents. Coney's amusement park is a celebrated staging area for a variety of snake charmers and scantily clad self-styled artistic dancers who like to enhance their bumps and grinds with cuddly pythons or boa constrictors.

The weirdest snake case in the ESD's history occurred in the winter of 1960 in an upper West Side furnished room where a fifty-seven-year-old man was found dead. The walls of the cluttered room were adorned with snakeskins. On the floor were four glass cases, each containing a snake—one a python that was twenty-two and a half feet long. A fifth snake—eight feet long—was squirming under the bed. For good measure, the man, who had worked as a night elevator operator in a Park Avenue apartment house, despite personal papers that showed he held a doctor's degree in science, had lived in the room with seven framed collections of butterflies, two house cats, four turtles, a pair of man-eating piranhas and a two-foot alligator, which was found dying in the bathroom sink.

Public works officials periodically protest that the city's sewers are alligator-free, but the ESD claims it is not rare to find the baby variety lurking in the murky depths, and once in a while even poking snouts up into toilet bowls in houses and apartments. But the classic tale, which the oldtimers remember with the most fondness and amusement, unfolded shortly before midnight one spring evening in a Brooklyn subway station, where an alligator, two feet long and very slimy, thrust its head up out of a refuse can as a train pulled in. When the train halted, the reptile slithered out of the can, crawled across the platform and boarded one of the cars. The passengers, mostly women, screamed and fled out of the train to the nearest exit. The agent in the station's change booth called police. When ESD men arrived, the alligator lumbered toward them with apparent unconcern. One policeman pounced on the creature and managed to keep clear of its snapping jaws while another got a lasso around the animal's mouth. The alligator was turned over to the ASPCA. Passengers who had been waiting on the subway platform later told police that shortly before the alligator made its subway debut, a man had put a large bundle into the refuse can and quietly walked away.

Whales, sea lions and eels are among the other aquatic animals the men have encountered on search and rescue missions. Harbor Unit launches have regularly towed small whales back to deeper waters after the mammals strayed in from the Atlantic. An acrobatic sea lion once threw Brooklyn's Sheepshead Bay boating and fishing area into mayhem for twelve hours until a police launch crew overtook the thrashing grayish-brown fugitive, which had leaped in and out of boats, outsprinted swimmers and dodged pursuing motorboats. Sea lions still are sighted periodically in the outlying Rockaways.

The ESD barely missed a battle with a three-foot-long, seven-pound eel that clamped its jaws around the left index finger of a Brooklyn housewife while she was preparing to skin it alive in her kitchen for dinner. When the housewife thrust her arm out the kitchen window and shrieked for help, neighbors came on the run. All fled, thinking she was lashing out at them with a whip. Before the ESD was called, a local precinct officer was sent to the home. The eel had loosened its grip and dropped to the ground. It was snared in the leather thong of a night stick and carted away, much to the consternation of the housewife, who said she had nothing else for dinner and that her husband would have to settle for scrambled eggs.

A wide variety of airborne creatures inhabit the city. The ESD is summoned to deal with them whenever they cause a nuisance or imperil humans and other animals. Most insect cases are shunned, since early skirmishes, especially with bees, ended in mind-boggling complications. One of the first bee incidents involved a swarm of some 35,000 rolled into a ball twenty inches in circumference on the branch of a silver birch outside a Bronx home. Policemen wearing rubber boots, raincoats and rubber gloves, with gas masks and potato sacks over their heads, approached the bees and tried to brush them off the branch. The insects clung tenaciously. The branch had to be sawed off and dumped with the bees into a barrel. An hour later, Sergeant John T. Egan telephoned the

ESD's headquarters to report that the bees had been trapped and asked his superior, Inspector Daniel A. Kerr, what should be done with them.

"Bring them back with you, and we'll figure that out later," Kerr instructed.

The insects were transported to the squad's quarters, where things literally hummed for the next few days while the Police Department's property clerk puzzled over the legal problem of disposing of confiscated bees. Growing impatient, the squad asked the ASPCA to adopt the bees, but the society demurred. It ruled that bees technically were not animals and therefore were outside its jurisdiction. Officials at the Bronx Zoo were queried on whether the zoo could use a supply of bees. The answer was a firm no. The problem was solved when the property clerk was pestered into agreeing that the bees should be destroyed—and they were.

Nowadays, the ESD prefers not to tangle with bees personally and employs amateur or professional apiarists when possible to catch swarms that alight uninvited on someone's doorstep or in public places. The apiarists usually charge a fee, plus traveling expenses, but some are willing to take the bees in payment. An eighteen-year-old Queens high school student and amateur bee-keeper helped corral ten thousand bees that escaped one spring day from a broken crate in Grand Central Terminal. Armed with a burlap sack, a smoke cylinder and a long acquaintance with bees and their habits, the tall, lanky youth entered the nearly deserted terminal with brave determination, stopping only to don a bee-catcher's veil. Within two hours, he had accomplished the apiarist's trick of locating the queen bees and brushing them into a sack so that the others would follow. The student, who picked up three stings in the process, charged a fee of seven dollars per swarm, observing modestly, "It's not much, considering."

When no apiarists are available and the bees are accessible, the men have found a healthy squirt from a fire extinguisher effective in freezing a swarm into a cluster that is then removed to a less crowded site, where the insects can fly free when they warm up.

One of the ESD's first bird safaris was a bizarre expedition against screech owls that overran a residential section of Queens and kept home owners awake with their nocturnal hooting. Fears spread that the birds also might attack neighborhood children, and complaints were made to the State Conservation Department, which sent a game warden to investigate. The game warden notified police, and the assignment was given to the ESD. Nine policemen, armed with rifles and searchlights, arrived in the neighborhood one hot July night to surround the grove of trees suspected of being the owl hideout. Before the hunters had a chance to aim the rifles, an owl family swooped down out of nowhere, almost daring them to shoot, and then vanished into the darkness. When the policemen raised the weapons and started firing, a hundred heads protruded from nearby windows and passers-by ran for shelter. Searchlights roaming through the branches soon confirmed by the reflection of round unwinking eyes that the owls had survived the salvo unscathed. New blasts of scatter shot riddled the leaves and tore the bark from trees, but failed to stir the birds beyond an occasional shift to more comfortable perches elsewhere in the grove. Certain that a long siege was in prospect, the marksmen took stations at the four corners and in the center of the grove while thoughtful neighbors supplied them with boxes to sit on as well as lemonade and cigars. The battle bogged down to an impasse, with policemen periodically sighting at distant targets and firing, and the owls hooting politely in response.

With the coming of midnight, windows that had been closed against the bombardment were flung open and sleepy heads demanded to know when the noise was going to stop. The weary owl brigade departed, but returned the next night to answer the hooting owls with gunfire from every vantage point. The owls gradually began to retreat, their exodus encouraged by loud shouting in which the policemen were aided by several small boys. The third night, not a screech was heard in the area, convincing the hunters that any owls that lingered had at least been frightened into perpetual silence. Screech owls have since become a rarity in the city, but other similarly curious creatures, such as bats, invade homes now and then.

Stringent ecological laws limit the ESD to nets, nooses and bare hands to capture birds threatened with extinction that live in outlying marshland preserves and sometimes stray into residential areas.

A novel entrapment technique was contrived when a flock of geese ran amok one chilly December day in the heart of Times

Square while being herded by a beautiful girl as part of a scene in a movie being filmed on location. Half the flock, their honks rising defiantly above the serenade of auto horns, goose-stepped up and down the center of the roadway, refusing to return to the sidewalk. Traffic came to a standstill and employees of the motion picture company stumbled here and there trying to round up the stray birds. An ESD truck en route to an official call was halted by the jam and added its siren to the din. The truculent birds kept marching. The policemen got out of the truck to disperse the geese and in short order were busy brushing feathers off their uniforms. Someone maintained enough calm to slip off to a nearby store for a bag of popping corn. He laid a heavy trail of kernels from the roadway to the sidewalk, and the birds followed. A moving van that had trucked the geese to their premiere was rushed in from a side street and the birds were hustled aboard.

In another runaway bird case, the ESD wound up rescuing an artist after he was stranded while pursuing his pet canary across rooftops on Manhattan's West Side. When the artist–bird-lover discovered the canary was missing from its cage in his studio, he had started searching and saw the bird resting comfortably on the roof of an adjoining Catholic church. While working his way across rooftops toward the canary, he slipped and fell into an enclosed shaft. ESD Officer Arthur Moretti was lowered in rope and sling to hoist the dazed artist out. The canary perched nearby and watched the proceedings with great fascination and puzzlement.

The ESD's concern for the tiniest and most insignificant life was warmly illustrated in the rescue of a baby sparrow caught between the panes of an apartment window on the lower East Side. The woman occupant of the apartment had gone on a trip, leaving the window open about seven inches from the top and bottom. The sparrow had landed on the frame and plunged into the space formed by the overlapping upper and lower panes. After frantic attempts to escape the glass prison, the sparrow weakened. The bird's mother and her other babies gathered seeds and bread crumbs and dropped them through the narrow crevice to prevent the fledgling from starving. For three days, the feeding process was maintained and the birds kept up an excited chorus of chirps for help on the fire escapes and window ledges of the building. A woman neighbor thought the sparrows were hungry, and threw out bread crumbs on the first day. The birds dutifully brought the food to their imprisoned kin. While hanging out laundry on the morning of the second day, the woman glanced up from her second-floor apartment window and saw the trapped sparrow. She called the ASPCA. An agent was sent out with the wrong street number and spent all day in a fruitless search for the address. On the third day, the woman called the ASPCA again. An agent showed up only to find that there was no passkey available for the apartment where the bird was trapped. The agent telephoned police. ESD Officer Harold Pritchard entered the apartment by vaulting from a fire escape landing to an open bathroom window. He went to the window where the sparrow was trapped, gingerly raised the upper part and lifted the bird out. The tiny creature was taken to an ASPCA shelter, where an examination showed no injuries. It was placed in a cage for several days of rest and rehabilitation so that it could be restored to health and vigor before being returned to its mother. Three days later, exhausted by its ordeal, it died.

One animal-rescue case, which may or may not have happened, depending on your degree of skepticism, was reported by an ESD squad on March 28, 1960, after a gorilla supposedly wandered out of its cage at Madison Square Garden. The official report follows:

Upon arrival was informed that a gorilla had escaped from his cage in Madison Square Garden and had entered a bar and grill across the street. Was also informed that about ten persons were in the rear of the premises. Members of this squad observed the gorilla standing at the center of the bar and persons cowering in the rear holding chairs and tables in front of them. Entered premises with lasso stick and, observing gorilla standing quietly, moved cautiously behind the bar, mixed a martini and placed it in front of the gorilla, who promptly drank it down and walked back across the street into the Garden to his cage. No other services rendered by this squad. Radio dispatcher notified from scene.

7. The Waterfront

Beyond the shoreline of the city's vast land area, where the Emergency Service performs its work among the sick, the injured and the deranged, stretch about one hundred and forty-six square miles of rivers, bays and inlets that are the maritime domain of the little-known Harbor Unit.

In the shadow of New York's towering skyline but well out of sight of its workaday world, the seagoing policemen serve aboard eleven 512-horsepower steel-hulled launches and a flotilla of smaller auxiliary craft that patrol the waters of the "City of Islands" twenty-four hours a day, making rescues, supervising marine traffic and guarding against fires and thieves.

On some tours, the 180 officers and men of the Harbor Unit encounter about as much excitement as fellow policemen pounding lonely beats ashore, but on others the routine is enlivened by swashbuckling adventures straight out of Joseph Conrad's novels.

Assignments run the gamut from smashing international smuggling rings and thwarting threatened bombings of foreign vessels and mutinies and labor trouble aboard ships, to rescuing human derelicts drowning off piers, foiling petty larceny in dry docks, aiding amateur Sunday boatmen in distress and corraling young-sters swimming in treacherous waters.

One unusual duty involves standing by in a boat as a precau-tionary measure when Greek-American youths dive to retrieve a crucifix thrown by a priest into the icy waters at the tip of Man-hattan in an annual religious ritual.

The unit's territory encompasses the largest police jurisdiction in the city, extending 578 miles—equivalent to the distance be-tween New York and Columbus, Ohio—along all the navigable waters in and around the five boroughs from City Island to Rock-away Point and from Yonkers to the tip of Staten Island, and all the way out to the two-mile limit in the Atlantic.

In year-round surveillance, the launches protect hundreds of freighters, tankers and passenger liners berthing in the harbor, which, despite a decline in marine traffic in recent years, still holds a commanding position as the nation's number one shipping termi-nus, with more than nine thousand vessels arriving and departing yearly. The volume amounts to roughly 20 percent of all the ships handled by major continental ports in the entire United States.

During summer months, the Harbor Unit's patrols cover thou-sands of pleasure craft that operate out of more than one hundred yachting bases and marinas, as well as miles of beaches crowded with millions of bathers.

Twenty-three islands not linked to the mainland by bridges or viaducts are circumnavigated by the launches daily to ferret out criminal activity and help persons in distress. Many are sites of hospitals, prisons and detention facilities for drug addicts and mental patients. A perennial trouble spot is tiny Buck Rock, 200 feet off the eastern shore of the Bronx, where fifteen to twenty fishermen, picnickers and sunbathers are rescued yearly after wad-ing out during dead low water only to discover within a few hours that a rapidly incoming tide has marooned them.

Since fifty-seven of the city's police precincts touch on water, the twin-screw diesel-powered police craft, based at seven stra-tegically located stations throughout the port, operate in close co-operation with police land and air forces and are linked through constant radio and ship-to-shore-telephone contact with the Harbor Unit's headquarters in the southeast Bronx, and the central police communications bureau in Manhattan.

Named after policemen killed in the line of duty, the launches are fifty-two feet in length. All fly the Police Department flag with five stripes, green and white, denoting the five boroughs, and twenty-four stars on a field of blue, which stand for the communities merged into the greater city. Each launch is tailor-made to meet the specialized conditions of the waterways it patrols. The bow of one, for example, is reinforced for icebreaking, and a crash launch that plies the waters off Kennedy International Airport has a shallow shrimp-boat draft that permits it to penetrate dense marshes on the field's southern border.

The hulls and decks of the launches are loaded with equipment to meet every conceivable kind of emergency—depth finders, radar, sonar, life-line guns, grappling irons to raise sunken bodies and automobiles, portable pumps to bail out sinking craft, first-aid kits, resuscitators, oxygen tanks, fire-fighting equipment, life preservers, signal flags, searchlights, public address systems, outboard motors, rowboats, lasso sticks to rope floundering animals, and heavy firearms, including machine guns and smoke and tear-gas bombs.

The most modern acquisitions include "night light" vision gear and a $6,550 portable underwater television camera for scanning large areas beneath the surface that would take divers hours to search. Enclosed in a cage that prevents underwater debris from interfering with its lens, the camera is equipped with a high-intensity light to illuminate its path and a special fin that stabilizes its course as it flashes pictures to a monitor screen located in the cabin of the launch.

Whenever the President of the United States flies into the city, the launches monitor the White House jet's landings and takeoffs over water. Other police boats lurk under bridges crossed on the President's route into Manhattan or inspect every inch of water off the lower East Side heliport when the trip from the airport is made by helicopter. Occasionally, the intense security leads to embarrassing errors. After one of the late President Johnson's visits, the Harbor Unit was forced to apologize to a woman one launch crew excitedly reported was loitering on the Triborough Bridge with a suspicious-looking black bag. The "assassin" turned out to be a blind mute, who had paused in confusion at the approach of the presidential motorcade.

The bulk of the Harbor Unit's personnel are policemen with previous experience in the Navy, Coast Guard and Merchant Marine, or as former tugboat operators or commercial fishermen. Many are sons or nephews of former Harbor Unit members, and all look like sailors and talk their jargon, with regulation uniform caps and guns the only marks that distinguish them as policemen. Their standard uniform while on patrol consists of blue denims with a furled-anchor insignia on the shirt sleeves, and all crewmen wear flotation jackets capable of keeping two two-hundred-pound men afloat.

Ocean-going masters' and harbor pilots' licenses are commonplace among the men, who must qualify under rigid Coast Guard standards as masters, mates, pilots, engineers or motorboat operators and demonstrate skills in first aid and as navigators, radio operators and marksmen.

Others are skilled mechanics, carpenters, steam fitters and electricians who staff the unit's own repair shop at Randalls Island in the Harlem River, which is equipped with dry-dock facilities and boat-basin machinery for overhauling propeller shafts and power plants and rebuilding damaged hulls.

Damage from half-sunken logs or drifting pieces of wreckage is a constant threat for the launches, particularly in the notorious waters of Hell Gate, where currents flood through a narrow two-hundred-yard channel toward Long Island Sound at three and a half knots and ebb toward the Battery at four and a half knots. An ever-present danger exists of collisions with the dark, cumbersome juggernauts of runaway barges or tugboats with car floats lashed to their sides, which sometimes swing wild in riptides.

While most Harbor Unit policemen now serve on the launches and auxiliary craft, in crews of two to six men, a few once pounded beats along Newtown Creek and the Gowanus Canal in Brooklyn, unsnarling freight, barge and tugboat traffic and warning away adventurous youngsters using the tributaries as handy swimming holes. The assignments were abandoned only a few years ago.

The Gowanus, known among old-timers as "Lavender Lake," was by far the toughest patrol. Foul fumes rose from its purplish, sewage-strewn waters and were a pungent challenge, but policemen assigned there claimed that time and patience inured them. One veteran, Officer Michael Harrigan, who rescued countless humans and animals and spotted the bodies of hundreds of drowning, suicide and murder victims during his fourteen years along the canal, grew thoroughly immune. "I was surprised when I saw passers-by holding handkerchiefs to their noses," he once said.

Despite the huge expanse of water for which the Harbor Unit is responsible, the launch crews display an uncanny ability for being in the right places at the right times.

Two launches towing a disabled sailboat were barely 150 feet away when a single-engine plane crashed into a 541-foot radio transmitting tower off the Bronx shore in a blinding rainstorm and spiraled into the waters of Long Island Sound on the afternoon of August 27, 1967. The bodies of two men floated to the surface and were retrieved after the plane sank fifty-two feet to the bottom.

Nine longshoremen were plucked from almost inevitable death by a launch crew that spotted them at the tip of a blazing pier in Brooklyn on the afternoon of December 3, 1956. Minutes later, the flames reached a cargo of primacord and set off a devastating explosion that killed ten persons and injured more than two hundred at the land end of the pier.

Another launch was cruising nearby when the last of four barges towed into the Hudson River off the upper West Side to stage a pre-Fourth of July fireworks display for a department store blew up in a flash of light on the evening of June 23, 1964, killing two crewmen. The launch raced to the flaming barge to pull three injured victims from the water as a crowd of about 500,000 on shore applauded the tragedy in the mistaken belief that the fiery explosion was the spectacular climax to the pyrotechnic exhibit.

Political fireworks nearly sank a Harbor Unit launch that was stationed in the East River on December 11, 1964, when a bazooka shell was fired by Cuban exiles at the United Nations Building, where the then Cuban Minister of Industry, Ernesto ("Che") Guevara, was speaking. The rocket zoomed across the launch's bow and arced into the water two hundred feet short of the Manhattan shore, sending a twenty-foot geyser into the air and rattling windows throughout the United Nations compound. The launch had been sent to the area after the FBI received a tip that the UN, which was under siege by demonstrating Cuban exiles, would be bombed. With the help of information supplied by the launch crew, detectives slogged through mud to a marshy lot on the opposite side of the river, where they found a homemade, self-timing telescopic-sighted mortar, decorated with a Cuban flag and still ticking. Police later said that the shell had been fired as a diversionary tactic to allow a black-garbed, knife-wielding woman among the crowd of protesters outside the UN to slip inside and assassinate Guevara. She was caught as she climbed over a fence to get into the building.

The Harbor Unit, one of the oldest organizational arms of the New York City Police Department, was incorporated into the Emergency Service in 1936, but boasts a rich and colorful history dating back to pre-Civil War days, when shorefront hideouts throughout the port were infested by pirates waging a reign of terror against sailing vessels and newer steamships.

The brigands bore such picturesque names as the Daybreak Boys, led by Patsy the Barber and Socco the Bracer; the Hook Gang, commanded by Slobbery Jim and Bum Mahoney; and included pirate subsidiaries of several shore gangs.

Their main entrenchment was a stretch of Hudson River waterfront on mid-Manhattan's West Side in a now teeming area known as Hell's Kitchen, which in those days was the site of slaughterhouses, fertilizer plants and soap works and a dumping ground for ashes and other refuse.

With driftwood from the river, timber from dealers' yards along the shore, rusted tin roofing and other debris, the pirates built a commune of dilapidated hovels, in which they plotted forays against arriving ships and cargo-laden wharves. One gang, known auspiciously as the Den of Forty Thieves, established headquarters on a wrecked lighter offshore and slipped out into the river under cover of darkness in rowboats to board moored schooners and engage the crews in swashbuckling sword and cutlass battles. The prize usually was valuable booty, but on some occasions the pirates jettisoned the crew and fled with the entire ship.

In one foray, the freebooters stormed onto a huge clipper ship off Governors Island, a half mile from the tip of Manhattan, clamped the captain in irons, herded the crew below and stripped the vessel of every article of value, including brass fittings and copper sheeting covering much of the woodwork.

Piers and warehouses were plundered by other buccaneers, who paddled under docks in small dinghys and drilled up through wooden flooring with brace and bit into huge hogsheads of Jamaica rum, vats of fuel and sacks of grain. The products were drained into containers, which were then carted off for lucrative resale. Watchmen patrolled the wharves, but most were unaware of the thefts, and whenever one did interfere, he was killed outright.

Besides cargo thefts, the pirates engaged in a number of sidelines. One was the smuggling of aliens, and there were few qualms about dumping the human cargo overboard when the danger of discovery was at hand.

Sea-gull wings, which sold for more than a dollar a pair for women's hat plumage and other finery, were another remunerative pirate industry, and thousands of the birds were shot while soaring over Spuyten Duyvil, at the northern tip of Manhattan. The killings were a crime punishable by a twenty-five-dollar fine— a high penalty in those days. Still another profitable pirate depredation was the ravaging of clam beds off Princess Bay, Staten Island, a rich breeding ground for the mollusks in the days before the waters became polluted. Amateurs frequently joined in the raids and among those caught on one occasion were a local sheriff, a clergyman and the superintendent of his Sunday school.

Following the lead of London's Metropolitan Police, twelve husky policemen in a fleet of five rowboats were assigned to patrol the harbor's Upper Bay and the lower Hudson and East Rivers to combat the piracy and thievery. On February 15, 1858, police commissioned an old sidewheel steamboat named the *Seneca* from which the rowboats could be launched with the men to intercept the pirates. The policemen, resplendent in specially designed uniforms, concentrated solely on law enforcement while the vessel itself was manned by civilian pilots, engineers, coal stokers, deck hands and cooks. The flamboyant buccaneering came to an end, spurred by intramural warfare among the gangs themselves.

The lighter that was headquarters of the Den of Forty Thieves was destroyed, and freebooters convicted of murder were hanged on a gallows on Ellis Island, then known as Gibbets Island. Twelve of the Daybreak Boys were killed in one of the final battles, but no accurate toll of the number of harbor policemen slain exists because the *Seneca*'s records were lost when the vessel was destroyed by fire in 1880.

Within two years, the *Seneca* was replaced by the *Patrol,* the first vessel specifically built and equipped for police use. A number of small steam-driven support launches later were added to the fleet as the patrol area was expanded toward the outer reaches of the port and the civilian crewmen gradually were phased out as policemen were trained to assume their duties.

While the *Seneca*'s drive effectively stamped out open piracy for a time on the city's waterways, it failed to quench criminal lust for the port's vast wealth, and the battle against thievery remains to this day one of the Harbor Unit's chief functions.

Croesus-rich, the waterfront stocked the goods of the world. Its piers were choked with products from every land under the sun: the silks and spices of the Orient, linens from Ireland, the wines of France, cargoes of rubber and other raw materials from India and Iran, from Spain and Portugal—all lucrative targets for thieves and smugglers.

The major pirate adversaries of the modern-day Harbor Unit were unscrupulous operators of junkboats—small, oil-smeared steam- or gasoline-driven vessels, with old automobile tires festooning their sides, that roamed berths and anchorages of the port buying unwanted equipment and other scrap from arriving merchant ships.

The junkboats originally were licensed by the city as a way of curbing harbor pollution from the dumping of old hawsers and other gear by growing steamship traffic that turned New York into the world's largest and busiest natural port.

Strict regulations required that the junkboat operators be citizens, operate only during daylight hours, carry no passengers and keep logbooks listing every transaction, including a description of the material bought, the ship involved in the sale and the exact time that the deal was made. But abuses resulted in a wave of plundering and smuggling that quickly overtaxed the Harbor Unit's forces.

Unlicensed gypsy boats began operating under cover of fog and darkness to steal shipments from docks and smuggle narcotics, gems, aliens and spies into the country. The gypsy craft often carried small rowboats for ferrying passengers to shore and for working as surreptitiously as possible while looting piers, which shippers installed with concrete decks to make them less vulnerable to pilfering from below.

A few of the junkboats were rigged with special gear to speed chuting of coal and other cargoes and many were powered by engines that could easily outrace Harbor Unit launches, which were then wooden-hulled steam-driven vessels. Efforts to combat the thefts were further hampered by an 1833 treaty that limited the unit's jurisdiction to the low-water mark of the then poorly policed New Jersey waterfront. When pursued, the gypsy boats invariably headed across the Hudson to the legal refuge.

The river pirates improvised a number of schemes to skirt detection by the harbor policemen. Coal-barge trains under way in the rivers were boarded by thieves who held crews at gunpoint while shoveling the fuel into sacks, which were dumped aboard fast boats that raced out in relays from various points on shore and carted off the booty. Metal-strapped bales of processed sheet rubber were shoved from pierheads into the water, where the buoyant bulks submerged only a few inches beneath the surface and could be strung together and left for later pickup or towed away invisibly. The trick also enabled the thieves to cut the bales loose and deny all, if overtaken by police, and return later to retrieve them when the coast was clear.

Angry prosecutors attempted to charge those who were caught with piracy on the high seas—a capital crime punishable by death —but the moves failed in the courts. Pier guards and crew members often cooperated in the thefts for a portion of the loot and covered up for their confederates, and defense lawyers commonly argued that the missing goods probably had been stolen from the ships on stops in foreign ports before arriving in New York.

The thieves enjoyed other legal loopholes, since conviction required positive identification of the stolen goods—a task the harbor policemen found next to impossible with such common items as coal and rubber, cocoa and unroasted coffee, especially when the shipment labels were destroyed.

World War I briefly interrupted the thievery. All junkboat licenses were suspended for security reasons. The boat owners went to work as longshoremen, in a sudden burst of patriotism, but returned in force after the conflict. By 1925, the problem had reached crisis proportions. Steamship companies and other maritime interests voiced public outrage after illegal junkboat operators resorted to open violence by boarding vessels and robbing them at gunpoint. One captain was wounded when a gang swarmed onto his ship off Saint George, Staten Island, and opened fire in the best tradition of the old-time buccaneers. A money protection racket also was put into operation, and shipowners were shaken down for immunity from thefts and threatened with violence if they reported the incidents or testified against defendants in court. Annual losses in the port climbed to one million dollars.

Hard pressed to combat the junkboats because of inadequate personnel and equipment, Inspector Elihu West, then commander of the Harbor Unit, attended a mass meeting of all maritime organizations at the New York Maritime Exchange and appealed for their support to wipe out the menace. The result was a swift doubling of the Harbor Unit's fleet from six to twelve craft with more powerful gasoline engines and a 25 percent increase in its personnel. This helped reduce river piracy to the vanishing point by 1930 as land-based police, shipping-company guards on piers and masters of arriving vessels cooperated in the campaign. Lured by new profits available due to Prohibition, the thieves gradually shifted to the bootlegging trade. (Pursuit of the rum-runners was considered mainly within the purview of the Coast Guard and federal agents. Rumor had it that the Harbor Unit developed a marked lack of enthusiasm for the work after one of its officers was wounded when a police launch was fired on by federal agents who mistook it in the darkness for a bootlegging craft.)

After repeal, the junkboat operators resumed business as usual and branched out from cargo theft to opium smuggling—some boats were seized with as many as six hundred packages of opium. They also looted a growing number of yachts and other small craft in the harbor. Marinas were invaded and boats stripped of everything from compasses and other costly nautical instruments to plumbing, rope, brass, iron, deck fittings, lanterns and even mooring buoys.

The marauders were banned again from the port during World War II by Mayor La Guardia, whose edict was strictly enforced not only by the Harbor Unit but by federal government craft that shadowed liners and troop ships, scouting for floating mines and warning away small boats and low-flying airplanes on possible sabotage missions.

Stiff opposition from government and shipping officials stalled attempts to reissue licenses after the war. The junkers shifted operations to land, using regular carting licenses to roam the piers, and harbor policemen were forced to switch tactics and go ashore to determine if the scavengers were legally clear.

Modern container ships, with cargoes sealed in huge metal boxes, have gradually reduced the loot available in the harbor, but a few unlicensed junkboats remain, operated by the offspring of families who have been in the business for decades. But no new licenses are issued and the boats gradually are dying out by attrition.

Protecting the port's commerce constitutes only one small aspect of the law-enforcement activities of the Harbor Unit, which cooperates closely with the Coast Guard and the U.S. Customs, Immigration and Public Health services in preventing smuggling of aliens and contraband and in intercepting travelers with contagious diseases. Federal and state conservation officials also rely on the unit for help in detecting oil spills.

Shotgun-wielding policemen aboard the launches frequently shepherd ships carrying millions of dollars in gold to a pier on Manhattan's lower East Side. The bullion comes from about seventy foreign nations, central banks and international monetary organizations. It is loaded into armored trucks for transfer to the Federal Reserve Bank in the financial district where it is stored in a vault eighty feet below the ground and nearly half the length of a football field.

While mutinies and labor trouble still occur from time to time aboard ships, the episodes are not as frequent or as violent as those during the early 1930s, when many foreign ships arrived in port with poorly treated Chinese, Hindu and Muslim crew members, who staged uprisings with clubs and knives over working conditions and the refusal of captains to allow them ashore because of stringent immigration regulations.

Tramp steamers smuggling Chinese aliens also were prevalent in that era, and Harbor Unit launches often spent hours trailing the ships and waiting in the shadows off docking areas to thwart unauthorized landings.

The recovery of bodies, guns, automobiles and other evidence from riverbeds by the unit has always figured importantly in solving crimes and apprehending criminals. In one famous case, a speedboat retrieved from the bottom of Jamaica Bay off Queens supplied the first concrete clue to the unprecedented escape of a precision-drilled team of eleven bandits who ambushed an armored car outside the Rubel Ice Company plant in Brooklyn at high noon on August 21, 1934, and fled with $429,000. Discovery of the craft provided a crucial link in tracing the robbers, who escaped in a car to nearby Gravesend Bay, boarded the boat and raced to Jamaica Bay, where they sank the vessel and switched to a truck for a getaway.

A majority of the bodies recovered by the Harbor Unit are so-called floaters, generally derelicts or others who have fallen into the water accidentally, committed suicide by drowning or been shoved to their death by gangland assassins. About 125 bodies are found each year, when they float to the surface. The bulk of them are fished out of the waters by Harbor Unit launches, mostly during the spring months. The warming action of sunlight on the waters thaws out the cadavers, which have lain frozen and preserved on the bottom during the cold season, and they rise through the buoyancy of gases generated in the stomach and other organs as the process of decomposition is renewed. The corpses usually are ballooned into grotesque shapes and horribly mutilated by crabs and other underwater life, and possibly for that reason there are far fewer women than men among the suicide victims.

An outstanding example of the criminal genre was Ernest ("The Hawk") Rupolo, a gangland police informer, whose body was pulled from Jamaica Bay on August 24, 1964. A bullet in the back of his head, numerous stab wounds and ropes wound around his neck, body, hands and legs testified eloquently to the underworld's opinion of the one-eyed, hook-nosed Rupolo, whose death marked the climax of a twenty-year vendetta by the mob, which had posted a ten-thousand-dollar price on his head after he turned police informer in 1944 to implicate Vito Genovese and five others in a ten-year-old gangland murder.

After the trussed body of trunk-murder victim Reuben Markowitz was found in the Harlem River on November 8, 1963, it
was thought at first that the ninety-dollar-a-week supermarket
clerk had somehow run afoul of a maniacal killer. But investigation disclosed that Markowitz had doubled as a bookmaker and
reportedly listed among his clients Mark Fein, a wealthy Park
Avenue businessman who owed him a crushing $23,898 debt
stemming from an unfortunate bet on the New York Yankees in
the 1963 World Series. As a result of the discovery, Fein was arrested and at a subsequent trial it was charged that, rather than
pay the debt, he had shot Markowitz and enlisted the aid of a
Titian-haired paramour to fold the body in a gold-trimmed black
metal trunk and dump it into the river. Fein was sentenced to a
thirty-year prison term.

Most crimes encountered by the Harbor Unit are far less sensational, but all have their peculiar earmarks. When a man being
questioned about passing a bad check bolted into the waters off
Staten Island in the summer of 1967, he was overtaken by a police
launch that had been alerted by radio. The policemen returned the
man to shore and learned to their dismay that the complainant in
the case would not press charges. But the suspect already had paid
a penalty of sorts—he had been stung by a jellyfish. Another
launch crew barely missed catching a homesick Scandinavian who
stole a thirty-seven-foot sailboat in Brooklyn's Sheepshead Bay
and set out on a voyage to his fatherland. After outdistancing the
police launch, the errant mariner was intercepted by the Coast
Guard halfway across the ocean in international waters, where he
could not legally be arrested.

Hardly the crime of the century but certainly a sign of the
emerging complexity of the Harbor Unit's work was the arrest
of a Queens secretary and law student during the summer of 1972
in a test case against a regulation barring nude bathing on the
city's beaches. Her appearance in the flesh on a small island off
the Sheepshead Bay beach drew outcries of "Pig," "Liberal" and
"Exhibitionist" from horrified women bystanders, and lecherous
stares from their husbands. A launch crew took the modern Go-
diva in tow and transported her to shore, where she was charged
with public lewdness, a class B misdemeanor punishable by up to
six months in jail. Protesting the arrest as "inhuman, illegal and

unconstitutional," she insisted that other people would do what she did "but they're too uptight." She was let go in court.

The Harbor Unit's law-enforcement tasks are closely entwined with its illustrious history in rescue operations, and few men who have served in its ranks performed in both areas as well as Scottish-born Officer James Bute, who retired in 1950 after a heroic career that began on September 8, 1934, while he was vacationing aboard the steamship *Morro Castle*. When the luxury cruise liner caught fire in a raging storm off Asbury Park, New Jersey, Bute leaped into the ocean to rescue scores of struggling passengers and assist them into nearby lifeboats.

Two years later, Bute earned the second of his seven bravery commendations by dashing into a burning home, rescuing a trapped woman and child, and returning to the blazing structure to save a man overcome by smoke.

The tale of intrigue for which Bute was best known began on the night of January 6, 1939, when he was aboard a launch that set out from the tip of Manhattan in a freak midwinter thunderstorm on one of the strangest cloak-and-dagger voyages in the Harbor Unit's history.

Bute was posing as the companion of undercover narcotics squad Detective John V. J. Sweeney, who had masqueraded as a rogue cop to infiltrate an "Italian connection" drug syndicate. Members of the syndicate, despairing of slipping opium shipments through tight customs inspections set up to curb a wave of narcotics smuggling that reached a critical peak before World War II, had recruited Sweeney to help them by using a police launch to ferry the drugs ashore from arriving ships. After a test by the gang, in which he was induced to take a police launch to Jersey City and bring back a small package from a ship for three hundred dollars, Sweeney had been asked to smuggle in 123 pounds of opium worth five hundred thousand dollars from an Italian freighter docked in Hoboken. He was to receive a five-thousand-dollar payoff for the mission.

When the launch came alongside the stern of the freighter, Sweeney, by arrangement, gave three signals with a flashlight and was answered similarly by someone on the vessel's fantail. Then four five-gallon cans containing the opium were lowered to the deck of the launch, which put about and moved toward a rendezvous with the smugglers at a deserted pier in Brooklyn. Through coded radio messages, the launch kept in touch with scores of federal and city narcotics agents strategically posted at various points to close in when the contraband was transferred. To give the officers ample time to station themselves in hidden places on the pier, Bute simulated an awkward landing, moving the launch in and out several times at the end of the dock. The police did not reveal themselves until the tins of opium had been handed over to four men waiting on the pier, who stashed it in a waiting car and started to drive off. As the vehicle neared the end of the pier, a police car shot across its path, forcing it to halt, and the darkness was shattered by the sound of gunfire as the smugglers attempted to flee. Bute was grazed on one finger by a bullet as he clambered onto the pier to cut off a retreat to the water by the smugglers, who were quickly surrounded and subdued.

Only three days after that coup, on January 9, 1939, Bute rescued a drowning man and boy whose boat had overturned. His later exploits included rescuing another man from drowning, capturing two men in a stolen car after a bullet-punctuated chase, and saving a woman and four children from a burning building.

Equally memorable in the Harbor Unit's history was a tall, raw-boned deep-sea diver named Tom Walsh, who served for nearly half a century as a civilian consultant in all sorts of underwater work.

Walsh was born in 1871, the same year the unit faced its first major ship disaster, when, on July 30, the Staten Island ferryboat *Westfield* was ripped by a boiler explosion after leaving its slip at the tip of Manhattan. The blast hurled scores of women and children overboard and sent hundreds of others running for their lives to escape scalding clouds of steam. One hundred died in the tragedy, but the calm and shallow water surrounding the ship enabled police to recover bodies of the victims by grappling. In those days, in deeper water, the police resorted to firing cannon over the surface in an attempt to dislodge bodies from the bottom when the depth and uncertainty about the bodies' location made grappling operations unfeasible.

By the time they tackled what still rates as the city's most appalling maritime disaster—the burning of the excursion steamer

General Slocum—the harbor police had turned to enlisting the aid of civilian deep-sea divers. Tom Walsh was among the first.

The *Slocum* had sailed from a lower East Side pier at 10 A.M. on the morning of June 15, 1904, for a picnic outing at Locust Grove, Long Island. Packing the vessel's three decks, according to a later police calculation, were 1,435 persons, but other estimates ranged much higher. More than half of them were children from the Sunday school of Saint Mark's German Evangelical Lutheran Church, their teachers, relatives and friends. There were scarcely any men in the party.

As the ship churned out of the swirling waters of Hell Gate and veered for Long Island Sound, a fire flared on its lower deck near the bow. The flames leaped upward and swept astern with lightninglike speed, burning scores to death where they stood. Hundreds of others, in uncontrollable panic, jumped overboard into treacherous currents racing toward Hell Gate. Captain William H. Van Schaick, the vessel's veteran skipper, who had carried an estimated thirty-five million passengers safely in his years at sea, stuck to the blazing wheelhouse and ordered the craft, by now streaming flames one hundred feet in the air, steered to a beaching on nearby North Brother Island. In the fifteen minutes before the ship grounded, scores of children were trampled to death as derelictions of the crew contributed to the hysteria, and for hundreds of yards in the wake of the doomed craft the river was dotted with struggling forms. When the vessel finally struck land, the hurricane deck collapsed, turning it into a blazing charnel house, and the stern was left jutting out into the water, confronting those trapped there who could not swim with the macabre choice of death by fire or by drowning. Within two hours, the police boat *Patrol* and other rescue vessels had recovered two hundred bodies drifting in the water or flung up on the river's bank or on the shores of nearby islands.

Walsh was among several divers who worked to recover victims remaining trapped in the riverbed. The operation was supervised by Marine Division Detective Edward Mulrooney, who years later was to become police commissioner.

By the time the operation was over, the toll had mounted to 1,020 persons according to the figures announced by the police—

62 missing, 897 identified dead and 61 others who were never identified and are still memorialized at anniversary services in a Queens cemetery where they are buried under a common monument. One hundred eighty were injured and only 235 escaped unharmed on the basis of the police count, but no definitive totals of the dead, injured and unharmed exist because the records of a federal inquiry into the disaster were ordered destroyed on the grounds that they would be too upsetting if they ever fell into the public's hands.

Walsh's work on the *Slocum* assignment so impressed Mulrooney that a close friendship sprang up between the two men and for years thereafter the diver was regularly recruited by police. He also served as wreckmaster for the Pennsylvania Railroad for twenty-two years and earned a reputation as the dean of New York divers.

The chain-smoking diver was the husband of a Texas Guinan dancer named Trixie DeWitt, and it was not unusual for him to show up for emergency work in dinner clothes, fresh from a party and often still exhilarated by the night's festivities. Two policemen would help him lace into two hundred pounds of helmet, boots and diving dress before he descended to muddy river bottoms in quest of bodies, guns or autos that had accidentally plunged off pierheads.

In the winter of 1927, Walsh groped in four feet of mud at the bottom of the Gowanus Canal for the body of missing four-year-old Billy Gaffney, whose disappearance had touched off a national sensation and still is a mystery to this day. Desperate for clues to the boy's whereabouts, police had enlisted Walsh's services when a spiritualist led them to the canal on the basis of information he said he had obtained by conducting a seance in the boy's nearby home.

Walsh played a key part in the search for bodies in the city's second-worst ship catastrophe, on September 9, 1932, after the forty-four-year-old excursion steamer *Observation* was blown to bits by an explosion of its patched boiler at almost the same location where the *Slocum* had caught fire twenty-eight years before. The 122-ton *Observation,* which normally cruised on moonlight voyages up Long Island Sound, had been temporarily hired out to transport laborers to work on the penitentiary being built on

Rikers Island. It was barely one hundred feet out of its berth when the explosion occurred. Forty ironworkers, who had cursed their luck because they had been refused employment in the 150-man working party aboard, watched in amazement from the pier as the double-decked vessel was shaken by a thunderous roar and disappeared in a spouting geyser of planks, dismembered bodies, dust, rigging and steam. Dead and wounded littered the wreckage-strewn water and a veritable shower of bodies scattered onto nearby vessels and piers. One victim was catapulted five hundred feet in an arc through the air and dashed against the fifth-floor window of a waterfront power plant before his limp body plummeted to the ground. Seventy-two lives were lost in the tragedy. Nearly all the bodies were recovered through the efforts of Walsh and Harbor Unit and land-based ESD grappling crews, who dragged the area for weeks, piling the dead on the wooden planking of the same pier that had been stacked with the corpses of the *Slocum* dead.

Walsh's successor, who was put under contract to the Harbor Unit in 1934, was equally colorful in several respects. A lean, lanky, blue-eyed and sandy-haired New Englander named John Turner, he was the grandson of one of the United States Navy's first hardhat divers. Turner's other claim to fame was his belated admission that after a diving career spanning roughly a half century he still could not swim a stroke, although he had made repeated and strenuous efforts to learn. His sinkability served him well, however, since he was responsible for locating numerous sunken automobiles and weapons that police needed for evidence and recovered nearly 1000 bodies from the city's waterways.

"I never got used to it," Turner once said, confessing that he would often wake up in the middle of the night and relive the ordeals of the body recovery assignments. "I shrank from it, and yet I knew I had to go through with it. Relatives, police, the whole city wanted to know."

One of the most ghastly recovery operations in the city's modern history fell to Turner's successor, Barney Sweeney, who was sent down in an unsuccessful effort to retrieve the last of eleven men, women and children when a car in which they were returning from a christening party went down a darkened dead-end street and plunged into the Harlem River from a bulkhead in the

Bronx on the night of November 3, 1963. "Longest underwater day I ever had," said Sweeney, who also upheld the idiosyncratic tradition of his predecessors by living only in high-rise apartments. "When I work I have to look up," he explained, "so I live where I can look down."

While grappling and hard-hat diving are still occasionally employed on some underwater assignments, the Emergency Service had begun to recognize the shortcomings of both as early as 1932, when an experimental program was started that led to the formation of its current team of scuba divers.

Grappling, the task least relished by the Harbor Unit, was largely a long, tedious, hit-and-miss operation that would involve days, weeks or even months of blindly dragging vast areas of water with no certain way of knowing how close the searchers were to the object sought or whether it had been snatched away by currents to an entirely different part of the harbor.

Diving partially solved the problem by putting the searcher on the bottom, where he could scrutinize hidden gullies and coves, but the scope of the diver's movements was limited by the burdensome weight of his lead-soled shoes, brass helmet and other heavy equipment, as well as the leash of rubber hose that supplied him with air from a pump on the surface.

In the spring of 1932, Officers Edward J. Kiernan and John Wynne, working under Inspector Dittman, began experiments with gear that would permit a diver to roam pretty much at will under the surface, carrying his own air supply with him. The idea for bulky apparatus was inspired by the success of the Momsen lung, a device invented in 1929 by the late Vice-Admiral Charles B. Momsen when he was a Navy lieutenant, to facilitate the escape of crewmen from sunken submarines. The Kiernan-Wynne contraption weighed forty-six pounds. Its main components were oxygen tanks and a standard Army gas mask adapted for underwater use.

Kiernan ran several successful tests in shallow waters around the city, but the device was first put to actual use on August 12, 1932, in the Delaware Water Gap, where George Martin, the twelve-year-old son of city Traffic Officer Felix Martin, had drowned while swimming. Attempts to grapple for the boy's body proved fruitless when the hooks caught in tangles of water plants on the river's soft bed. Dittman, Kiernan and Wynne volunteered to help. With Dittman and Wynne holding ropes attached to his body, Kiernan donned the breathing rig and descended four times into twenty-five feet of water for periods ranging up to ten minutes before he located the boy wedged between two rocks. He dislodged the body and brought it to the surface.

While the equipment represented the first experimental breakthrough toward formation of the Harbor Unit's Scuba Squad, the idea of training a specialty team of skin divers did not get under way in earnest until years later, after the 1959 crash of the turboprop airliner into the East River. That disaster forced the hiring of several civilian hard-hat divers at great expense and kept the Harbor Unit's launches diverted from other assignments for more than two weeks in the search for bodies.

Officer John Kuzyk, a nineteen-year veteran in the Emergency Service who worked on the plane catastrophe, approached Walter Klotzback, then an assistant chief inspector, with a suggestion that a scuba program be started on an experimental basis. Klotzback, always amenable to any and all plans to improve rescue techniques, was adamantly opposed because he felt that the lives of personnel would be endangered in the murky waters around the city by all sorts of underwater death traps, ranging from ragged automobile and boat wrecks to sharp-pointed pier pilings that sometimes lurked just beneath the surface. As further grounds for his opposition, Klotzback cited accident and rescue figures, which showed that a growing number of amateur skin divers had been killed or had come close to drowning while exploring the city's rivers and bays.

Kuzyk reluctantly accepted the decision, but after Klotzback's retirement he renewed the idea with Captain John P. Lowe, then the Harbor Unit commander. Convinced that the perils of scuba diving were due more to inadequate training than to inherent dangers, Kuzyk worked with Officer Vito Marrone, then conducting skin-diving instruction at the YMCA, to develop a tentative program for presentation to Lowe. He eventually gave conditional approval to both men to utilize scuba gear for several assignments. After the policemen demonstrated that the work could be done with relative safety, Lowe sent a recommendation to officials at police headquarters. Final approval for a full-scale program was given by Police Commissioner Howard R. Leary.

Forty policemen responded to the initial call for volunteers for the squad, but only eight, including Kuzyk and Marrone, outlasted an exhausting three-day series of qualifying examinations set up by Chief Police Surgeon Stephen McCoy. McCoy, an experienced diver himself, was determined that the members of the squad represent the hardiest physical specimens as well as the best trained, to reduce the possibility of mishaps.

After a week of intensive training at the New York State Police Diving School at Bolton Landing, Kuzyk and Marrone mapped out a program of stamina and swimming tests for the candidates, including swimming nearly half a mile nonstop on the surface and swimming eighty feet under water twice in succession—both to be quickly followed by running a mile, performing thirty push-ups, fifteen chin-ups, forty sit-ups and one hundred leg jumps—all within one day. After pool orientation in the use of aqualungs, the fledgling divers worked out in the surging underwater currents of the Atlantic Ocean, swimming with black tape pasted over their face-mask visors to adapt them to the kind of underwater "Braille" necessary for searching the inland waterways of the city, which pollution had turned into a land of blackness.

Within three months after the Scuba Squad was officially established, in May, 1967, the members had been cited thirty-one times collectively for bravery and excellent police work, including helping the FBI recover a case of guns thrown into the Hudson and retrieving several victims of drowning and submerged auto wrecks.

The squad has since been expanded to include policemen from other units of the department with special aptitude for underwater work. When not engaged in diving, the men serve on their regular assignments and none receives premium pay for scuba tasks. Operations of the squad have resulted in saving upward of $250 a day that would normally be paid out in fees to civilian hard-hat divers.

One of the ace lifesavers in the Harbor Unit's early days was Officer William Neumann, who acquired his aquatic skills the hard way during his boyhood, in the last-one-in's-a-rotten-egg, rough-

and-tumble swimming off the waterfront docks of Manhattan, where he grew up. Before joining the force in 1919, Neumann ran up a record of six rescues of drowning persons—a background that earned him quick appointment to the Harbor Unit. During his career, Neumann won five official citations for bravery—four for saving drowning victims and a fifth for pulling a man from the path of a subway train. In all, he accomplished sixteen rescues—on one occasion hauling a man from the Hudson in the morning, going back on duty and pulling a woman from the river the same afternoon.

Other Harbor Unit policemen have risked their lives by plunging into fiery waters surrounding stricken ships to save crew members. On July 26, 1944, Sergeant Irving Feinstone joined three other policemen in leaping into flaming waters to rescue seven workmen. The men had jumped overboard after an oil slick around the liberty ship S.S. *Champ Clark* was set ablaze by a spark from a workman's acetylene torch while it was undergoing repairs at an upper West Side pier.

Officer Kenneth Craig plunged into a similar inferno to rescue a floundering crew member on June 2, 1973, after the tanker *Esso Brussels* was rammed by the freighter *Sea Witch* near the Verrazano-Narrows Bridge in a spectacular holocaust that claimed sixteen lives.

Drownings and reported submersions average about five hundred a year at beaches and elsewhere along the city's waterways and well over a fifth of the victims are pulled from the water alive and are resuscitated. Many of the cases have strange overtones.

A young couple strolling along the banks of the Harlem River in the moonlight one fall night began arguing and the woman, in desperation and anger, leaped into the water. Her companion jumped after her. The pair still was in midstream when a launch arrived in response to a call from a passer-by on shore. The angry couple was fished out, revived with oxygen and whisked off to a hospital for examination—still arguing.

A suitor was told to "go jump in the river" after he repeatedly telephoned to beg forgiveness from his beloved, and finally he took the advice literally. Boarding a ferryboat for New Jersey, he plunged overboard one hundred feet from the Manhattan shore. The crew of a nearby Harbor Unit launch dragged him out before he sank. One officer, a marine matchmaker of sorts, asked the young Romeo why he had jumped. Told the tale of unrequited love, he offered to call the young lady to try to patch up the shattered romance. It all turned out to be a sad mistake. The distraught lover had been calling the wrong number—and the wrong girl.

Midsummer madness was the only motive the ESD could attribute to the escapade of a guitarist who led them on a wild chase across the East River after he was spotted perched on an offshore rock happily strumming his favorite tunes. When urged to return to safer ground, the marooned minstrel stood up, stripped down to a pair of swimming trunks, threw his clothing and guitar into the water and then plunged in himself, paddling vigorously toward Welfare Island. A launch and a helicopter came to the rescue, along with land-based ESD Officers Edward Mansfield and Eugene Flood, who leaped in after the man. Mansfield and Flood were hardly a match for the musician, who soon demonstrated that he could swim as well as strum. The launch fished both policemen out of the water as their quarry straggled onto the island's shore with enough strength left to start a grueling set of push-ups. Other ESD policemen, who had sped by car over the bridge to the island, overtook and subdued the fugitive, taking him directly to the Welfare Island hospital psychiatric ward for observation.

The Harbor Unit once labored under severe handicaps in attempts to control a tremendous proliferation of private pleasure boats in the city's waterways that began during the late 1930s and has grown steadily in the ensuing years.

Klotzback, who served as Harbor Unit commander for a time, once compared the regulations controlling small boats up until 1957 to laws applying to "stench bomb" throwers, which called for proof of "culpable willfulness in creating a condition hazardous to life and health." The available statutes in the city made it almost impossible to enforce the law against reckless and speeding boat owners, and a state law governing motorboating covered only inland waterways as far south as Tarrytown in Westchester County. Through Klotzback's efforts, the law was extended to the city in 1957.

To help enforce it during the summer months, when the Harbor Unit's work load is heaviest, an auxiliary fleet of five twenty-six-foot fiberglass speedboats, each manned by two policemen and capable of speeds up to twenty-eight knots, supplement the patrols of the regular launches.

The smaller boats, first acquired by the unit in June, 1962, watch the city's beaches for swimmers in distress and for reckless, hot-rodding small-boat owners menacing bathers. The radio-equipped craft now bear the legend POLICE—NYC in huge letters on their sides as the result of complaints that unmarked boats were being used by the police to trap small-boat owners in indiscretions. But unmarked craft are available for undercover operations against smugglers.

The auxiliary fleet's duties have mounted enormously, with a yearly average of six deaths from small-boat accidents, and one hundred boat fires and collisions. Nearly one thousand other boats require assistance when they experience motor trouble, run aground or start to sink. Close to a half a million dollars' worth of stolen marine equipment, including radios, binoculars, outboard motors, anchors, brass fittings and other accessories, is recovered each year. The seagoing policemen also average six arrests annually and issue more than three hundred summonses for such violations as reckless navigation, speeding, dumping garbage in the water, illegal docking, unregistered operation, inadequate and unsafe equipment and water-skiing without the required observer.

To reduce accidents and deaths, which usually occur when boats are caught unexpectedly in severe storms because they lack radios to receive reports of impending bad weather, the regular launches carry triangular red pennants, eighteen inches wide and three feet long, and raise them on their masts at the first sign of approaching squalls. The pennants were supplied to the Harbor Unit in 1963 by the U.S. Weather Forecasting Service, which now transmits a constant stream of reports to the launches via the communications bureau through a program set up with the cooperation of the U.S. Commerce Department.

On May 21, 1972, the first class of sixty-five concerned citizens graduated as the initial members of the Harbor Unit's new Marine Auxiliary Police Section. The citizen mariners assist the launches in patrolling the waters around marinas, yacht clubs, beaches and other such areas.

While the average New Yorker knows little about the Harbor

Unit's everyday exploits in rescue and law enforcement, the police-men enjoyed widespread notoriety for a time after inaugurating shark patrols off Coney Island on August 24, 1960. ESD marks-men aboard launches, with helicopters conducting aerial surveil-lance overhead, began tracking the killer fish after the sharks in-vaded coastal waters and attacked two swimmers. The patrols are still in effect, but one ESD rifleman, after observing the surging mass of humanity from a launch off Coney Island's beach one day, insisted:

"There are no sharks at Coney Island. They're afraid to come in here. You see that mob on shore there? Those people would eat the sharks alive, and the sharks know it."

8. Flying Flatfoots

The Emergency Service and the Harbor Unit pursue their daily rounds beneath an umbrella of helicopters whose gnatlike presence is the bane of lawbreakers and a harbinger of hope for the sick, the injured and the marooned.

While the Harbor Unit is one of the oldest branches of the New York City Police Department, the Aviation Unit is among the youngest, dating its first tentative operations back to nearly three years before Lindbergh's historic transatlantic flight. The first 120 police pilots, all fresh from military flying during World War I and serving on their own time without pay, started dawn-to-dusk aerial patrols over the city on July 22, 1924.

The missions were flown in seaplanes borrowed from the U.S. Naval Aviation Reserve unit based at Fort Hamilton, Brooklyn, and the goals were to curb pollution from ships dumping oil and garbage into the harbor waters, and to combat a growing number of low-flying private pilots who were "buzzing" and stunting over the city's densely populated areas. The tasks quickly branched out to include detection of riverfront thefts and smuggling activities and the sighting and rescue of drowning victims, but friction developed when the Navy complained about increasing police use of the planes. The jurisdictional dispute forced the police pilots to end the patrols within a matter of months, and for the next five years the dangers from low-flying and reckless aviators grew alarmingly. Buzzing incidents over New York Giants baseball games at the old Polo Grounds, the Goldman Band concerts in Central Park and other places of public assembly stirred widespread concern but went unchecked, with the police powerless to intervene. Cocksure barnstormers scoffed at the public criticism of their antics and at least one, in a flamboyant gesture of defiance, went so far as to threaten to discard his engine muffler and create even more of a commotion.

It was not until the summer of 1929 that the newly appointed police commissioner, Grover Whalen, acted decisively to crack down on the menace. Whalen had gained firsthand experience at a weekend polo match in Westbury, Long Island, where several women in his party nearly fainted in fright when low-flying pilots harassed the crowds. But his outrage reached a fever pitch a few weeks later when three persons were killed by reckless pilots in a single weekend. A motorboat owner was run down and killed in Jamaica Bay off Queens by a hedge-hopping pilot, who claimed he had become lost in fog and thought his plane had scraped a log in the water. The other victims were two children crushed to death by a seaplane making a forced landing on the beach of Coney Island. The pilots in both accidents were arrested and Whalen unleashed a public blast at the U.S. Commerce Department for refusing to tighten its existing regulations barring planes from flying below one thousand feet over the city or stunting over populated areas at any height. The federal agency insisted that its power to revoke licenses was adequate to deter the aerial lawbreakers, but Whalen charged that enforcement of the penalties was lax and he announced a campaign to enact his own regulations and organize a permanent police air force to ensure compliance.

On September 26, 1929, Whalen named Arthur N. Chamberlain, a newspaperman and World War I aviator, to a $4,500-a-year job as his assistant secretary to supervise the planned Air Service Division. The commissioner, who had been air-minded since 1927, when he served as manager of Admiral Richard E. Byrd's transatlantic expedition, used his uncanny showmanship to generate public interest and support for his uphill struggle to win the city's financial backing for the project.

A fortuitous opportunity came less than a week later, on October 4, 1929, while Whalen was on his way down New York Bay aboard the municipal tugboat *Macom* to greet Prime Minister Ramsay MacDonald of Great Britain aboard an arriving ship. The welcoming committee included William F. Carey, president of the New York Air Terminal Corporation, who voiced interest in Whalen's plans and said he would loan the police one of his planes if needed. Returning to his office later in the day, Whalen learned of an incident the night before during which a barge captain named William Mehaffey was killed in a brawl with a tugboat captain after their vessels collided in darkness in the East River off Fort Schuyler in the Bronx. The skipper of the tug, William G. Baker, had reboarded his boat after the fight and was well on his way to his destination in Boston by the time crewmen discovered Mehaffey's body in the barge cabin and notified police. Instantly recognizing the dramatic possibilities of overtaking Baker by air, Whalen arranged to borrow one of Carey's fleet of orange-and-black Loening amphibians. While the plane was warmed up at Glenn Curtiss Airport, on what is now the site of La Guardia Airport in Queens, a search party was organized for the pursuit. The air posse included Chamberlain, Detectives Thomas Malone and George McCartney and two police officials who were to succeed Whalen as commissioners—Deputy Chief Inspector Edward Mulrooney and Lieutenant Arthur W. Wallander.

The chase was a Mack Sennett production from the outset, but nonetheless accomplished all its intended purposes. Speeding under motorcycle escort to the East River, the policemen boarded a motorboat in such haste that the pilot assigned to fly the plane nearly was left stranded on the dock. A jouncing voyage up the river to the airport was followed by a jarring takeoff into howling winds that swept Long Island Sound.

Within two hours, a tugboat resembling Baker's came into view off New Haven, Connecticut, but turned out on closer inspection to be a different vessel with a somewhat similar name. After more circling, the airborne detectives sighted Baker's tug off New London, Connecticut, steaming north at six knots with two barges in tow. When the pilot said he was afraid to land because the water was too rough, a decision was made to fly to New London and secure a boat to pursue Baker by sea. On landing in New London's harbor, the amphibian struck an air pocket and nearly overturned, but the drenched policemen managed to straggle ashore and commandeer an open surfboat. When the boat's engine sputtered and hammering waves at the mouth of the harbor poured gallons of water over the gunwales, the wet and shivering policemen returned to the dock and switched to a seventy-five-foot Coast Guard vessel that was used for chasing rumrunners. It was hardly an improvement, for the rum-chaser's engine quit in short order and an eighty-five-foot rescue vessel had to be sent out to tow it back. Baker's tug meanwhile made steady progress and vanished over the horizon. Exhausted, the searchers adjourned after reporting their troubles to Whalen by telephone.

Whalen went through the formalities of ordering a teletype message issued to warn Boston police that Baker was en route and should be detained on arrival, but he was not content to let the matter rest there. Photographs of the search party, under headlines hailing the city's first "Aerial Manhunt," had been splashed across the front pages of the newspapers and the image of the department obviously was at stake. At the crack of dawn the next day, Whalen routed his men from their hotel beds with urgent orders to resume the chase by air. Reboarding the amphibian, the policemen had to wait a full hour before the craft warmed up and soared aloft. The plane dropped perilously close to the water several times as it climbed out over the Atlantic at eighty-four miles an hour.

An hour later, Baker's tug was observed chugging out of a canal to Massachusetts Bay and the amphibian settled into the water nearby with the policemen shouting and gesticulating so excitedly that the tugboat captain thought the plane was sinking and raced alongside. The searchers clambered aboard the tug and identified themselves, and Baker, with seeming unconcern, accepted the news that he was under arrest for murder. When asked by Mulrooney to waive extradition and return to New York, Baker eyed the amphibian bobbing in the water and was instantly enthralled. "You know, I've never been up in one of those things," he said. "I think I might just go along with you."

Leaving the tug under command of his mate, the captain boarded the plane with his captors. The trip back to New York was comparatively smooth except for a minor emergency after the craft ran low on gas over New London and was forced to land and refuel. When the plane touched down safely at North Beach, near Flushing Bay, a little under three hours later, Whalen was on hand with a welcoming committee, including a huge contingent of newspapermen. As cameras clicked and reporters dutifully recorded his remarks, the commissioner deftly skirted the more discouraging aspects of the flight and vigorously proclaimed the occasion the opening of a new era of air power in police work. Baker, somewhat jumpy by now over the reason for his return, cooperated to the extent of thanking the pilot for a pleasant trip. "Airplanes have it all over tugs," he assured the reporters as he was whisked off for arraignment on the homicide charge.

Whalen soon was swept up in a storm of protest from Massachusetts authorities for what they charged had been an "air invasion" of their state. The officials refrained from filing formal court action, barraging Whalen instead with a series of blistering statements accusing him of violating political etiquette and legal procedure in permitting Baker's return without extradition. Stubbornly defending the action, Whalen displayed signed affidavits from each member of the mission swearing that Baker had surrendered and agreed to return without duress. Surprisingly, the commissioner drew support from Baker's own lawyer, a one-time Brooklyn district attorney, who refused to criticize the arrest. "To protest would only be to criticize an attempt to modernize methods of handling crime," he said. "We need every modern method we can get to stop getaways by criminals." Citing Baker's willingness to return voluntarily as proof of his innocence, the lawyer went on to win acquittal for the tug skipper by demonstrating that Mehaffey died accidentally when he fell and struck his head in the struggle.

Confident that Baker's speedy capture had fired the public's interest, Whalen pressed ahead with his plans for the Air Service Division despite the city's delay in answering his request for $100,-000 in emergency funds to finance the venture. More than one hundred policemen had applied for transfer to the new unit. By October 24, 1929, ten of them—one a World War I pilot and the others with considerable civilian flying experience—began training at Roosevelt Field, Mineola, Long Island, marking the first attempt in the nation to form a regular municipal police air force. To expedite the flight instruction, Whalen acquired an amphibian from department store heir Rodman Wanamaker II, whom he named a special aide and put in charge of the new unit's equipment and personnel. Wanamaker, a private pilot and avid aviation enthusiast, conveniently poured some of his personal fortune into the program while city officials argued over whether to approve Whalen's plea for money.

The commissioner's program won attention and praise from Admiral Byrd and war ace Captain Eddie Rickenbacker, both of whom predicted that similar air-police units eventually would be established in every great city in the country. One thrust of Whalen's campaign focused theatrically on the need for aerial police to capture criminals who were using private planes in growing numbers to flee the city, but he also stressed the other potential uses. Nationwide support mounted steadily for his war against dangerous fliers as officials in other affected areas joined in urging action to stamp out the menace. The drive picked up renewed impetus when a publicity-seeking lion-tamer parachuted into the Central Park Zoo from a private plane that crashed into a nearby apartment building, killing the pilot. The tragedy prompted Whalen to insist on a stringent local code that would keep pilots at a minimum altitude of seven thousand or ten thousand feet while flying over the city. Meanwhile, unexpected difficulties plagued the air unit's training program, which was threatened with collapse at one point when instructors "washed out" five of the initial candidates on the grounds that they lacked qualifications to become good fliers. Wanamaker reviewed the findings and rejected them, claiming the evaluations had been made on the basis of questionable standards that overrated previous flying experience. He restored the "washouts," contending that prior experience actually could be a liability in some cases since pilots with extensive air time tended to be less flexible and might adapt less easily to the teaching of new tactics necessary for police duties.

By December 21, 1929, the pilot training had progressed sufficiently to establish the first police air base at North Beach, and Whalen attended ceremonies there to christen two city-purchased

Savoia-Marchetti amphibians. The open-cockpit, high-winged bi-planes, powered by a single ninety-horsepower engine above the top wing, were baptized with bottles of ginger ale that were shattered over their icicle-covered noses while a police band played "In the Good Old Summertime."

Designated PD-1 and PD-2, the planes were fitted out with guns, tear gas bombs, sirens and first-aid kits. Although the craft had seats for three men, their limited lifting power made it impossible for them to take off with a crew of more than two. The third, unoccupied seat came to be known as the "angel seat"—reserved for a heavenly presence that the pilots hoped somehow was helping them to stay aloft.

A third Savoia-Marchetti and a Loening later were integrated into the fleet. Regular patrols officially started on March 29, 1930, with a force of twelve police fliers under Wallander's command. An appropriate telephone number—NIghtingale 4-1661—was set up for the public to register complaints against reckless aviators.

Within days the first summons was issued by Officer Peter Terranova to a pilot flying below one thousand feet over Van Cortlandt Park in the Bronx to watch aviation ace Frank M. Hawks complete a transcontinental glider flight under escort into the city by the new police airmen. The offending pilot's license was revoked for thirty days and he was fined $250 at Whalen's request.

During the unit's first year of operation, plane crashes in populated areas and complaints about low-flying aircraft, which had risen to as many as two hundred to three hundred a year, virtually vanished, but a few pilots searched for ways to circumvent the law. One commercial aviator flew above the minimum altitude in a plane with loudspeakers that blared down popular songs and advertising messages to Sunday strollers. Frustrated police legal experts were powerless to stop the nuisance, but an irate West Side clergyman succeeded by denouncing the practice from his pulpit. The businessman who had chartered the plane canceled the flights under public protest.

The work of the fledgling police airmen was perilous from the start and there were several narrow brushes with death. One pilot, Otto Kafka, who later excelled as one of the unit's top aviators, nearly was decapitated by the whirling propeller of a plane he was cranking up after a practice forced landing near Roosevelt Field.

Two other pilots were injured when their amphibian developed motor trouble and plunged to a hard landing in Flushing Bay near North Beach. A similar plane, carrying Wallander and a copilot, nosed over in twenty-five feet of water while taking off at Port Washington, Long Island, but both men escaped with minor scratches and were rescued by a passing boat. The plane was salvaged to fly again.

Victims of less serious mishaps were awarded a special booby prize, which consisted of a gilded tomato-can top and an authoritative-looking tin star dangling from a safety pin. Recipients included one pilot who bumped a beaching ramp and another who showed up for work on his day off.

The planes swiftly showed their rescue potential by saving a crewman washed overboard from a yacht off Hart Island in Long Island Sound on May 7, 1930. The rescue—the unit's first—was accomplished by Officers Thomas Mason and Francis Diefenbach, who landed their amphibian nearby and hauled the sailor from the water.

Ground communication with the aircraft was pioneered by Mulrooney soon after he succeeded Whalen as commissioner. On November 26, 1930, he spoke from police headquarters to the crews of two planes through a telephone hookup with a radio station in New Jersey. The experiment's success led Mulrooney to announce that he would explore the feasibility of installing two-way radios in police cars on the ground, which still were without short-wave equipment at the time.

A bizarre extortion plot that Whalen's most inspired showmanship could not have duplicated provided the air unit with a timely opportunity to dramatize its prowess at crime detection. The plot was hatched after a thousand-dollar reward for information was offered by the family of a New York Central Railway clerk who had vanished on November 19, 1930, after leaving his home in Queens. The family received a telephone call from a man who said he knew where the clerk was and could guarantee his safe return if the money was sent to him by two carrier pigeons that had been left in a cardboard box at a nearby cigar store. He instructed that a family member band a five-hundred-dollar bill to the leg of each pigeon and then turn the birds loose, and promised that the missing clerk would be returned after delivery of the ransom.

The family notified police and the Air Service Division arranged to put a plane aloft to trail the birds after they were released. It was a ploy worthy of Sherlock Holmes but it failed in a comedy of errors when the pigeons refused to cooperate. One interrupted his homeward journey by joining a bevy of his feathered kin on a rooftop and flying off with them. The other made an unscheduled landing in a cemetery, where it blended in with the color of the tombstones and disappeared.

Fortunately, the extortioner had an ample supply of the birds and sent another pair, with a second demand for money. An ingenious police tactician came up with the idea of painting the birds' feathers bright orange to make them easier to track as they skimmed over the rooftops to their coop. On the second try, two planes stalked the pigeons straight to a Queens loft and alerted police on the ground, who closed in to arrest the owner. As it turned out, the "Pigeon Plot" was simply an effort to exploit the family's reward offer and had nothing to do with the clerk's disappearance.

The air unit's early successes in rescue and law enforcement failed to impress budget-conscious city officials, who were more concerned about the deepening impact of the Depression on the city's economy and viewed the operations as too expensive and not all that essential. Their mood was reflected in gradual fund cutbacks. The unit's flying hours dwindled from a high of one thousand in 1930 to only four hundred in 1933, when it shifted headquarters to Hangar No. 4 at Floyd Bennett Field, where it still rents facilities from the Navy for a fee of one dollar a year. Regular patrols were canceled and the planes went up only in emergencies. One involved rescue of the crew of the Navy blimp J-3, which plunged into the Atlantic on April 4, 1933, while searching for survivors from the crash of the Navy dirigible *Akron* off Atlantic City, New Jersey. The mission was flown by Officers Joseph W. Forsythe and Otto Kafka, who landed their amphibian in a trough between ten-foot waves so that the blimp's crew could cling to the wings and hull of the plane while it taxied them to shore.

The heroic feat exerted little influence on the air unit's faltering fortunes, and by the end of 1933 Police Commissioner John F. O'Ryan, a Mulrooney successor, was considering phasing out the operations. On January 31, 1934, O'Ryan reached a decision to scrap the Air Service Division, but he retained two of its planes and incorporated them into the Emergency Service on March 20, 1934, as a subsidiary Aviation Bureau. The other planes, which had cost the city $14,000 when new, were sold at auction two months later for only $620.

O'Ryan's successor, Commissioner Lewis J. Valentine, attempted a year later to reactivate the air patrols to deal with the city's worsening traffic congestion problem, but his pleas fell on deaf ears despite several dramatic rescues performed by the remaining pilots. Late in September of 1935, Officer Richard Ryan doffed his shoes and flying goggles and plunged thirty feet from the hatchway of a Savoia-Marchetti piloted by Terranova to aid two swimmers foundering in eight-foot waves off Coney Island. The plunge became necessary when Terranova found it impossible to land the plane in the trough of the waves, which were coming fifty feet apart. Ryan helped both swimmers ashore and was later decorated for bravery for the feat, but the Aviation Bureau faded into virtual oblivion over the next few years. By 1938, the remaining two planes had been disposed of as "antiquated" and scores of police pilots marked time on the ground.

It was not until the pending opening of a newly built commercial airport at North Beach, which later was to assume his name, that Mayor La Guardia made another effort to restore the air unit by promoting the city's purchase of two new planes and staging a publicity-geared ceremony at the airport site.

"We will find before long that the Aviation Unit will be performing such valuable and essential work that we will wonder how we ever got along without it," the mayor told assembled police airmen after returning from a ten-minute flight in one of the new planes with Valentine and Yankee baseball player Lefty Gomez while the police band played "Come, Josephine, in My Flying Machine."

La Guardia accurately prophesied that the unit would prove a boon in controlling the rising tide of commercial and recreational air traffic as well as the thousands of cars jamming the city's highways. He also predicted its future role in crime investigation, aerial photography and fire fighting. But even La Guardia's contagious enthusiasm could not overcome the deadening lull that set in with the outbreak of World War II, which restricted the unit to obsolete craft and skeleton crews as equipment and personnel were diverted into the military. Operations switched from Floyd Bennett back to La Guardia on September 25, 1942, and nine pilots were left to fly a single amphibian. Shortly after the war ended, two military Grumman amphibians were purchased as surplus for fifteen thousand dollars but they were swiftly supplanted by the helicopter, whose advent signaled the start of an entirely new chapter in the Aviation Unit's history.

The whirlybirds already had demonstrated their effectiveness and versatility in off-coast antisubmarine patrols and rescue missions late in the war, and on August 10, 1947, the city's Board of Estimate authorized purchase of the first police helicopter for $25,-000. The craft was officially placed in service on September 30, 1948, after members of the revitalized air unit underwent intensive training at the plant of the manufacturer, Bell Laboratories, at Niagara Falls, New York. Captain Gustav Crawford, who had been appointed the unit's new commander, personally flew the Bell 47-D copter to the city, establishing New York as the first municipality in the world to own such equipment. By 1950, three more whirlybirds were acquired and two years later the last of the fixed-wing planes was sold at public auction.

The helicopters flew only emergency assignments at first, but regular daylight patrols were started on June 25, 1953, with Lieutenant Anthony Fiore and Officer Thomas R. Williams manning the controls on the first flight. The switchover to the innovative craft greatly expanded the unit's duties in rescue, law-enforcement and allied fields.

A year later, the helicopter fleet had grown to six, and older models were traded in under a still existing policy that calls for updating equipment periodically so that no chopper remains in service more than five years. The helicopter swiftly showed many unique, built-in advantages over fixed-wing planes. Besides an ability to hover low and come to a practical standstill as a floating platform in midair, it required only ninety seconds to warm up and fly, compared to the minimum of ten minutes necessary for conventional planes. It also needed very little storage space and could land almost anywhere and fly in weather that might keep other light planes on the ground. Its speed and hovering capability were invaluable for racing to the scenes of reported emergencies and assessing the extent of the trouble. But as with all human inventions endowed with seemingly miraculous powers, the helicopter proved to have some drawbacks too. One disadvantage was limited usefulness for nighttime patrols, since the city's skyscrapers, bridges, smokestacks and high wires pose hazards for low-flying craft. The craft usually patrol only up to 11 P.M. A second disadvantage is the lack of automatic-pilot equipment, which results in fatiguing demands on the operator to constantly coordinate five separate controls regulating the craft's speed and direction. Two or three hours at a time at the complex job is considered the safety limit for most pilots.

Six copters now cover a territory encompassing 319 square miles. It contains more than 6,000 miles of streets and highways, as well as the developed river- and harborfront areas and beaches, marinas and other installations, which they patrol in coordination with the Harbor Unit, as part of the Air-Sea Section. The jurisdiction also takes in all airports and skyports within the city boundaries from which itinerant fliers and student and military reserve pilots operate.

The craft are flown and maintained by a close-knit band of thirty-four men. All are carefully chosen volunteers. Candidates for flying duties hold commercial pilot licenses, which require a minimum of two hundred hours of in-flight training, and both pilots and mechanics receive intensive on-the-job instruction. Despite skills that could command big salaries elsewhere, the unit's members receive the same base pay, according to rank, as regular gun-toting policemen on the force, except for the pilots, who are rewarded with an increment amounting to five dollars a week.

The unit's staff consists of one captain in command, who is a qualified copter pilot, two lieutenants, four sergeants and twenty-seven officers, all either pilots or licensed mechanics. One lieutenant and two of the officers also are licensed by the Federal Aviation Agency as helicopter instructors. The other lieutenant is qualified by the FAA as an aircraft inspector and supervises two sergeants and ten officers, who are experts in aircraft maintenance.

To ensure that the mechanics are constantly up to date on the latest maintenance and repair procedures, periodic leaves are granted to rotating pairs of men to attend a four-week instruction course at Fort Worth, Texas, and a further two-week session in turbine engines at Indianapolis, Indiana. On returning, the teams conduct training programs to familiarize their fellow mechanics with the newest developments. The excellence of the mechanical staff is consistently evident in the high trade-in prices commanded by the older aircraft resold for newer models. As an added incentive to assure safe performance of the copters, the mechanics regularly fly in them as observers.

"If they're going to fix them, they're going to fly them," one veteran pilot explains. "It's not a bad way to keep everybody on his toes and make sure everything's in tiptop working order."

To the occasional criticism by policemen in other sections of the force that their flying comrades have "contract" or soft-berth jobs, one veteran replies, "If you're a cop in a prowl car that breaks down in Times Square, you can pull over to the curb for a fast check. But how can you pull over to a cloud?"

With neither premium pay nor insurance against the hazards of the work in the Aviation Unit, the ultimate safeguard is spelled out in a motto emblazoned on a plaque adorning the wall of the headquarters, which reads: THERE ARE OLD PILOTS—AND THERE ARE BOLD PILOTS—BUT THERE ARE NO OLD BOLD PILOTS!

Considering the tens of thousands of hours logged, the safety record of the unit is exceptional. Only four pilots have died in accidents—two in a crash into the East River near the Brooklyn Bridge in 1967, two others in a flaming plunge onto the front lawn of a Queens home in 1970.

Each chopper logs upward of nine hundred flying hours yearly, including daily, programmed patrols and others during morning and evening rush hours and on weekends to help direct and control the great choked streams of traffic moving into and out of the city. All the craft are fitted out with radio and some with television transmitters that enable them to communicate directly with the motoring public over the municipally owned radio station, WNYC, and to telecast jam-ups, accidents and breakdowns to police and traffic department officials. During a mass transit strike in 1966, all the whirlybirds went aloft simultaneously, flying expanded dawn-to-dusk patrols to untangle huge traffic jams when subway and bus riders turned to car travel.

Little escapes the view of the police airman, whose vantage point from several hundred feet of altitude permits scanning of traffic conditions over a distance as far as sixty-one blocks in any direction. The craft rarely drop lower than two hundred feet while traffic-watching unless something very special occurs, but the occasions do arise, particularly during summer weekends. When one Sunday motorist bogged down in nightmare traffic on a Brooklyn highway walked off disgusted, and the abandoned car he left backed up traffic for a mile, Lieutenant Kenneth C. Johnston swooped down in his helicopter to within twenty-five feet of the fleeing man's head and waved his arms to signal him back to the vehicle. Hand signals are favored over copter loudspeakers in traffic situations because, as one pilot puts it, "The public-address system gets drivers all shook up and they think it's an air raid or something and go smashing into each other."

Besides traffic control work, the choppers perform a variety of sideline chores for city and federal government agencies, which save taxpayers a substantial amount of money in view of the hundred-dollar-an-hour cost of hiring commercial whirlybirds. The unit's aerial photographers average one assignment weekly, snapping aerial shots of land and water sites involved in legal proceedings or proposed as building, land-fill or dumping areas. The photos are requested by such city agencies as the Planning Commission, the Board of Estimate, the Bureau of Real Estate and the Department of Water Supply, Gas and Electricity.

The city's Air Pollution Department regularly enlists the choppers to gather high-level samples of air and, until ecological concerns halted the practice, the craft helped spread insecticides over infested marshes to curb mosquitoes and other insects. Detecting smoke violators as well as vessels illegally dumping oil or garbage is still another responsibility of the copter service, which also aids in locating and trailing dye markers in waters surrounding the city to provide data for the U.S. Department of the Interior on tide directions and pollution trends.

Since the helicopters usually are first to arrive at air-crash scenes, their aerial photos and pilot observations prove indispensable to federal authorities inquiring into the causes of the accidents. As part of an ongoing program to prevent accidents and enforce air safety standards, the unit annually inspects nearly a score of seaplane bases, heliports and private airports in the city, using two police radio cars it keeps on hand for ground investigations. The findings, including any violations, are reported to the city Department of Marine and Aviation for correction or disciplinary action.

Except for a brief resurgence of reckless flying for one year immediately following World War II, when homecoming military pilots chartered small aircraft to buzz the homes of friends on weekend larks, low-flying complaints have remained uniformly few due to the unit's strict enforcement of section 435-16.0 of the city's Administrative Code. The law prohibits pilots from making reckless maneuvers or violating federal statutes calling for altitudes no lower than one thousand feet above the highest obstacle.

Low flying generally costs the culprit a fine of at least fifty dollars and the violations are reported to federal authorities for further action. In the more flagrant cases, the fine can go as high as five hundred dollars and also carry a jail term of up to one year. The same law stipulates that forced landings are excusable only when due to engine failure or other mechanical problems, but even these circumstances do not absolve pilots who are violating low-flying or other regulations.

When the law was passed, it included a prohibition against another kind of landing after a parachutist, intent on making aerial movies, bailed out of a light plane over Manhattan on May 31, 1947. The 'chutist got away scot-free because no specific regulation existed against his type of antic, but when he made a second jump on August 20, 1949, he was fined fifty dollars under an ordinance that was passed after his first leap. An emergency police crew spent hours disentangling the chute from a chimney atop an East Side building where he had landed. The law also forbids other dangerous nuisances, such as the towing of aerial advertising banners.

Curbing reckless fliers is only a small part of the unit's wide range of law-enforcement activities, which include detection of vandalism and boat thefts along the city's docks and marinas and surveillance of suspects transferring narcotics and other illegal contraband from arriving ships and airlines. The FBI and the Federal Bureau of Narcotics and Dangerous Drugs often request cooperation in the latter cases. Mechanics once spent an entire night repainting a helicopter blue so that it would blend with the sky while trailing a car suspected of ferrying smuggled narcotics from airliners at La Guardia. Federal agents in unmarked cars on the ground were linked by radio with the camouflaged copter, which advised them on the car's location as they pursued it through heavy traffic. The agents were able to move in to make arrests at the opportune moment.

The unit's photos of crime scenes aid in investigations and prosecutions by the police as well as by the district attorneys' offices. In one case, aerial photos and observation of buildings and terrain in a Bronx neighborhood where a teen-age girl had been shot and critically wounded by sniper fire helped ballistics experts and homicide squad detectives to correlate trajectory angles and other factors that exactly pinpointed the origin of the bullets. Analysis of the data resulted in the arrest of a boy who police said had been firing a rifle at random out of an apartment house window.

Not the least of the helicopter's assets is its strange, clattering presence, which has a potent bulldozing effect on crowds when it sweeps down low over riot scenes to keep ground forces constantly informed on potential trouble spots. Many a lawbreaker or fleeing fugitive has frozen in his tracks at the sight of the weird contraption zeroing in on him from above. When inmates escape from the penitentiary on Rikers Island, copters join the Harbor Unit launches in hunting the fugitives; the downwash of their rotors flattens marsh reeds on the perimeter of the island and exposes any jailbreakers hiding in them. The Department of Corrections routinely calls on the whirlybirds for periodic aerial security checks of various prison grounds. The choppers conduct similar searches of large ground areas for evidence in criminal cases, in far less time and with much greater effectiveness than is possible with ground search parties. One such search uncovered an abandoned bicycle that figured as an important link in the slaying of two children and led to the capture of a suspect.

The first time helicops witnessed a crime from the air, chased the fugitives and arrested them was in the winter of 1958, when Sergeant Harold Behrens and Officer William Reis spotted five youths scurrying around a car in a vacant lot near Aqueduct race track in Queens at a time in the afternoon when most youngsters were in school. At the sight of the whirlybird, the boys piled into the car and roared off at breakneck speed. Squinting through binoculars, Behrens recorded the car's license-plate number, radioed police headquarters and was informed within minutes that files showed the auto was stolen. The fleeing car hit speeds of up to one hundred miles an hour, five miles faster than the top speed of the piston-engine copter, but the chase narrowed when the car slowed down in heavy traffic. "Pull over to the side of road," Behrens boomed through the chopper's loudspeaker as the helicopter dropped low over the car. The frightened youths swerved around the blocking traffic and sped off again, only to crash into a tree a short distance away. Unable to touch down in the obstructed terrain, Behrens and Reis flew back to the race track, borrowed a car from a guard there and rushed back to the scene in time to seize three of the youths. The others had escaped.

The youths' auto was one of more than one hundred stolen cars and hijacked trucks that the unit recovers each year. Its crime-fighting potential has rapidly expanded with the pace of techno-logical and tactical advances. The pilots use their traffic-scanning television equipment to flash pictures of crime scenes back to central screens at headquarters for evaluation by top police officials. A high-intensity bluish-white light called the Spectro Night Sun is installed on one of the choppers to sweep heavily forested sections of the city after darkness and detect or scare off muggers, purse snatchers, rapists, vandals and other troublemakers. The five-thousand-dollar light can illuminate an area the size of an entire baseball field with a soft glow from a height of three hundred to six hundred feet, or brighten a space comparable to a baseball infield with a glare as intense as daylight.

Patrols now include "skywatch" search-and-apprehend missions, during which a copter stays in the air for two-hour stints over pre-designated areas in continual radio communication with a fleet of radio cars on the ground. Each radio car bears an identifying three-foot-high numeral on its roof that is clearly visible from five hundred to eight hundred feet altitude, so that the aerial observers can single out the vehicle and dispatch it to sites of suspected criminal activity. The patrols are effective and economical in spotting auto thieves, car-strippers and housebreakers on roofs, in back alleys and at other sites of high crime incidence, since one copter can inspect in four minutes an area that would require a radio car an hour and a half to cover.

A bank-robbery suspect was arrested in Brooklyn with the help of a helicopter in the summer of 1972, not long after police began asking landlords and businessmen to paint abbreviated street ad-dresses—in yellow or white letters at least twenty-four inches high and with strokes at least three inches wide—on the rooftop of at least one building in every block in the city. Word of a holdup alarm received from the bank was flashed over the police radio and picked up by Officer Kenneth Otten, who flew to the scene and was able to pick out the bank building from its rooftop iden-tification before the suspect had a chance to escape. As the whirly-bird swooped down, the man froze. "He heard the propeller noise and thought the bank was surrounded by police," said Otten, who hovered over the bank until radio-car officers arrived to take the frightened suspect into custody.

Emergency and rescue missions comprise only a small amount of the unit's work, but take precedence over every other type of operation.

The copters respond to all major multiple-alarm fires to relay aerial reports on the spread of the flames, and sometimes they take Fire Department officials aloft for a better view on how and where to deploy men and apparatus most efficiently. The whirly-birds also serve as fire-watchers during dry spells by scouting for blazes in remote woodland regions. When poison gas escaping from a cracked container in a factory threatened to engulf a Man-hattan neighborhood, a chopper flew to the roof of the plant, hooked the lethal cargo to a line and raced out to the open sea to dump it into the waves. During the boating and bathing season, the unit maintains daily patrols over public beaches and water-ways used for recreational boating and aids the Harbor Unit in hunting down sharks.

A wild black dog that had bitten several children in Queens was captured with the aid of a helicopter on March 25, 1958, after the animal eluded two radio-car policemen by loping off into a dense marshland. The police officers called for two more radio cars, but the ground search proved futile. Sergeant Behrens, who only three weeks before had captured the boys in the high-speed stolen-car chase, was patrolling over the area with a mechanic, Officer Frank Waluk, when both saw the circling radio cars and landed for a routine check. Told about the missing dog, Behrens and Waluk whirled back up to two hundred feet, spotted the animal and

FLYING FLATFOOTS   215

tracked it, relaying radio reports on its location until the policemen on the ground cornered and subdued it about three and a
half miles from where the children had been attacked.

Under a "missions of mercy" program, the helicopters make
special flights to transport eyes, kidneys and other organs for
transplant operations. On January 10, 1973, a chopper piloted by
Officer Edward Schellhorn flew to Valley Stream, Long Island, to
pick up two kidneys that had just been removed from a donor and
rushed them, along with three doctors, to Montefiore Hospital in
the Bronx, where the organs were transplanted into a critically ill
person. A month and a half later, Officer Vincent Driscoll flew a
similar mission to the Jersey Shore Medical Center in Neptune.
The helicopter sped back to Manhattan with a pair of eyes for a
corneal transplant. Surgeons were able to begin the operation less
than two hours after the eyes had been taken from the donor.
Driscoll accomplished the mission in exactly one hour and seven
minutes.

Every helicopter is equipped with first-aid materials, wire basket
stretcher, an inflatable life raft and a rope ladder, and a pair carry
electric hoist machinery that is capable of lifting several hundred
pounds. The copters serve as aerial ambulances under a program
initiated in 1961 when, in conjunction with the city's hospitals department, all medical facilities were surveyed and seventy-nine
sites near them were designated as suitable landing areas. Contingency plans exist for airlifting seriously ill and injured persons
to hospitals when ground ambulances face delays in traffic and for
rushing medical supplies and personnel to accident scenes cut off
by storms, floods or disasters.

During a record snowfall in February, 1969, the helicopter
crews airlifted one pregnant woman, numerous cardiac cases and
several kidney-disease patients in need of lifesaving treatment to
hospitals.

The first use of a police helicopter as an aerial ambulance actually occurred on the windy and overcast afternoon of June 28,
1951, when the ESD's Aviation No. 6 fluttered aloft from Floyd
Bennett on a rescue mission unprecedented in the city's history.

The helicopter's destination was the Episcopal Cathedral of
Saint John the Divine, on Manhattan's Morningside Heights, where

a steeplejack lay twisted in pain on the roof after having fallen thirty feet from a ladder that had snapped under his weight while he was painting a steel scaffold.

The worker had fractured his right hip and crushed his right leg and several ribs in the plunge, but he remained conscious through it all. While two fellow workers comforted him, a third raced down a long winding stairwell inside the cathedral for help.

Two emergency squads responded but they could not remove the injured man by way of the spiral steps because the route was too narrow to maneuver him down on a litter without worsening his injuries. Blood was oozing from his mouth, and it was feared that he had suffered internal damage, although most of the blood appeared to come from several teeth he had broken.

Swinging the steeplejack over the roof's edge in a wire basket and lowering him 170 feet to the street with ropes and pulleys was considered, but the idea was abandoned when he balked at the long, lonely descent. Stiff twenty-mile-an-hour winds buffeting the area also presented the risk of battering him against the building's side.

At 12:45 P.M., an urgent request for a helicopter was flashed to the Aviation Unit's hangar at Floyd Bennett after Inspector Klotzback arrived and suggested that the steeplejack be taken from the roof by air. Captain Crawford, a pilot since the scarf-and-goggles days of the twenties, was on duty when the call came in and he lumbered out onto the field as Aviation No. 6 was towed out of the hanger on a dolly. Crawford, an Irish-Swede whose striking good looks epitomized the Hollywood image of a crackerjack pilot, wasted no time changing the work clothes he was wearing sans underwear. He climbed into the chopper's plastic bubble cockpit with his copilot, Officer John T. Jordan, and within ninety seconds the whirlybird was airborne and soaring northward over Brooklyn and Manhattan.

The helicopter negotiated the seventeen air miles to the cathedral in ten minutes and hovered overhead while Crawford peered down from the transparent cockpit to size up the challenge before him. The available landing space on the roof was scarcely thirty feet square and obstructed by the scaffold, which rose between the cathedral's uncompleted 160-foot-high twin towers of Saint Peter and Saint Paul. The copter's tip-to-tail length was forty-one feet, but Crawford figured that a section of the tail could be left hanging in midair over the roof's edge while he balanced the craft by gunning the engines. The chief danger was the rotors, which cut a circle thirty-six feet in diameter and could send the chopper crashing down the cathedral's side if the tips struck the scaffold or towers.

Confident that he could land safely, Crawford carefully calculated the drift from the strong winds lashing the craft and eased the helicopter in so that it settled down in a grotesque position with one pontoon resting lengthwise along the parapet, less than two inches from the edge, and the rotors spinning barely two inches from the surrounding towers.

The steeplejack's broken hip was adjusted in a splint and he was secured in the wire basket stretcher, which was lifted onto one of the helicopter's pontoons and strapped down tightly. Crawford placed a jacket over the injured man to shield him from the wind and Jordan debarked from the craft to lighten the load. At 1:17 P.M., seven minutes after its arrival, the copter backed away from the roof while crowds gaped and cheered at the breathtaking spectacle from the street. Three minutes later, Crawford glided to a smooth landing on a stretch of grass in Riverside Park, sixteen blocks to the south, and the steeplejack was transferred to a waiting ambulance and rushed to a hospital.

The helicopter's rescue potential had been explored by Captain Crawford long before he saved the injured steeplejack from the cathedral. Fascinated with aviation since early childhood, Crawford quit a job with a honey-processing firm to learn flying in Kansas during the twenties. He worked briefly as a commercial pilot at New York City's first private airfield on Staten Island before joining the police force. After a stint on foot patrol, he was accepted into the Harbor Unit, which put him in line to move into the newly evolving Air Service Division in 1933. A veteran of rescue exploits in fixed-wing planes, Crawford was quick to appreciate the helicopter's singular characteristics. In the winter of 1947, when the unit still was without its own copter, he borrowed a whirlybird from the Coast Guard to search for a little girl lost in a blinding snowstorm. After three ground crews had tramped for hours through icy swamps in a futile ground search, it took Crawford, at the time the father of three small children, less than an hour to locate the missing child, wandering cold and hungry but unharmed in a nearby graveyard.

The helicopter's unparalleled ability to scour vast regions with speed and thoroughness at low altitudes was instrumental in saving two brothers who otherwise would have frozen to death in desolate, wind-swept marshes bordering Jamaica Bay in March of 1952. The youths, one eighteen and the other fourteen, were marooned after setting out in a rented rowboat with a rod and reel that had been given to the younger boy for his birthday. The boat's oarlocks broke, and the youths paddled into the marshes a half mile from International Airport, but were afraid to walk inland through the weeds because of the danger of slipping and drowning in numerous hidden tidal channels that honeycombed the area. They spent all day trying without success to erect a crude shelter against the biting winds and to light a fire for warmth while waiting for help. Darkness brought a rapid drop in temperature that turned their clothing into suits of armor made of ice. At dawn the next day, after their parents and police had searched the marshes and turned up no trace of the youths, Sergeant Behrens flew over in a copter and found them without difficulty. The pair was flown to Floyd Bennett and rushed to a hospital for lifesaving treatment.

Although the fleetest of the copters can fly forward at only up to 140 miles an hour and dart backward and sideways at much lower speed, quicker takeoffs and landings and maneuverability more than compensate for their relative slowness when compared to conventional aircraft. Merely twenty minutes was required to rescue a student pilot from the icy currents of Jamaica Bay in December, 1948, when his amphibian flipped over in a cross wind as it skimmed the choppy water on a practice landing. Unsnapping his safety belt, the student climbed onto one of the plane's ice-sheeted pontoons, but began to lose his grip when his hands went numb. He was sinking beneath the surface when Captain Crawford arrived in a chopper with his copilot, Officer John J. Murphy, who pulled the young man to safety.

For persons who plunge through thin ice in winter accidents, the copters provide a much faster and less hazardous rescue method than the standard procedure of extending ladders to the victims across the frozen surface. A woman who mistook Brooklyn's Prospect Park lake for a snow-covered field and crashed through the ice on December 20, 1964, was evacuated within minutes by a copter after she had been shivering in waist-deep water while a land crew struggled to reach her. When victims are trapped under the ice, the whirlybirds aid the searchers by jouncing pontoons on the crust to break through to the water below.

The tornadolike downwash from the helicopter's rotors that endows the craft with powerful built-in lifting capacity also plays ingenious roles in rescue work. When a fisherman was mired up to his neck in mud after stepping out to free his rowboat, which had run aground in black slime 150 feet from the Jamaica Bay shore, Sergeant Behrens and Officer Gerald Crosson improvised an aerial derrick to extricate him. Behrens balanced on the chopper's pontoon to circle a rope under the victim's armpits and Crosson gunned the engines to lift the craft and yank him free.

A propelling whirlpool kicked up by the rotor downwash nudged two dazed men drifting on an ice floe in the middle of the Harlem River back to within a few feet of shore after Lieutenant Theodore Cavooris spotted the pair from his helicopter in February, 1971. Radio-car patrolmen on the riverbank completed the rescue by tossing a line to the men and reeling them in. Unhurt, the pair left the scene in such haste that no one ever found out for certain who they were or how they had wound up on the strange voyage. A significant clue was supplied by one policeman, who noted, "Their breath was melting the ice."

The rotor downdraft has been utilized in similar fashion to shove scores of youthful mariners back to shore when they ventured into the city's rivers and bays on makeshift rafts, but its most stunning accomplishment was the rescue of five men and an eleven-year-old boy after they abandoned a flaming cabin cruiser on August 19, 1958, in Rockaway Inlet, less than two miles west of the Aviation Unit's Floyd Bennett hangar. The six escaped in the cabin cruiser's dinghy, but strong winds threatened to sweep them back into the blazing vessel because they had no oars to row out of danger. Sergeant Behrens arrived overhead in a helicopter and directed a blast of air from the rotors that thrust the dinghy out of range of the inferno.

Long hours of practice have made the pilots adept at guiding life rafts dropped from the copters to floundering victims by skittering them across the surface with downwash. A high degree of accuracy is achieved even in riptide currents.

The use of the hoists aboard the helicopters to haul victims to safety poses risks because the craft are intrinsically unstable due to lack of adequate control surfaces. The choppers develop a wobble at low speeds and the hovering maneuver is sometimes akin to trying to balance on top of a rubber ball. The phenomenon almost resulted in tragedy in the summer of 1959 during the rescue of a ten-year-old boy and his companion after their rowboat capsized off Coney Island. One boy, in panic that he would be left behind, insisted on clinging monkeylike to the neck of his friend while both were drawn up thirty feet to the copter on the hoist cable. The shifting weight nearly side-slipped the chopper into the water, but Lieutenant Johnston averted a disaster by skillfully working the controls to restore the craft's equilibrium.

The space and weight limitations of the early helicopter models often made it necessary for one crewman to stay at the point of rescue until the pilot flew the victim to safety and then returned. The unit's first chopper ran into weight-lifting problems on the evening of June 20, 1949, while rescuing two young men clinging to an overturned sailboat off Coney Island. After landing, Sergeant Behrens could not maneuver to the youths because the sailboat's mast threatened to pierce the copter's pontoons. Life rings with ropes attached were hurled to the thrashing pair and the co-pilot, Officer Walter Smith, dragged them in. When the extra weight of the two new passengers prevented the craft from rising from the water, Behrens taxied to an arriving police launch and jettisoned Smith, the heaviest of all aboard. He then flew the soaked youths to shore. The power and size of the helicopters have improved steadily since those early days, with turbojets replacing the piston engines.

The pontoons on the older models are now designed with separate watertight compartments that guarantee buoyancy if punctured, and the newer jets are equipped with landing skids that contain built-in flotation gear, which can be inflated by controls in the cockpit for landing on water. Pontoons seldom are used nowadays to transport the sick and injured because of the complex problem of working out proper load distribution and the danger of exposing the victims to accidents. Two policemen and a drowning man they had rescued from Jamaica Bay were nearly killed one winter day in 1972 when the victim toppled back into the water from a pontoon as the helicopter taxied to within a dozen feet of shore. The chopper heeled over as the sudden change in its center of gravity sent the float on the opposite side plunging beneath the surface. The pilot, Officer Peter Mandleur, was trapped in his seat belt in the cockpit under five feet of water, and his observer, Officer Thomas Cardi, was sucked under the pontoon on which he had been crouching to hold the rescued man. An off-duty fireman and two radio-car patrolmen on shore witnessed the accident and waded out to cut Mandleur loose from the cockpit and drag Cardi and the drowning victim from beneath the float.

Pontoon rescues usually are favored only in cases where carrying frantic persons inside the cockpit would expose the craft to even greater jeopardy. An ailing sixty-seven-year-old hospital patient was lashed to a float by Behrens and Officer Anthony Schiano, who fished him from the East River after he had scaled a fence and plunged into the water from Welfare Island on May 2, 1957. But Schiano taxied all the way back to the island rather than risk taking off in the swirling currents of Hell Gate with the flailing 190-pound victim.

A swimmer paddling across the Hudson River on the afternoon of April 11, 1954, was given wide berth by Officers Robert Volmut and Sam Leonowich after he displayed great reluctance at the prospect of being rescued. The man was halfway to New Jersey when Volmut settled the chopper into the water and Leonowich shouted an encouraging, "Hello, take it easy." A rope line and life preserver were thrown to the man but he angrily pushed both aside and waved the helicopter away. When Leonowich straddled one of the pontoons and tried to corral him, the swimmer fought furiously to break loose and the whirlybird nearly tipped over in the battle. Leonowich finally succeeded in looping a line around the swimmer's wrist and then set him adrift. The copter taxied at four miles an hour to shore, towing the resisting man at a safe distance in its wake. He was removed to a nearby hospital for submersion treatment and then to Bellevue for psychiatric observation.

In shunning indiscriminate use of the pontoons, police pilots also take into account the unsettling psychological impact that a ride on the floats could have on the rescued person. "Not only is the practice not safe under certain conditions," one veteran pilot explains, "but if the victim is unconscious and happens to come around and find himself over the Empire State Building, he'd really be shocked. He might think he was going to heaven."

In view of the balance dangers and the risks of overturning in rough water or striking submerged objects or small boats, the pilots also are encouraged to avoid landing whenever possible and to substitute a number of midair rescue tactics instead.

The most deadly landing hazard ever faced by a police pilot was a huge pool of high-octane gasoline that spread over the surface of Jamaica Bay where an Air National Guard plane crashed on November 26, 1958. Lieutenant Johnston arrived to find that the pilot had been hurled clear and was clinging to a floating tire in the ever-widening patch of explosive fuel, which Johnston realized could be set off in a flash by the heat of his helicopter's exhausts. Gambling with death, Johnston swooped close enough to the wreckage to drop a line to the pilot, and towed him out of the gasoline-coated water, narrowly averting a holocaust.

Two boys, isolated by the incoming tide at the tip of a 150-foot jetty off Coney Island on October 10, 1951, were saved by Sergeant Behrens and Lieutenant Johnston, who were unable to land on the sharp rocks. Instead they lowered a life vest on a rope so that each youth in turn could strap it on and wade to safety through the raging surf while the helicopter moved along above, keeping the line taut so he would not tumble.

A "sky-hook hitch" was used to rescue two young men whose rowboat was swamped on August 7, 1955, in the Atlantic Ocean off the Rockaways when gale-force winds suddenly struck the area. Crabbing the helicopter down to a midair standstill just above the ten-foot wave crests, Officer Thomas R. Williams and Sergeant Behrens threw a line and life ring to the struggling men. The victims held on and the helicopter slowly "ski-towed" them to shore.

Of all the Aviation Unit's feats over the years, few, except perhaps Richard Ryan's early aerial rescue leap, match Sergeant Behrens' daring acrobatic performance in overtaking a runaway speedboat in Jamaica Bay on June 19, 1949. The sixteen-foot boat was abandoned by its two passengers after one fell overboard in rough water and the other, realizing his companion could not swim, dived in after him without stopping to shut off the engine. With its tiller jammed, the boat careened wildly through a flotilla of cabin cruisers, sailboats and rowboats, throwing the entire bay into bedlam. A police amphibian and a Coast Guard plane flew to the scene but were powerless to halt the mayhem, and the craft's speed and erratic course made pursuit by other boat owners impossible. A helicopter arrived with Sergeant Crosson at the controls and Behrens as copilot. Climbing out onto a pontoon, Behrens knelt and firmly gripped its supporting strut as hurricane-force winds tore at his clothing. Crosson dropped the chopper toward the speedboat, and Behrens swung down from the pontoon, hanging by his hands from the strut as torrents of water from the boat's wake surged upward, drenching him from head to foot and sending salt spray gushing over the plexiglass cockpit. Barely able to see through the spray, Crosson glided the copter to a position above the boat, hovering for an instant until Behrens released his grip and plummeted into the vessel's cockpit. Behrens struggled to his feet, turned off the engine ignition and grabbed the boat's wheel to steer it away from other vessels until it rocked to a halt.

9. ESD—The Forward Operation........

With a record of nearly one million responses to cries for help in a history spanning more than four decades, the Emergency Service preserves a unique position as one of the few law-enforcement–rescue agencies of its kind in the world.

No other major city in the United States or abroad operates an emergency organization of the ESD's size and scope. The overwhelming majority assign the burdens of all rescue work, except riot incidents, almost exclusively to firemen.

Studies aimed at shifting the tasks to fire fighters in New York have always ended in recognition that the city's sheer massiveness and its giant grab bag of troubles demand a catchall force like the ESD, with the versatility to tackle a wide spectrum of situations involving law enforcement, rescue, or both.

Unlike many other great metropolitan areas, such as San Francisco or Tokyo, New York has never had to worry about natural disasters. Its geological underpinning of bedrock and its topography of hilly terrain are built-in bulwarks against "act of God" catastrophes such as earthquakes and floods.

But like every other place on earth, the city enjoys no immunity from the acts of man and their consequences, and the vicissitudes

224

of the human condition make New York essentially a metropolis of manmade emergencies, which in many ways are exasperatingly more complex, varied and unpredictable than the malevolent forces of nature.

"Handling an emergency in New York is like opening a can," one ESD veteran explains. "Inside that can is another can, and inside that another, and so on. . . ."

With human beings as the catalysts, the city's perils are multiplied by vast commerce and industry, old urban ills such as weakened and dilapidated housing, and all the dangers inherent in the marvels of modern technological progress. No other city has more tall buildings (nearly a hundred in Manhattan alone that tower above four hundred feet); more public transportation (close to eight hundred miles of subway, elevated and commuter train lines and bus routes); more bridges (over sixty, ranging from the Verrazano-Narrows—the world's longest suspension span—to a variety of small bridges across inland waterways); more tunnels (twelve for subways and trains and four for vehicular traffic); or more streets and arterial highways (a network stretching well over six thousand miles).

The future is expected to spawn new breeding grounds for trouble, with hydrofoils skimming the waterways, monorail systems streaking around the perimeter of Manhattan, people-moving sidewalks, aerial tramways arching among the five boroughs and a proliferation of commuter helipads and STOL (short takeoff and landing) airports.

Sophisticated and heavy-duty rescue gear will be needed to save victims of accidents involving these new modes of transportation, and a number of devices are being researched and tested. The latest is a compact four-thousand-dollar power tool with jawlike arms that can tear apart crumpled automobile, train and airplane wreckage within seconds. The push of a button by a single operator sends hydraulic fluid surging from the tool's small gasoline-driven compressor to power the extended arms with ten thousand pounds of spreading force. The multipurpose apparatus can also be utilized for lifting the crushing weight of trailer trucks and elevator cars and for a variety of other entrapment cases. Despite its speed and force, the equipment generates almost none of the heat and friction that have always posed dangers when circular saws and acetylene torches are employed at rescue scenes near accumulations of gasoline, oil and other flammables.

In the resuscitation field, the ESD is studying the development of techniques that simultaneously supply heart-stimulating massage and life-giving oxygen. Strangely enough, the procedure incorporates principles that were intuitively known during the frontier days of the last century, when drowning victims were draped across jogging horses, which supplied the rhythmic motions needed to expel water from the lungs and restore heart action.

For faster response to emergencies, the ESD has commissioned a new fleet of compact, jeeplike vehicles with a low-slung chassis design that will afford greater clearance and stability while weaving at high speeds through traffic-choked streets. Giant helicopters are envisioned for the Aviation Unit when budget allocations make their purchase possible and engine improvements reduce the current nine-hundred-dollar-an-hour operating cost. The whirlybirds will serve as aerial cranes to perform such tasks as lifting debris from building-collapse sites and snatching disabled automobiles from clogged highways. In the Harbor Unit, hydrofoil craft may someday augment the regular fleet for greater speed and mobility.

By far the most horrendous future dangers facing the city are those born of the atomic era—the risks of death-dealing radiation accidents and the nightmarish possibility of a cataclysmic enemy nuclear attack. In a master mobilization plan drawn up in 1962 for major disasters, the ESD occupies the number one position as the "forward operation" to spearhead search and rescue efforts. The policemen are candidly pessimistic about what, if any, meaningful action can be taken in the event of a direct hydrogen bomb strike on the city, but the fatalistic view has not deterred them from formulating elaborate contingency plans for controlling crowd panic, restoring vital communications links and attempting to reestablish viable conditions in any peripheral areas that might remain intact in the aftermath of an atomic holocaust.

The unit's extensive array of RADIAC (Radioactivity Detection Identification and Computation) equipment also is geared to cope with potential accidents at any of hundreds of university research installations, hospital laboratories and industrial plants throughout the city that employ radioactive materials in their work. The relatively minor incidents thus far have called for containment of small amounts of radiation spillage and for recovering cartridges of deadly atomic particles that slip from trucks or are found discarded in vacant lots or other public places after being stolen in burglaries of factories and research laboratories.

A tiny radioactive isotope, an eighth of an inch long and three thirty-seconds of an inch wide, caused detouring of traffic and evacuation of all residents of the first eight floors of a nearby housing project when it was found in a street excavation on the upper East Side on December 20, 1972.

The pellet had escaped through a break in a cable while workmen were using an x-ray device to test the weld on a thirty-inch underground gas main. It was lifted from the pit by ESD policemen, placed in a can of sand, then transferred to a brick-lined lead container and finally into a bomb-disposal truck for removal.

The policemen detailed to the work carry dosimeters and ion chambers to measure radiation levels and mark off danger areas for evacuation. All wear ray-absorbing film badges designed to record the amount of radiation each man receives during any particular job. The specially coded badges undergo laboratory analysis after each incident so that policemen threatened with dangerous overexposure can be withdrawn from the work. The ESD maintains close liaison with the Atomic Energy Commission to update training and methods for handling nuclear mishaps, which are expected to grow in importance in coming decades with increasing use of atomic reactors to generate power.

Many other of the ESD's future challenges are simply projections of old problems that call for reevaluation and improvement of current law-enforcement–rescue techniques. Shootouts, especially those involving hostages, are the subject of ongoing study, with the emphasis on weaponry and fire power being supplanted by psychological-warfare "game plans" that are carefully rehearsed and orchestrated to break down the emotional resistance of barricaded gunmen and pressure them into surrender.

Ironclad tradition is expected to prevail in only one area—the task of talking jumpers out of suicidal leaps. There are no plans for formal psychiatric training of policemen for this work. "After all, we've done pretty well on our own up to now," one veteran rescuer comments. "Why argue with success?"

Some very tentative and speculative thought has been given to the idea of devising large and quickly inflatable air mattresses that can be spread on the ground to catch jumpers, but the major problem to be solved is how to develop apparatus to contain the victim when he bounces.

In the area of personnel, the ESD's all-male makeup happily faded into oblivion in late 1973 when a woman police officer named Ann Morrissey became the first female to join the ranks of the rescue forces as a nursing specialist.

While the ESD in the past has undergone several phases of reorganization to consolidate its operations, the current trend leans toward decentralization aimed at bringing each squad closer to the problems and needs of the individual communities within its jurisdiction. The so-called borough-wide organizational concept received its first pilot test on Staten Island where Emergency Squad No. 5 was accorded separate status to work out its own methods for dealing with the island's peculiar range of emergencies, which encompass everything from fiery explosions in natural-gas storage tanks to animal rescues in remote rural areas.

In other squads throughout the city, field representatives now visit the precincts within the territory to survey and discuss potential emergency problems with each commander so that the ESD will know in advance where and how it can supply the most effective help when needed. The program represents the kind of innovativeness, efficiency and competency that has always earned the ESD the confidence and respect of the fellow policemen it serves as a backup force as well as millions of citizens whose lives it has touched over the years.

The image has been fostered by action rather than words, since the ESD has never spent much time in publicity fanfare. In fact, with the exception of spectacular cases that draw heavy coverage by the newspapers and other media, the unit's operations more often are cloaked anonymously by general references to "police" and "rescue workers" that deprive it of specific credit.

One of the few organized efforts by the ESD to familiarize others with its work is little known to the public at large since it involves entertaining and informative shows that are staged from time to time at Randalls Island exclusively for schoolchildren. The series was begun in 1966 under the direction of Sergeant Joseph

Emru as part of an overall "Know Your Police" program. For many children from neighborhoods where "cop" is a curse word, the shows provide a rare opportunity to watch policemen acting in the positive role of heroes rather than in the terrifying framework of ghetto violence and arrests. After a faltering start, in which intricate rescue work and highly technical terminology proved beyond the children's understanding, the shows were revamped to play up action-packed helicopter and suicide-net rescues and to simplify expressions like "extricate" and "resuscitate" to more colloquial phraseology.

Although seldom attracting public recognition for the thousands of heroic and humanitarian tasks it performs each year, the ESD has managed throughout its history to win and hold the universal admiration of public officials, reporters and other insiders for its dedication and professionalism.

After the 1973 sniper incident in New Orleans that wound up in a Wild West-type shootout, one newspaperman summed up the reaction of his fellow journalists by observing: "A thing like that could never happen in New York. They'd send those guys from Emergency Service and the whole thing would be wrapped up beautifully with no one getting hurt in the process." The comment was prophetic. A week later, the Brooklyn sporting goods store takeover and the safe release of the hostages underscored the reporter's point. Inspector Freeman, the man largely responsible for the outcome, thereafter traveled thousands of miles to share the ESD's knowledge with policemen in other cities, including New Orleans.

The ESD's professional image has been further enhanced by the unusually large percentage of coveted police decorations awarded to its members for bravery and excellence and by a remarkable record of integrity that has kept it free from scandal.

"It's the most corruption-free outfit in the entire department," says Lieutenant Matthew L. Byrne, of the Police Department's Legal Division, who formerly served in the ESD's ranks. "The reason is simple. All these men are volunteers, professionals who could probably command much higher earnings in civilian life. You naturally get a very high caliber of man. You can be sure they're doing the job because they love it, and not for any other reasons."

An electric shock went through the ESD following an incident in 1958 when two officers were accused of selling nine rusty pistols to a gunsmith for three hundred dollars after finding the weapons they said they thought had been discarded in a cardboard box in a garage near the Bronx police property clerk's office. Mystified fellow officers denounced the act as "incredibly stupid," and Inspector Klotzback was extremely upset when he heard the news—the reputation of the ESD was a matter of great pride to him. The offending officers were suspended forthwith and later fired, but the judge who heard their case imposed suspended sentences when he read their records, which had been spotless up to that time and contained numerous citations for excellent police work.

Despite its seriousness, the episode failed to diminish the esteem that the ESD has held before and since among officials and others with intimate knowledge of the men and their deeds. Its files are crammed with testimonials to that esteem from representatives of foreign embassies that have been searched by the policemen after bomb scares, from spokesmen for prison guards saved with ESD help after being taken hostage in riots and from police and fire rescue units elsewhere in the nation and overseas that have benefited from ESD instruction and advice.

The most stirring tributes of all, however, come from thousands of ordinary citizens whose lives have been salvaged in unforgettable ways by the policemen. These messages more than any others show that heroism and simple kindness are virtues that are still much admired and appreciated in a city whose citizens sometimes appear to thrive on nothing more than tough-crusted indifference.

Seldom a day passes without at least one telephone message or letter arriving at the office of the police commissioner or at the ESD's headquarters lauding the policemen for their work. One tells of the forthcoming marriage of a young girl saved by an ESD crew after her lower right arm was severed and her right leg mangled in a fall under a subway train. Others are sent by persons who have been restored to health after suicide attempts, heart attacks and rescues from entrapment.

Even during the tumultuous upheavals of the late 1960s and early 1970s, when militant antipolice sentiment peaked across the nation, the flow of gratitude was uninterrupted. At the height of that period, while law-enforcement officers were being barraged, particularly in the ghettos, with hostility and the epithet "pigs," a letter from Harlem praised ESD Officers Anthony C. Napoli and Francis W. Twormey for their efforts in reviving a woman stricken by illness in an office in the heart of the black community.

"We are proud of these policemen and want both of them to know it," the letter from the woman's friends read in part. "We appreciate it. Please tell them that we said so. Everybody is somebody."

Typical of other expressions of gratefulness was one from a Manhattan clothing store executive commending two ESD officers for "working incessantly" to save the life of a business partner who had been felled by a massive coronary.

"They refused to give up on him and through their great efforts were able to restore life in him," the message read. "What little life he has at this moment is due to the wonderful work of these two men. We believe that when your department performs good work that this should be brought to the public's attention as well as all the detrimental remarks that people both read and hear about."

The letters frequently are poignantly intimate, mingling gratitude with a need to share personal heartbreak by reliving it with the policemen who were involved. One recounts the thoughts of a father as he watched a small army of policemen in his West Side apartment capture his berserk son:

I have been a resident of New York City for the past twenty-two years, and somehow time passed by without any incidents in which either my family or myself needed the assistance of the police. Then one morning about a week ago everything changed.

Little were my personal sorrows in comparison to the catastrophic events at eight-thirty that morning when the peace was broken in my home. My son, aged twenty, became violent because of my insistence on his going to work. (He gets psychiatric care every week.) He literally went berserk and I saved myself in time to call your assistance.

The emergency squad appeared on the scene in no time. Although I was extremely bewildered, I followed all the details of what I believe was a two-hour siege of my apartment. My son demolished everything and appeared to be in a most dangerous condition, throwing bottles as soon as your men tried to open the door.

Repeatedly the commanding officer of the squad cautioned his men on the use of tear gas. The teamwork and the patience these men showed on the job was something that filled me with admiration and deep gratitude for their extreme concern to care so much for the life of the young man and introduce nothing in their strategy that would have upset him more and could possibly have caused him to lose his last control.

In the front line were two of your men who kept talking to my son, and who finally after patient and convincing persuasions brought him out voluntarily.

As a father and citizen of New York, where you are called on to settle so much grief and misery, allow me to express to you and especially to Patrolmen John Maddock and John Leonard, my deepest gratitude. . . . Our lives were out of balance, but your men were there and saved us.

More than any others, rescues of children prompt possibly the most intense feelings of gratitude. One note in the form of a Christmas card contained the snapshot of a slightly toothless three-year-old girl who had been cut loose and revived by ESD Officers Robert Maroney and Emanuel Cavallaro after she was nearly strangled to death by a Venetian blind cord she had looped around her neck while playing in her upper Manhattan apartment. When she was rushed to the hospital, doctors said the girl would have died or suffered irreversible brain damage, except for the quick action of the police. Penned inside the card was a note from the girl's parents, which read: "Thanks to you and others like you, the smile is back. Our daughter will be home soon and as far as anyone can tell will one day soon be fully recovered. I know you see tragedies almost every day, but I hope that knowing your work does so much good will balance out the sadder cases. I hope you understand that words are not enough to thank you, but they are all we have and our prayers for your long and happy life."

The card obviously is treasured as one of the prized mementos of his police career by the stocky, red-haired Maroney, and the case has an interesting footnote. About four months after saving the girl, Maroney and Cavallaro were passing her home while on patrol and dropped in to see how she was doing. They found to their consternation that she had caught the chicken pox.

"Well, that's life," Maroney says. "If it isn't one emergency, it's another."

Appendix A: Equipment for Emergency Service Station Wagons

2 portolights
1 life preserver
100-foot ⅜-inch rope
200-foot ½-inch rope
100-foot ¾-inch rope
2 resuscitators
2 blankets
7 oxygen cylinders (medical type)
1 first-aid kit with board splints
1 cot stretcher
1 back board with footrest
1 body bag
2 all-service gas masks
2 gas mask filter canisters
2 Scott Air-Paks
1 pair rubber boots
1 Morrissey life belt
1 grappling iron with hooks
2 bulletproof garments
1 pair gas-tight goggles
1 journal jack
1 Porto-Power jack (4 ton)

2 pairs utility work gloves
1 open-end wrench set and socket drive
1 pair tinner's shears
1 entrenching shovel
2 rope snaps
1 pair rubber wading boots
1 pair rubber electrical gloves
1 pair glove protectors
1 audio hailer
1 animal lasso stick
1 bolt cutter
1 wire cutter
1 ring cutter
1 knife file
1 claw bar
1 pinch bar
1 cross-cut handsaw
1 ax (6 pound)
1 box for small tools
1 claw hammer
1 machinist's hammer
1 hatchet
1 pair side-cutting pliers

1 pair diagonal pliers
1 Stillson wrench
1 cold chisel
1 screwdriver (10 inch)
3 Phillips screwdrivers
1 monkey wrench
1 refrigeration ratchet
  wrench

10 film badges (radiac monitoring)
1 ion chamber (radiac monitoring)
1 Geiger counter (radiac
  monitoring)
1 dosimeter (radiac monitoring)
2 portable radios

Appendix B: Equipment for Emergency Service Trucks

1 acetylene cutting unit
2 acetylene cylinders
1 ammunition box
2 augers and handles
1 ax (6 pound)
1 ax (8 pound)
1 back board
20 film badges (radiac equipment)
1 claw bar (Kelly tool)
1 Z bar (fixed)
1 Z bar (split type)
1 battery booster cable
1 Morrissey belt
2 wool blankets
1 block and fall (200-foot 1-inch line)
2 snatch blocks (8 inch)
2 boat hooks
1 body bag
1 bomb blanket
1 pair wading boots
7 bulletproof vests (ceramic)
7 sets car openers

600 cartridges (.223 caliber)
1,800 cartridges (.38 caliber)
500 cartridges (9 mm.)
300 cartridges (12 gauge No. 4 buck)
200 cartridges (12 gauge 00 buck)
500 cartridges (12 gauge rifle slug)
6 cartridge clips (9 mm.)
1 cold chisel
1 wood chisel
4 traffic cones and reflectors
1 bolt cutter
1 maul and rivet cutter
1 pipe cutter
1 wire cutter
1 cutting tool ("can opener")
1 dosimeter
1 electric drill (½ inch)
1 drill index
1 extinguisher (foam type)
1 extinguisher (CO_2)
1 knife file

1 first-aid kit (large)
1 funnel (1 gallon)
2 gas masks (M.S.A.)
6 gas masks (tear gas)
1 tire gauge
1 Geiger counter
2 generators (2.5 kw.)
6 pairs leather-palm gloves
6 pairs neoprene gloves
2 pairs electrical gloves
2 pairs electrical gloves with leather protector
1 pair chipper-type goggles
8 pairs tear-gas goggles
6 pairs clear-lens goggles
1 pair welder's goggles
5 grappling-hook sets (6 hooks per set)
1 line-thrower gun (Remington .22 caliber)
2 machine guns (9 mm.)
8 shotguns (12-gauge Ithaca)
6 Remington antisniper guns with binoculars and scopes
4 tear-gas guns (1.5 caliber)
1 hacksaw frame and 6 blades
6 pairs handcuffs
1 claw hammer
1 machinist's hammer
1 sledge hammer
1 hatchet (2 pound)
1 jack hammer (electric)
1 ion chamber
1 chain jack (15 ton)
1 journal jack (15 ton)
1 journal jack (25 ton)

1 Porto-Power jack, hydraulic (4 ton)
1 screw jack (10 ton)
1 screw jack (15 ton)
3 junction boxes
1 set high-pressure keys
1 set subway-exit keys
1 ladder (28 foot)
1 ladder (10 foot)
1 life net (ground and wall)
2 life preservers (kapok)
1 life ring
6 1000 watt lights
2 500 watt lights
1 flashlight
4 portolights (6 volts, dry cell)
1 retrieving magnet
16 oxygen cylinders (16 cubic foot)
2 oxygen cylinders (110 cubic foot)
10 electrical pigtails
1 pair chain pliers
1 pair diagonal pliers
1 pair side-cutting pliers
1 pair slip-joint pliers
2 Nottingham pole connectors
2 portable radios
1 Stephenson resuscitator
4 reels electric cable
1 ring cutter and blades
200-foot ⅜-inch rope
200-foot ½-inch rope
200-foot ¾-inch rope
1 15-foot wire-towing rope
4 rope snaps

1 partner-rescue saw
1 all-purpose saw
1 chain saw (gas-driven)
1 circular saw
1 cross-cut saw (20 inch)
1 3-foot cross-cut saw
1 herringbone saw
1 pruning saw
1 ripsaw (26 inch)
1 5-inch screwdriver
1 8-inch screwdriver
1 12-inch screwdriver
1 Phillips screwdriver (No. 1)
1 Phillips screwdriver (No. 2)
1 Phillips screwdriver (No. 3)
1 pair tinner's shears
1 entrenching shovel
2 long-handle shovels
3 short-handle shovels
2 rubber sleeves
2 cot stretchers (army type)
1 folding stretcher
1 wire stretcher (Stokes basket)

2 Scott Air-Paks
20 tear-gas cartridges (short range No. 203)
20 tear-gas grenades (Spedeheat No. 112)
10 tear-gas grenades (smoke No. 108)
5 tear-gas grenades (blast dispersion No. 121)
12 tear-gas projectiles (Flite-Rite No. 230)
4 tear-gas projectiles (Flite-Rite blast dispersion)
10 tear-gas projectiles (short range No. 219)
6 tear-gas vests
1 screw wrench (Allen set)
1 box wrench
1 hydrant wrench
1 monkey wrench (12 inch)
1 open-end wrench set
1 socket wrench set
1 refrigerator ratchet wrench
1 12-inch Stillson wrench
1 24-inch Stillson wrench

The following pieces of equipment are stored in quarters:

1 excavation barrel
1 bomb container
1 battery charger
1 dosimeter charger
1 large grapnel (60 pound)

1 horse belt
1 pantograph pole
1 aluminum rowboat
1 5-foot cross-cut saw (2 man)

Appendix C: Use of Wall Net

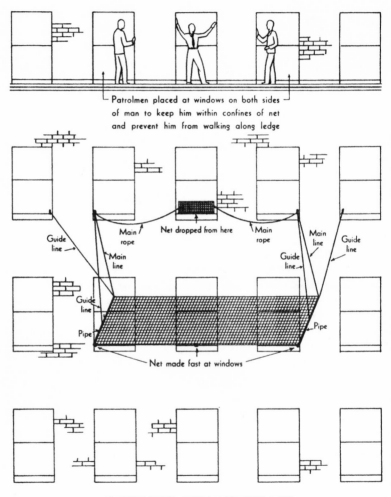

Patrolmen placed at windows on both sides
of man to keep him within confines of net
and prevent him from walking along ledge

Guide
line

Main
rope

Net dropped from here

Main
rope

Main
line

Guide
line

Main
line

Guide
line

Guide
line

Pipe

Pipe

Net made fast at windows

DIMENSION OF NET: LENGTH, 30 FEET; WIDTH, 20 FEET

FBI Law Enforcement Bulletin, 1949

238

Appendix D: Ground Net Diagram

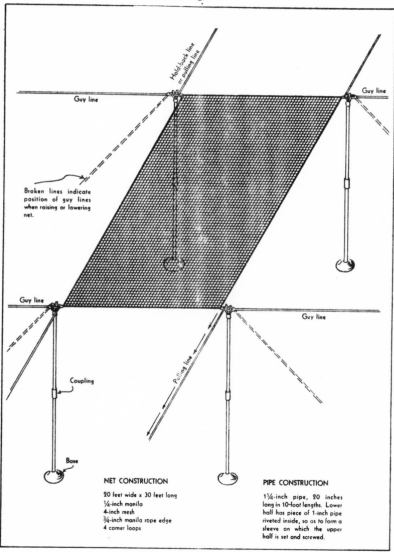

Hold-back line or pulling line

Guy line

Guy line

Broken lines indicate position of guy lines when raising or lowering net.

Guy line

Guy line

Guy line

Pulling line

Coupling

Base

NET CONSTRUCTION

20 feet wide x 30 feet long
¼-inch manila
4-inch mesh
¾-inch manila rope edge
4 corner loops

PIPE CONSTRUCTION

1¼-inch pipe, 20 inches long in 10-foot lengths. Lower half has piece of 1-inch pipe riveted inside, so as to form a sleeve on which the upper half is set and screwed.

FBI Law Enforcement Bulletin, 1949